DEVIN ALEXANDER

75+

Amazing Recipe
Makeovers of Your
Fast Food
Restaurant
Favorites

Book design by Carol Angstadt
Cover photographs by Ben Fink
Front cover recipes: Pizza Hut Supreme Personal Pan Pizza (page 133); Dairy Queen Brownie Earthquake (page 209); Hardee's 1/3-Lb Western Bacon Thickburger (page 33); and KFC Twister (page 98)

Library of Congress Cataloging-in-Publication Data

Alexander, Devin.
   Fast food fix : 75+ amazing recipe makeovers of your fast food restaurant favorites / Devin Alexander.
      p.   cm.
   Includes index.
   ISBN-13 978-1-59486-310-3   paperback
   ISBN-10 1-59486-310-5   paperback
   1. Convenience foods.   2. Nutrition.   I. Title.
TX370.A54   2006
642'.1—dc22   2005035751

Distributed to the trade by Holtzbrinck Publishers
2   4   6   8   10   9   7   5   3   paperback

We inspire and enable people to improve their lives and the world around them
For more of our products visit **rodalestore.com** or call 800-848-4735

To my grandmother,

Florence DeLess,

who has been my culinary inspiration

as long as I can remember.

I LOVE YOU, NAN.

CONTENTS

FOREWORD

Dressed in their best on Sunday mornings, most Catholic teenagers of my generation went to church; I went to Wendy's.

As a child, if I was too sick to go to church on Sunday, I had to make it up by attending mass during the week. If my brother and I fought, my mother dragged us to weekday services. "You must not be close enough to God if you're acting like that," she'd say. And though I weighed in excess of 175 pounds my freshman year in high school, I was dying to make the cheerleading squad. So my mother suggested I go to church to say a novena (9 consecutive days of attending church to make a specific plea to God through prayer). Though I had never liked church and I was the furthest thing from a morning person, I was desperate. Not having had the foresight to consider that even if I had made the squad, I wouldn't have fit into the uniform, I woke up an hour-and-a-half earlier than usual (the sun wasn't even up) to attend mass before school for 9 very long and tiring days. When I didn't land a spot on the squad, I was mad at my mom; I officially hated church; and I was convinced that God had it in for me.

Soon thereafter, my brother, Brent, my little sister, Leslie, and I started walking "to church." Our scheme was simple: We would figure out a subtle way to confirm that our parents were going to attend the noon service, and then we would announce our plan to "attend" the 10:30 one. We'd arrive on the church steps just in time for us to send Leslie inside to listen to the sermon and pick up a church bulletin (the evidence required to satisfy our parents). She'd then skip out on the rest of the service and rejoin us for our weekly jaunt to Wendy's, which happened to be conveniently located just behind Sacred Heart Church. Leslie would relay the brief overview of the sermon and identify the priest as I religiously ate my sacred Frosty and french fries.

Of course, my devotion to fast food wasn't limited to Wendy's alone. Because my dad traveled on business a few days a week, my family enjoyed fast food nights regularly. Though I loved my dad, I remember looking forward to his trips, because that meant there would be a fast food menu in my immediate future. And speaking of memories, I'll never forget the first time my mother drove her new Mercedes convertible through the McDonald's drive-thru. Before then, we didn't have a lot of money, so I remember her giggling with a childlike spirit, as if she was getting away with something. She thought that because she could afford a Mercedes, she should no longer be buying 99-cent cheeseburgers.

Heck, fast food was such a part of my childhood that the only picture that exists of all my grandmother's grandchildren is in front of a statue of Ronald McDonald. All eight of us still have a copy of the photo, as do our mothers. My cousins all want to return and retake the same picture, now 27 years later. I'm torn.

By my junior year in high school, I was officially a fast food junkie who needed a daily fix. Lucky for me, juniors and seniors were allowed to leave during our half-hour lunch period, so we'd pile into the cars of anyone old enough to drive (I was only 15) and rush to McDonald's, Burger King, or Wendy's to avoid the soggy pizza and french fries our cafeteria offered.

Shortly thereafter, however, my love affair with fast food came to a screeching halt. I was attending a precollege summer theater program at Carnegie Mellon University, when I experienced my first real crush. His name was Matt, and his feathered hair and gorgeous smile melted me. It seemed that he had a crush on my roommate and best friend—a perfect-looking, thin girl named Audrey. She swore she wasn't interested. I believed her . . . until the night the three of us went to McDonald's after a James Taylor concert. I knew my affection was one-sided when Matt reached across the table and started hand-feeding his french fries to *her*. Horrified, I didn't know what to do, so I tried to distract myself by eating more than usual that night. When I looked up and saw that they were kissing, I was ill. I don't think I said another word all evening.

When I woke up the next morning, I still felt sick. I rolled over and saw Audrey lying there, looking perfect as always in her skimpy little lace teddy. I was convinced that Matt would have liked me if I weren't so fat, and I resolved to lose weight. I went cold turkey off fast food, and it didn't hurt that the mere mention of McDonald's continued to make my heart ache for years. I have not touched fast food since (well, until the making of this book, that is).

I must admit that I was a little worried about the prospect of losing weight. After all, when I was supposed to be going to church and creating merit with God, I was sneaking off for fast food. What were the chances (by this point, I was fully plagued with Catholic guilt) that God was suddenly going to award me my wish to be thin, when I still didn't understand why I wasn't granted my wish to be on the cheerleading squad? But much to my surprise, by simply eliminating fast food from my diet, I lost more than 25 pounds.

After a few years and a couple more crushes, I was able to throw away the photos of Matt and Audrey. And I started craving hamburgers, french fries, and the Burger King Chicken Parmesan Sandwich I had always loved, but I was determined not to give in to my cravings. Clearly having an inherent talent for cooking (the incredibly gifted Italian grandmother mentoring me didn't hurt), I soon realized that I could re-create my favorites at home with a fraction of the fat. In fact, I was so successful in doing this that I would swear on a Bible (still plagued with Catholic guilt) that I have truly not since craved actual fast food, which, in part, enabled me to lose an additional 25 pounds. I do still crave (and indulge in) chocolate and my made-over fast food counterparts, but I have not even considered walking through the doors to visit Ronald, Wendy, or Jack for a meal since that heart-wrenching night in 1988. It occurred to me while revisiting chain after chain to collect the fast food favorites necessary to create this book that I have never driven through a drive-thru. That's right, never. Never ever. I wasn't old enough to drive when I swore off fast food. And I hadn't been back since.

I hope this book brings you the comfort, peace, and health (and even greater popularity!) the food has brought me.

GET YOUR FAST FOOD FIX

I consider myself a fast food admirer. I love the way fast food tastes, and I admire the folks who've spent countless hours creating the irresistible flavor combinations that we Americans can't wait to find in drive-thrus. Actually, I consider these people artists of sorts, and I, for one, really appreciate their work.

Fast food had been a regular part of my diet for most of my teenage years. However, when I stopped eating it, I lost 25 pounds. When I kept it out of my diet and made a few other changes, I lost another 25. In recent years, I've heard many stories similar to mine. Meanwhile, movie hits like *Super Size Me* advise us that eating a steady diet of fast food might cause maladies from sluggishness to liver failure. Bestsellers like *Fast Food Nation* warn us that feces might be found in our meat supply. So we Americans slowly but surely started to wonder more and more about the hazards of eating fast food. But just as we were starting to realize that it might be a good idea to steer our cars a bit more frequently to grocery stores instead of through drive-thrus, the fast food chains responded. They started offering healthier options, which has been great. But one major problem remains: cravings. When plagued with visions of a Big Mac, will a McSalad do the trick? When you're dying for a Cinnabon, will an apple hit the spot? Probably not. And when we're told we "can't" or "shouldn't," we want something even more—after all, it's human nature.

That's where this book comes in. It gives you options. It's a "go ahead, have it your way—really" cookbook. And "have it your way" every day if you want. Each of the fast food favorites in this book is a solution for satisfying the most-common fast food cravings. I'm hoping that we as a nation will be able to turn our backs on supersizing but will still get our Fast Food Fix with ingredients we select ourselves in the portions that our bodies need.

Fast Food Fix Promises

To give you the best creations I possibly could, I decided to make some promises about the recipes before I wrote another word of this book.

1. The serving size of every recipe contained in this book is at least as big as the original version, but it will contain considerably fewer grams of fat, calories, and chemicals.

I did my best in every case to buy three of each item from different locations of each chain. I broke down the recipes by first weighing and measuring each item and then its component parts on two scales. I re-created them by looking at the weights provided by the nutritional data sheets in conjunction with the serving sizes that were in front of me. Then, after I tested my versions, I purchased a final sample (when at all possible) to make sure my versions looked as large and weighed as much as the originals (in many cases, mine are significantly larger).

2. The recipes will use only common ingredients and employ basic cooking techniques with instructions as to how to cook the food properly to yield optimum results.

Though I can't promise that every item called for will be available wherever you shop, I did make sure key ingredients were available nationwide. In a few cases, it makes sense that it was harder to find ingredients for regional recipes outside the local area—grocery stores tend to stock popular, regional items. In the end, I was happy to learn that though 96% lean ground beef isn't sold everywhere, I found it in at least one major grocery store in each city I visited, and it was in all Trader Joe's stores and even in Wal-Mart Supercenters.

3. If the inspiring fast food item contains beef, the Fast Food Fix version will also contain beef—no substituting "girly veggies" for "manly beef."

There isn't even the slightest hint of a disclaimer here. I feel strongly about this promise and stuck to it throughout. I don't even believe in substituting turkey bacon for bacon, so I didn't do it.

I do not purport or intend to "trick" anyone into believing he or she is eating "the real thing." The *Fast Food Fix* versions model the same basic ingredients, flavors, textures, and feel as the favorites they re-create, but they're guilt-free.

It's also worth pointing out that in most cases, I've written recipes for single servings. My logic for this is pretty simple: These are recipes to help you satisfy real fast food cravings, so if you are the only one in the house hankering for a chili burger, you can easily fix it for yourself. This strategy also let me re-create the most exact flavors possible. However, in the interest of convenience, I've also made sure that all sauces yield enough for four servings (most of them store very well). By all means, if you are cooking for more than one person, feel free to multiply the recipes as necessary.

Whose Favorites?

You may have perused the Contents and wondered why the Wendy's Single isn't included but Back Yard Burgers' Black Jack Burger is. Or you may wonder why Dunkin' Donuts is and Krispy Kreme isn't. Rest assured, the task of compiling the list was a process that involved a wide range of people.

A group of colleagues and friends and I started by listing what we considered to be the most popular fast food dishes available. I then broke them down by type and researched their nutritional values. Some fell off the list because the makeovers just wouldn't save enough fat or calories to make it worthwhile to spend the time and energy re-creating them. For instance, Boston Market used to have corn bread that resembled mini-loaves. Over the past couple of years, they reformulated their corn bread to have a smaller size and a different shape. The new, smaller version has only 120 calories and 3.5 grams of fat. Even if I were to cut the fat by 75 percent, you'd be saving only about 2.5 grams. Meanwhile, also on our list was Dunkin' Donuts Corn Muffins, which one of my friends swears by. I was able to eliminate 153 calories and 15 grams of fat from that jumbo muffin and found that opting for a standard-size muffin will set you back only about 2 grams of fat per muffin. Since the flavors are similar, it was a no-brainer. I skipped Boston Market's version and included the muffin from Dunkin' Donuts.

Other items fell off the list because I just didn't feel I could duplicate them as similarly as I would have liked. Unfortunately, I worked on at least 30 recipes that never saw these pages. For instance, though the Wendy's Single is extremely popular, it doesn't have a sauce or any truly identifying characteristic other than its square shape that could make the lighter version come to life. The Big Mac, on the other hand, was a slam dunk as soon as I was able to perfect the sauce.

Others got bumped, so to speak, because they were too similar. I did my best to provide a diverse menu, of sorts. If you're a big bacon fan, you'll find a burger you love. There are thin fries, curly fries, crinkle fries, Cajun fries, etc., which I found preferable to making a new version of the regular straight-cut fries I found in almost every restaurant I visited.

The pizzas are heavy on meat toppings because the veggie toppings don't add or subtract much. If you'd prefer a mushroom onion pizza, you can skip all of the toppings on the pizza from your favorite fast food pizza restaurant and follow the directions for the dough, sauce, and cheese, then top it with mushrooms and onions to your heart's content.

But Who *Really* Has the Time to Make Their Own Fast Food?

You may be apt to argue that the point of going to a fast food restaurant is that it's fast. But really, how fast is it? In traffic-congested Los Angeles, where I currently live, it can take longer to get to most drive-thru restaurants, wait in line, order the food, pay, and drive home than it does to make many of the dishes in this book.

Granted, there are exceptions; having pizza delivered to your door is immensely less time-consuming than making any of the pizzas in this book, and the Cinnabon Classic Roll takes much longer to make than it does to pick up. But for the most part, I would argue that it's definitely worth the little bit of time it takes to make your own food rather than wading through traffic. But to help you save even more time, I've provided "Drive-Thru" options for a number of the dishes, and I've noted which dishes take less than 30 minutes to prepare (look for the clock symbol at the top of those recipes). Hopefully, once you've employed a few of these options, you, too, will make and take the time.

Do You Really Save Money Eating at Fast Food Restaurants?

I know that a lot of people may have the impression that groceries are expensive and ordering fast food is not. It may seem that way, but is it true? We are constantly inundated with fast food deals for 99-cent Fish Fridays and Taco Tuesdays where you get three tacos for 99 cents, so we think that fast food costs less. But unless you eat those items and only those items used to draw you in, I've found that eating fast food doesn't necessarily pay.

Now I will be honest . . . until I actually sat down and factored out the individual cost of the dishes I was making, I didn't realize that it really is no less expensive to eat at the drive-thru. But item after item, it became more and more obvious that making the food at home was the way to go for me and my wallet. Consider this:

A medium serving of McDonald's French Fries costs approximately $1.49 plus tax (again, in June 2005 in the Los Angeles area). Now consider the cost of the ingredients needed to make them.

* Extra virgin olive oil costs $10.99 for a 16.9-ounce bottle of my favorite brand (though you could certainly find other brands cheaper), which will give you more than enough oil for 100 servings of my fries for 11 cents each.
* Baking potatoes cost around $2.99 for a 10-pound bag, which will give you about twenty 8-ounce servings for approximately 15 cents each.
* A container of salt goes for around 59 cents and would be enough to season hundreds of servings of fries, but for the purpose of this exercise, let's say that salt would set you back one cent per serving.

So by my calculation, you could make one serving of McDonald's French Fries for about 27 cents. At that rate, you could make a serving of fries for each member of a family of five and still save pennies over buying one serving at McDonald's.

Now let's consider the Big Mac. At the McDonald's near my home (where I'll be doing the grocery comparison), a Big Mac costs $2.15. To make one in your kitchen, you would need:

✳ Three ounces of 96% lean ground beef, which at $4.99 per pound translates to about 94 cents per serving

✳ One (3½-inch) sesame seed hamburger bun plus one bottom bun, which would cost 33 cents if you bought a package of eight for $1.79

✳ One slice of 2% milk American cheese, which would cost 24 cents if you bought a 12-ounce package for $3.89

✳ A tablespoon of condiments (low-fat mayonnaise, mustard, ketchup, and relish), which would set you back about five cents tops

✳ One teaspoon of sugar and a pinch of salt, which for the purpose of this exercise we'll say costs one cent, though it's likely far less

✳ Two teaspoons of freshly minced white onion, which costs four cents at most

✳ One-third cup of shredded iceberg lettuce, which would cost about 11 cents if you bought a head for $1.29

✳ Two dill pickle rounds, which would cost about six cents if you bought a 16-ounce jar of them for $2.59

Going by these estimates, which are all based on buying name-brand products in standard-size jars at regular (not sale) price, the total cost of a Big Mac made

IN SEARCH OF THE BEST DEAL

Did you know that a Big Mac costs different amounts at different locations even within the same city in the United States? I had no idea. I called five (randomly selected) locations of McDonald's in Manhattan (in June of 2005) and found that a Big Mac costs $3.15 plus tax at one location, $3.25 plus tax at another, $3.57 plus tax at two locations, and $3.79 plus tax at another. On the same day, I found two locations in the greater Los Angeles area with different prices. At one location, the Big Mac costs $2.15 plus tax, and at another, it costs $2.39 plus tax. What surprised me more, though, was that in my hometown of Wyomissing, Pennsylvania, the Big Mac costs $2.75 plus tax. Because groceries are considerably less expensive in Wyomissing and the surrounding areas, and the cost of living is less than it is in Los Angeles, I was surprised to learn that you pay even more for a Big Mac in Wyomissing than you do in Santa Monica (near Los Angeles).

at home with the leanest beef, low-fat mayonnaise, light American cheese, and fresh produce is $1.78.

Next, let's consider a Starbucks Mocha Frappuccino. To indulge your sweet tooth with this tasty concoction at home, you would need:

* One-half tablespoon of instant coffee granules, which would cost eight cents if you bought an 8-ounce jar of them for $6.39
* One teaspoon of sugar, which we'll say costs one cent, just as we did in the earlier example
* One-half cup of fat-free half-and-half, which would cost 37 cents if you bought a 1-quart carton for $2.99
* Two tablespoons of chocolate syrup, which would cost 14 cents if you bought a 16-ounce can for $1.59
* One-third cup of fat-free whipped topping, which would cost 22 cents if it came from a 7-ounce can that you bought for $2.99

The grand total for your homemade version of Starbucks Grande Mocha Frappuccino would be about 82 cents. If you were to walk into a Starbucks in my area and order that same drink, you would pay $3.55. That means you could make the same size of my version for a family of four for less than buying one.

I could go on here listing everything from Domino's Cheese Pizza to Burger King's French Toast Sticks, and from KFC's Popcorn Chicken to Long John Silver's Crunchy Shrimp Basket, but you get my point.

Essential Tools

There are plenty of fun cooking tools and toys you can buy to stock your kitchen. But there are only a few that I would urge you to invest in that will really assist in your efforts to eat healthfully. Though I've tried to design the recipes in this book so they don't require too many tools, I would strongly recommend the following:

Nonstick Skillets

A couple of good (not to be mistaken with expensive) nonstick skillets of varying sizes are definitely worth the cost. Without them, food sticks or falls apart, leaving finished dishes cooked improperly or looking unappealing. Unfortunately, even the best pans lose their nonstick properties over time (even if they have a "lifetime warranty"), so an easy way to see if they're still good is to make an omelet over medium to medium-high heat using only a light squirt of nonstick spray. If the egg sticks, it's probably time to replace your pans.

Nonstick Baking Sheets

Like the skillets I just mentioned, all nonstick baking sheets can lose their nonstick properties over time. If you use cooking sprays, you may find that your baking sheets become slightly sticky—this is because a thin layer of spray residue has been baked onto the pans.

If you don't want to invest in new ones (or don't have any at all), you can line a baking sheet with parchment paper and spray that with nonstick spray (though it's not recommended that you do this when cooking at temperatures over 425°F). Another option is purchasing a silicone baking mat to line your pans, though you'll have to play with it and adjust cooking times and temperatures to achieve the proper level of crispness in the recipes.

If you're purchasing new baking sheets, I prefer to use ones that have a gray finish. If you use black ones, make sure to decrease cooking temperatures by 25°F—just like it is hotter to stand on a blacktop driveway than a (white) concrete side-walk when the sun is beating down (and burning your feet), a black coating on your pans will accelerate cooking where the food is in contact with the black coating.

Olive Oil Sprayer

I've heard a lot of debates between proponents of olive oil sprayers versus the cans of cooking spray that you buy at the grocery store. I am a huge fan of the sprayers except when baking sweets—then I always use a butter-flavored cooking spray.

I like the sprayers that you fill yourself for a number of reasons:

1. I know exactly what is being put on my food when I fill the sprayer myself—extra virgin olive oil. Prefilled sprayers often have added ingredients, such as grain alcohol and/or propellant, that I don't necessarily want to put on my food.

2. I can control flavor better. I like to fill the sprayer with my favorite full-bodied, extra virgin olive oil and then spray my food lightly for added flavor with little fat. There are a number of recipes in the book that were modeled after dishes that have a truly oily taste. By using a strongly flavored olive oil spray to finish them off, mine, too, can have a similar (but better) flavor. In my travels, doing cooking demos and teaching cooking lessons, I have had some clients say that they found that the sprayers can become clogged. However, that's never been my experience. I got my first sprayer more than 9 years ago and had it until last year when the cap broke. I'm now on my second, and neither cost me more than $10.

Kitchen Scale

Though I've tried to make the recipes in this book as user-friendly as possible even if you don't have a kitchen scale, I would highly, highly (that's two *highlys* on purpose) recommend purchasing one. Whether you're making the recipes in this book or just trying to live a healthy lifestyle in general, using a scale is one of the best ways to develop a sense of portion control. Your eyes can

WEIGHTS/MEASURES AND CONVERSIONS

Though I highly recommend you purchase a kitchen scale, below you will find rough measurements of weight equivalents in case you don't have one. (I still want you to be able to use the book!)

Ground Meats

½ ounce = 1 tablespoon

1 ounce = 2 tablespoons

2 ounces = ¼ cup

4 ounces (¼ pound) = ½ cup

⅓ pound = ⅔ cup

6 ounces = ¾ cup

8 ounces (½ pound) = 1 cup

12 ounces (¾ pound) = 1½ cups

Finely Shredded Cheddar Cheese

½ ounce = ¼ cup

1 ounce = ½ cup

2 ounces = 1 cup

3 ounces = 1½ cups

4 ounces = 2 cups

5 ounces = 2½ cups

6 ounces = 3 cups

8 ounces = 4 cups

Finely Shredded Mozzarella Cheese

½ ounce = 2½ tablespoons

1 ounce = ¼ cup + 1 tablespoon

2 ounces = ½ cup + 2 tablespoons

3 ounces = 1 cup - 1 tablespoon

4 ounces = 1¼ cups

5 ounces = 1½ cups + 3 tablespoons

6 ounces = 2 cups - 2 tablespoons

8 ounces = 2½ cups

deceive you, but a scale never lies. Use one faithfully and your portions will never accidentally expand (or decrease) over time. In regard to this book, I weighed and measured everything precisely so that the finished dishes will not only look the same as the originals, they should taste the same. For example, I seasoned the allotted 7 ounces of raw potato curls to make the Arby's Curly Fries with enough seasonings so that my testers and I believed they were seasoned as closely as humanly possible to the Arby's original. If you "ballpark it" and end up using only 6 ounces, you may end up having fries that are too spicy or that are dripping with too much egg. If you use 8½ or 9 ounces of potatoes, they may be too bland to accurately mimic the original. Also, there are many dishes in which the cooking times are based on the size or the weight of the meat. If you don't use a scale, it's especially important to watch for the signs of doneness called for in the recipes.

Fine Shredder for Cheese

When you're trying to reduce calories in a nice cheesy dish, this tool is essential. By shredding cheese finely, you can cover more surface with less cheese, ensuring that you get some in every bite without using it in excess. Plus, low-fat cheeses melt better if they are finely shredded.

You can pick up a fine shredder for a few dollars, or you can save prep time by purchasing a food processor with a fine-shredding attachment. I have both. If I want a bit of cheese on a salad, I'll use the handheld. If I'm making a pizza, it definitely saves time (and often my fingers) to use the food processor.

Meat Mallet

A meat mallet is another tool I consider an absolute essential. You can save fat and calories by tenderizing lower-fat meats with a meat mallet instead of using fattening accompaniments to tenderize them. Be sure to buy a mallet that is heavy and has a flat surface on one side and a toothed surface on the other. The flat surface allows you to pound chicken and fish without ripping them to shreds, while the toothed surface tenderizes steaks. If you don't have a mallet, in a pinch you can use the bottom of a heavy frying pan or even a heavy rolling pin.

What's the Best Way to Make Smart Substitutions?

Before I answer that question, let me be clear about one thing: I believe in eating what I really want to eat. For instance, if I were to have a Burger King Fish Filet sandwich, it wouldn't bother me to skip the cheese. However, if you take the tartar sauce from my sandwich, I would barely consider it a Fish Filet Sandwich. You might feel the opposite. These are the considerations to make in order to truly enjoy your foods while optimizing your health.

To help give you the same options, you'll notice that within a number of recipes, I've offered "Even Better" suggestions to help you make the finished dish healthier by adjusting portion size or by using lighter ingredients to cut fat

EASY WAYS TO CUT AND SAVE

Cut from recipe	Save
½-ounce slice of American cheese	50 calories, 2.5 g fat, 1.5 g sat. fat
1 ounce low-fat Cheddar cheese	60 calories, 2.5 g fat, 1.5 g sat. fat
1 ounce low-fat mozzarella cheese	60 calories, 2 g fat, 1 g sat. fat
1 slice center-cut bacon	25 calories, 2 g fat, 1 g sat. fat
1 tablespoon light mayonnaise	45 calories, 4.5 g fat, 0.5 g sat. fat
1 tablespoon low-fat mayonnaise	25 calories, 2 g fat, 0 g sat. fat
1 tablespoon light sour cream	18 calories, 1 g fat, 1 g sat. fat
1 teaspoon extra virgin olive oil	42 calories, 5 g fat, <1 g sat. fat

Substitute	
Whole wheat bun for white bun	Add 2 g fiber
Whole wheat English muffin for a white English muffin	Add 1 g fiber, 1 g protein
1 tablespoon low-fat mayonnaise for 1 tablespoon light mayonnaise	Save 20 calories, 2.5 g fat, 0.5 g sat. fat
4 ounces extra-lean ground turkey for 4 ounces 96% lean ground beef	Save 10 calories, 3 g fat, 1.5 g sat. fat
4 ounces extra-lean ground turkey for 4 ounces extra-lean ground pork	Save 16 calories, 2 g fat, 1 g sat. f

and calories further, without affecting taste. Just remember, if these changes feel burdensome and will make you crave the full-fat original, then ignore them and enjoy the recipes the way they are written. If you're on the fence, jump in and give one or two a try. Also, check out the list on page 11 to see how some across-the-board substitutions can help you save a lot of calories in the long run.

In Search of the Right Numbers

If given a choice, every time I ordered a sandwich or any item for this book, I always asked for the restaurant's standard version by saying, "the way they are supposed to be made." I had hoped that this strategy would yield the most-consistent results as I began to build my own versions and compare nutritional data. However, once the process was under way, I was surprised to see how much variability some franchises had not only among serving sizes but also in their reporting of nutritional data.

In fact, during the 9 months I spent collecting information, the analyses for more than 25 percent of the dishes in this book appeared to have changed; some lost fat and calories while others gained them. Granted, many of the items gained or lost only a few calories or a gram or two of fat, but it's surprising how much of a difference a few calories or fat grams here or there really make. For example, if you add just 100 calories per day to your diet every day for a year, you'll gain (on average) 10 pounds. If you subtract 100 a day, you'll lose (on average) 10 pounds that year. So if you're serious about watching calories, cooking for yourself really is the best way to know what you're eating.

Same Day, Different Source, Different Data

While it was amazing to me to see how nutritional data for certain items changed from day to day, sometimes I found conflicting sets of data at the same time. For example, one day I was searching for nutritional data on El Pollo Loco's Web site. When I used their meal calculator and selected their plain Cheese Quesadilla, it said that it is 6 ounces and has 494 calories, 36 g protein, 43 g carbohydrates, 43 g fat, 13 g sat. fat, and 2 g fiber. But then, when I downloaded the pdf version of their nutritional guide, it said that the same item weighed less (5.7 ounces to be exact), but had almost 50 more calories and 17 fewer grams of fat. So what's going on here? Is it 5.7 or 6 ounces? I thought that by ordering a few quesadillas, my questions would be cleared up. But instead, when I ordered them, they averaged only 5.4 ounces, which is different than either of the above.

I had a similar experience with Jack in the Box's Fish and Chips. When I clicked on the "Chicken and Fish" box to get the nutritional analysis for the Fish and Chips, a window popped up listing the dishes, including the Fish and Chips. It said, in addition to a disclaimer, that the Fish and Chips weighs 303.2 grams, has 887.3 calories, 18.4 g protein, 62.3 g carbohydrates, 62.8 g fat, 13 g sat. fat, and 4.3 g fiber. Seconds later, when I used the "Build Your Meal" calculator on the same site and selected one order of Fish and Chips (again with no amendments), it said that the Fish and Chips weighs 252 g and has 681 calories, 18 g protein, 60 g carbohydrates, 41 g fat, 10 g sat. fat, and 4 g fiber. That's a difference of 51 g in weight, 206 calories, almost 22 g of fat, and 3 g of sat. fat, yet there is a difference of only 2.3 carbohydrates and 0.4 g of protein. The ironic thing, again (yet this is even more extreme), is that the average serving we actually received was 231 grams, which is considerably smaller than either listed. So basically, one version has relatively the same nutrient value as the other but is much more laden with fat. My mind jumps to the same place: "What am I actually eating?"

Sometimes It Just Doesn't Add Up

On several occasions, in an effort to provide the most-exact comparisons possible, I was surprised to find the nutritional analysis didn't always match up with the foods I was trying to re-create. For example, when I purchased my first three

Subway Chipotle Southwest Cheese Steaks (from three different Subway locations), I pulled the sandwiches apart, then rebuilt them as I always did. They looked great and tasted great. But when I ran the numbers in my nutritional program, mine had more calories and more fat than Subway's data suggested their sandwich actually has. Never mind that I used low-fat mayonnaise, light cheese, and the leanest beef possible—mine was more. How was this possible, I thought? Where did I go wrong?

I used a fine-tooth comb to go back over everything, but I was still stumped. So I went back to Subway's data sheet. When I compared the nutritional data for a complete sandwich to its component parts, I couldn't get the numbers to add up—in fact, the only conclusion I could draw was that maybe I'd made a mistake about the ingredients (most likely the amount of meat) in the sandwich.

So I took my scale and returned to Subway. Knowing that the meat is pre-portioned at my local Subway, I walked in, put my scale on the counter, and asked the sandwich specialist if I could weigh the meat. He immediately said, "It's 4 ounces." I said, "Do you mind if I weigh it?" He put the bag of meat on my scale, and we were both right. It was 4 ounces, cooked weight.

Knowing how many calories are in 4 ounces of even the leanest cooked meat (or even $3^3/_4$ less the onions and peppers, assuming that Subway would use the leanest beef possible) still left me wondering how this sandwich could possibly be correct as listed. So I spoke with Subway's customer service department and learned that the standard formula for a 6-inch steak sub is $2^1/_2$ ounces of meat and not 4 ounces.

At the time, I was surprised. Since all of the restaurants I'd visited had served my sandwich with 4 ounces of meat, I had been expecting to learn that there was an error in printing and that I was correct. So as a follow-up, I decided to call more than a dozen different Subway restaurants across the country to ask how much steak they put into this sandwich. And while 4 ounces seemed to be the standard in California, elsewhere in the country, most of the time restaurants reported being closer to the $2^1/_2$-ounce "standard."

Assuming these responses are correct—how I wish I could have carried my scale into all of them—I'm not convinced that there are $2^1/_2$ ounces in most Subway Chipotle Southwest Cheese Steak Sandwiches. Are you?

Of course, Subway was not the only restaurant that made my mind work on overdrive.

Popeyes Cajun Battered Fries were another source of major research. According to their Web site, they serve 88 grams of their regular (sometimes referred to as small) french fries (to my knowledge, they serve only Cajun Battered Fries). At the Popeyes on Santa Monica Boulevard and 26th Street in Santa Monica, this is not the case. Repeated ordering of these fries over months and months yielded an average order of 132 grams, not 88 grams. They serve them in a box that they line with paper. Even with the paper, the box looks pretty empty with 125 to 150 grams of fries in it, which is probably why the sizing is off. Wanting

BEWARE THE DISCLAIMERS

As you might expect, given the surprising variations I found in my own sleuthing for this book, most fast food restaurants provide a disclaimer of sorts on their nutritional data pamphlets and/or on their Web sites. I'd really like to list the actual phrases used among the various fast food restaurants, but in the interest of respecting their copyrights, instead, I'll strongly encourage you to visit their sites and read the disclaimers there on your own. In the meantime, however, below you'll find a brief summary of the collective content:

✳ Products were tested on a certain day in one area only (other locations of the same chain may have varying data).

✳ Product builds may change from time to time.

✳ Data may vary due to change in supplier.

✳ Data may vary if food is obtained from local suppliers.

✳ Data may vary if food is obtained from various suppliers.

✳ Data may vary based on the season of the year.

✳ Data may vary based on recipe revisions.

✳ Data assumes that franchise owner complies with procedures.

✳ Data is not applicable if product is purchased in Hawaii.

✳ Serving sizes may vary due to portioning.

✳ Serving sizes may vary due to product assembly.

✳ Serving sizes may not be the same as size of serving tested.

✳ The restaurant setting makes it impossible to provide precise data.

✳ Products may vary due to "other factors."

to make sure that this was not the case everywhere, I drove out of the areas of my regular travels. When I arrived at a second Popeyes, I was served 99 grams of fries, which filled the paper sleeve they were served in. Phew, I thought. It was only one location that was off. But then I proceeded to a third Popeyes, where my fries were again served in a box. The woman flattened the paper (at the first Popeyes it was scrunched to make the box fuller) and filled it about halfway. When she handed it to me, I asked if that was the smallest size she had. She said it was and charged me the price for the regular serving, not the large. I was anxious to return to my kitchen, knowing that this one was just going to be blatantly off (which I knew only because I had weighed differing amounts within days). It weighed 211 grams.

So, basically, if I were to have ordered those fries for the first time and didn't weigh them, I would have thought that I was eating 261 calories, 3 g protein, 34 g carbohydrates, 12 g fat, 5 g sat. fat, and 3 g of fiber. Instead, I would have actually been eating more than twice that amount (626 calories, 7 g protein, 82 g carbo-

A QUICK GUIDE TO THE SYMBOLS

You'll find that this book is loaded with dozens of hints and suggestions to help make the recipes as easy to follow as possible. Plus, the tips have symbols next to them so they're quick to find. Here's a rundown of what each symbol means:

All recipes that you see with this symbol can be made in 30 minutes or less. There are 58 of them in this book!

Drive Thru Looking for a way to make the dish even faster? The drive-thru tips shave even more time off the clock, making some recipes speedier than old-fashioned take-out.

Even Better It's always possible to make a good thing even better. If you're keeping a close eye on your calories, look for these tips to find ways to make your fast food favorites even lower in calories.

Before You Start Especially if you're new to cooking, look carefully for these tips beforehand. This is where you'll find really helpful information about where to find special ingredients at the grocery store, as well as how to work around any equipment challenges, like not having an extra-large nonstick skillet.

hydrates, 29 g fat, 12 g sat. fat, 7 g fiber). That's a difference of 365 calories, 17 g fat, and 7 g sat. fat!

Now please do not think that I am suggesting that any of these companies print any of this information with malicious or ill intent. I do not think they are trying to deceive us. No one is sitting around saying, "Hey, if we serve a bigger order of fries, we can make them all fatter." From their perspective, it is really tough, perhaps even impossible, and expensive to stay on top of everything. They need to constantly change suppliers so they get better or competitive pricing; crops change; they can't control whether an employee had a really bad day and wasn't quite as diligent as they'd hoped; and they can't ensure that chicken breasts of the exact same size are available day after day.

And it's not just the companies listed above. In my research, I was shocked at the discrepancies of certain items when ordering them just once. Most of the time, most would be the same, but every once in a while, some item would be ridiculously off. In these cases, my assistants and I tried to go to even more chains to see just how off they were. If we just couldn't figure out what they were supposed to look like, we re-created the final versions to have relatively the same number of grams of protein and carbohydrates as the serving we received.

Apparently, it's with good reason that some companies go so far as to say that their data should not be depended on to reveal concrete information. I don't know about you, but I feel much better about leaving my scale in my kitchen, enjoying fast food flavors, and knowing that my body will feel great when I do so. I hope you do, too.

HERE'S THE BEEF

There's nothing like a juicy, succulent burger . . . especially if it's a lean one that you won't feel guilty about enjoying. Though we're led to believe that fat is what makes a burger great, it's simply not true. With a few cooking tips, you'll be shocked at how great a burger made from extra-lean ground beef can taste!

What Goes Into the Perfect Burger?

Burger Buns

When you go to the grocery store, you'll notice that the labels on some packages of buns actually read "hamburger buns," while others that look similar (but are usually larger) are called "sandwich buns." If you're a stickler for nutritional analyses and want to duplicate the restaurant versions as closely as possible, it's best to try to find the correct buns. Since I don't actually expect anyone else to carry a tape measure to the grocery store (I really did), I've read the packages carefully to help you find the right one. When the recipe calls for:

Hamburger bun or sesame seed hamburger bun: Look for packages that simply say "hamburger buns" or "sesame seed hamburger buns," respectively. These buns are generally 3½" in diameter; they tend to be easy to find and are generally available in sesame seed, white, or whole wheat varieties.

Sandwich bun or sesame seed sandwich bun (about 5"): Look for packages labeled "sandwich buns" or "sesame seed sandwich buns," respectively. They are clearly considerably larger than the buns labeled "hamburger buns."

Restaurant-style sesame seed bun (size varies): In some cases, the bun that will really make the perfect sandwich falls somewhere between 3½" and 5". And oddly enough, in all my research, I found that these buns were most often labeled "restaurant-style" or sometimes "Texas style."

Kaiser-style hamburger bun (about 4"): Unlike standard kaiser rolls, usually found fresh-baked in the bakery section, kaiser-style buns are generally found bagged with the hamburger buns. Often, the packages will simply say "sandwich buns" or "bakery buns." But you'll be able to tell that they're kaiser-style, because they will have the distinct "pinwheel" look of kaiser rolls versus the smooth top of a hamburger bun.

Cheese

Although most available light cheese singles found in grocery stores are ¾-ounce each, it seems to me that most fast food restaurants use ½-ounce cheese slices on their burgers and sandwiches. In cases where the recipes call for ½-ounce slices, if you don't find them readily available, simply purchase ¾-ounce slices and then put only two-thirds of the slice on your sandwich or burger. It will still cover most of the surface area of the burger or sandwich, and you won't have to go on a wild-goose chase.

HOW TO COOK THE PERFECT BURGER

I like to think of three Ss when I'm cooking a burger: Salt, Sear, and Smash (as in, don't!).

1. Salt—true, we need to watch our sodium intake, but a little salt on the outside of these burgers won't hurt (unless you have high blood pressure or your doctor has told you not to eat salt, in which case, listen to him or her, not me). Salt acts with the proteins in meat and seafood to help it plump and become juicier. You need only a little, but it makes a huge difference, so if you don't have a good reason to omit it, don't.

2. Sear—I always recommend cooking a burger on medium-high heat. This technique sears the burger nicely and helps to guarantee the best flavor and texture. If the burger starts to get too charred or browned on the outside (this will really happen only if you make thick burgers and like them pretty well done or in the case of turkey or chicken burgers, where they must be well done), lower the heat to medium or medium-low after both sides are seared. The most important thing to note is that when you place a burger in a pan or on a grill, it should make a sizzling noise (test the heat by first putting a few drops of water in the pan). If you don't hear a sizzle, remove the burger immediately and wait until your cooking surface is hot enough.

3. Smash . . . as in, don't!—How many times have you been to a barbecue only to watch some sexy guy (or gal) quickly become unsexy because he (or she) is smashing the juice out of the burger you're waiting to eat? Okay, maybe that's happened only to me . . . and a few of my boy-crazed, foodie girlfriends. Seriously, though, there is a widespread misconception that smashing burgers is a good idea because it will remove the excess fat. True, it does, in fact, remove some of the fat . . . along with most of the juice. The whole goal is to keep the juices in the burger. If you're buying the leanest cuts of meat (you should be; you're worth it!), there isn't a whole lot of fat in there. However, there is enough juice that if you treat the burger right, I promise you'll need a napkin to eat it (my personal test of a good burger).

Bacon

I always buy center-cut bacon. It is meatier and thus contains less fat than standard or thick-cut bacon. I also always cook my bacon well. Not only do I actually prefer it crispy, but more of the fat gets removed if it is cooked until it is crisped. Most fast food restaurants cook their bacon way too little for my personal taste. It's more chewy than crispy. The recipes contained within this book are written to mimic the original dishes as closely as possible, so the recipes generally instruct that the bacon not be cooked until it is crisped. However, if you're like me and you prefer your bacon to be cooked more, I encourage you to do so.

MCDONALD'S: BIG MAC

SAVE: 174 CALORIES, 19 G FAT, 7 G SAT. FAT

The key to re-creating the Big Mac is obviously perfecting the sauce. Some say it's simply Thousand Island, but the clever folks at McDonald's deserve much more credit for this masterpiece we crave.

In order to re-create the sauce, I had to ensure that I had a supply that I could taste on its own—away from the other great flavors this burger stacks. So I requested "extra on the side." The friendly woman behind the counter didn't flinch. She quickly produced a sundae cup half-filled with the neon, salmon-colored sauce. When I took a big sniff, all I could smell was a chemicalesque aroma. Tasting, on the other hand, yielded that wonderful flavor. Several tastings and I was convinced. The secret ingredient? Mustard. Simple yellow mustard. Add that and a pinch of sugar to a Thousand Island–style sauce, and you'll be surprised how closely it resembles the real deal.

> 3 ounces 96% lean ground beef (about 1/3 cup)
>
> 2 pinches of salt
>
> 1 sesame seed hamburger bun + 1 bun bottom
>
> 1 slice (1/2 ounce) 2% milk yellow American cheese
>
> 1 tablespoon + 1 teaspoon + 1 tablespoon McDonald's Big Mac Sauce (opposite page)
>
> 1 teaspoon finely chopped white onion
>
> 1/3 cup shredded iceberg lettuce
>
> 2 rounds dill pickle

DIVIDE the beef in half. On a sheet of waxed paper, shape each half into a 4" patty. Season both sides with salt. Transfer the waxed paper to a plate. Place, uncovered, in the freezer for 5 minutes.

Preheat a large nonstick skillet over medium-high heat until drops of water sizzle when splashed on the pan. Place the patties in the pan. Cook for 1 to 2 minutes per side, or until no longer pink. Meanwhile, place the bun top and bottoms, cut-sides down, in the pan. Cook for about 1 minute, or until toasted. (If the pan is not large enough to hold the patties and the buns, first cook 1 patty with the bottom bun and then start assembling the sandwich while the others cook.) Just before the patties are cooked, place the cheese on 1 patty.

Place 1 bun bottom on a plate. Spread on 1 tablespoon sauce. Place the cheeseburger, cheese-side down, on the bun. Spread 1 teaspoon sauce on the second bun bottom and place, sauce-side down, on the cheeseburger. Top with the remaining 1 table-spoon sauce, the onion, lettuce, pickles, the remaining burger, and the bun top.

MAKES 1 SERVING

386 calories, 26 g protein, 44 g carbohydrates, 11 g fat, 3 g sat. fat, 2 g fiber

Original McDonald's Big Mac: 560 calories, 25 g protein, 47 g carbohydrates, 30 g fat, 10 g sat. fat, 3 g fiber

DRIVE-THRU It's easy to throw together a Big Mac–like burger in minutes once you have the sauce made. So to save time, make a big batch of the sauce, omitting the onions (they are the only ingredient that will spoil quickly). Refrigerate the sauce in a plastic container for up to 1 month. When you're ready to enjoy a burger, simply add the correct quantity of onion to the amount of sauce you're using.

EVEN BETTER Save time and calories by omitting the second bun bottom and simply making 1 patty instead of 2 with the 3 ounces of beef. This way, you'll need only 1½ tablespoons of sauce. You'll be left with a more nutritionally balanced burger. Plus, you'll still have room for some fries or a side salad, all the while still enjoying that great Big Mac flavor ... in minutes.

The revised version will have 310 calories, 24 g protein, 31 g carbohydrates, 9 g fat, 1 g sat. fat, and 1 g fiber. You'll save 250 calories, 21 g fat, and 9 g sat. fat over the original.

MCDONALD'S BIG MAC SAUCE

⅓ cup low-fat mayonnaise

2 teaspoons dill pickle relish

2 teaspoons ketchup

2 teaspoons sugar

2 teaspoons yellow mustard

1 tablespoon + 1 teaspoon finely chopped white onion

IN a small bowl, combine the mayonnaise, relish, ketchup, sugar, and mustard. Stir to blend well. Cover and refrigerate for up to 1 month.

Stir in the onion just before serving.

MAKES ABOUT ⅔ CUP, ENOUGH FOR 4 SERVINGS

Each serving: 49 calories, trace protein, 6 g carbohydrates, 3 g fat, trace sat. fat, trace fiber

IN-N-OUT BURGER: DOUBLE-DOUBLE WITH ONION

SAVE: 282 CALORIES, 26 G FAT, 13 G SAT. FAT

Though In-N-Out is found only in California, Nevada, and Arizona, it has a huge presence. Known for its fresh ingredients with no preservatives, it's a bit of a secret society . . . when I made it up to In-N-Out's drive-thru window, it appeared that they serve only a few menu items. Later, I learned that they serve many more options. You just have to know to ask.

The oddest thing, though, was that when I arrived at In-N-Out for the first time, I couldn't believe my eyes. The line was so long, you'd think they were giving the burgers away. It took me 43 minutes to get my burger in hand. Forty-three minutes for fast food . . . not including driving time. Based on the quality and taste, I can see why In-N-Out is all the rage in California, but I grocery shopped for and cooked my version of the burger in less time. Mine also happened to have the fresh ingredients but 26 fewer grams of fat.

> 4 ounces 96% lean ground beef (about ½ cup)
>
> Pinch of salt
>
> 1 hamburger bun
>
> 1 tablespoon In-N-Out Secret Sauce (opposite page)
>
> 1 slice tomato (¼" thick)
>
> ¼ cup coarsely chopped iceberg lettuce
>
> 2 slices (½ ounce each) 2% milk yellow American cheese, divided
>
> 1 slice onion (¼" thick)

DIVIDE the beef in half. On a sheet of waxed paper, shape each half into a 4" patty. Season both sides lightly with salt.

Preheat a large nonstick skillet over medium-high heat until drops of water sizzle when splashed on the pan. Place the patties in the pan. Cook for 1 to 2 minutes per side, or until the patties are browned but still slightly pink inside. Meanwhile, place the bun top and bottom, cut-sides down, in the pan. Cook for 2 to 3 minutes, or until toasted.

Place the bun bottom, toasted side up, on a plate. Top with the sauce, tomato, and lettuce. Place 1 burger over the lettuce. Top with 1 slice of cheese and the onion. Place the remaining burger over the onion. Top with the remaining slice of cheese and the bun top.

MAKES 1 SERVING

388 calories, 33 g protein, 30 g carbohydrates, 15 g fat, 5 g sat. fat, 2 g fiber

Original In-N-Out Burger Double-Double with Onion: 670 calories, 37 g protein, 39 g carbohydrates, 41 g fat, 18 g sat. fat, 3 g fiber

DRIVE-THRU If you're a follower of the **Double-Double,** mix up a big batch of the sauce and store it in your refrigerator so it's ready to go on demand. That's the only part of this burger that really takes any time.

IN-N-OUT SECRET SAUCE

¼ cup light mayonnaise

2 teaspoons ketchup

2 teaspoons drained dill relish

IN a small bowl, combine the mayonnaise, ketchup, and relish. Stir to blend well. Cover and refrigerate for up to 1 month.

MAKES ¼ CUP, ENOUGH FOR 4 SERVINGS

Each Serving: 50 calories, trace protein, 2 g carbohydrates, 4.5 g fat, <1 g sat. fat, trace fiber

WENDY'S: BIG BACON CLASSIC

SAVE: 176 CALORIES, 15 G FAT, 7 G SAT. FAT

Everyone knows that Wendy's burgers are square, right? So imagine my surprise when I arrived home with my first Big Bacon Classic and the burger was rectangular. Granted, in my days of frequenting Wendy's, I'd never ordered one. Maybe they weren't all square? Perhaps they just had square edges.

I called a local Wendy's to inquire and learned that, in fact, all of Wendy's burgers are square. Hey, I got a bum burger. I drove to another chain and picked up another Big Bacon Classic. When I opened the wrapping, I started to wonder if I was in the Twilight Zone. The second burger was rectangular. How could that be? I decided to proceed, regardless, and broke apart the burgers: weighed them, measured them, etc. I took a guess at the proper dimensions, put the patty in my frying pan, and . . . uh . . . my perfectly square patty morphed into a rectangle as it cooked.

I think you, too, will enjoy watching this burger go from a square to a rectangle every time. Oh, and I should mention that I was surprised at how little mayonnaise and ketchup are on this burger.

3 ounces 96% lean ground beef (about $\frac{1}{3}$ cup)

$\frac{1}{8}$ teaspoon salt

2 slices center-cut bacon

1 kaiser-style hamburger bun (about 4")

1 slice ($\frac{1}{2}$ ounce) 2% milk yellow American cheese

1 large leaf iceberg lettuce

1 slice tomato ($\frac{1}{4}$" thick)

5 pieces from 1 slice small white onion ($\frac{1}{4}$" thick)

1 teaspoon light mayonnaise

$\frac{1}{4}$ teaspoon ketchup

5 rounds dill pickle

ON a sheet of waxed paper, shape the beef into a $4\frac{1}{2}$" square patty. Lightly season both sides with salt. Transfer the waxed paper to a plate. Place, uncovered, in the freezer for 5 minutes.

Lay the bacon slices in a small nonstick skillet set over medium heat. Cook, flipping occasionally, for 4 to 6 minutes, or until cooked but not crisp. Transfer to a paper towel–lined plate to drain. Cover to keep warm.

Discard the bacon fat. Off the heat, carefully wipe the skillet clean with several thicknesses of paper towels. Preheat the pan over medium-high heat until drops of water sizzle when splashed on the pan. Place the patty in the pan. Cook for 1 to 2 minutes per side, or until no longer pink.

Place the bun bottom on a plate. Top with the burger, cheese, bacon, lettuce, tomato, and onion. Spread the mayonnaise on the cut side of the bun top. Dollop on the ketchup. Place the pickles over the mayonnaise mixture. Flip onto the sandwich.

MAKES 1 SERVING

404 calories, 31 g protein, 42 g carbohydrates, 14 g fat, 5 g sat. fat, 4 g fiber

Original Wendy's Big Bacon Classic: 580 calories, 35 g protein, 46 g carbohydrates, 29 g fat, 12 g sat. fat, 3 g fiber

WHITE CASTLE: SLYDERS

SAVE: 262 CALORIES, 38 G FAT, 11 G SAT. FAT

White Castle Hamburgers, also known as Slyders, are much smaller than most burgers, which is part of White Castle's signature. But how many Slyders does the average person eat per sitting? And how many *should* the average person eat per sitting? I asked a clerk at one White Castle near Nashville, Tennessee, who voiced a strong opinion: "There's no way I could answer that."

Having never previously been to a White Castle, I decided to use the menu as a guide. If you order Slyders as part of a meal, 1 regular fries and 1 regular drink is served with 4 Slyders; 2 regular fries and drinks are served with 10; and 4 regular fries and drinks are served with 20. Thus, I've deduced that a typical serving is between 4 and 5 Slyders . . . though a couple of my friends who frequent White Castle have confessed that they've been known to eat upward of 10 in a sitting if they weren't eating fries. I can see where one would want to do that based on the unique, wonderfully oniony taste of these baby burgers, but . . . wow!

> 5 ounces 96% lean ground beef (about 1/2 cup + 2 tablespoons)
>
> Salt and ground black pepper
>
> 1/2 cup water + additional, if needed
>
> 1 1/2 tablespoons dehydrated minced onion
>
> 5 square dinner rolls (about 2 1/2")
>
> 5 rounds dill pickle

LINE a medium baking sheet (one that will fit in the freezer) with a sheet of waxed paper.

Divide the beef into 5 equal portions. On the baking sheet, shape each portion into a 3 1/4" square patty. With a drinking straw, cut 5 holes from each patty—one in the center, and one halfway between each corner and the center hole. Press the straw straight into the patty, then twist to cut each hole. Lightly season both sides of the patties with salt and pepper. Place, uncovered, in the freezer for 5 minutes.

In an extra-large nonstick skillet, combine 1/2 cup water and the onion. Cook over medium heat until the mixture slowly comes to a boil. Boil, stirring occasionally, for about 3 minutes, or until the onion is soft. A thin layer of water should remain. If needed, add up to 2 tablespoons of water. Place the patties in a single layer over the onion. Cook for about 1 minute, or until the bottoms are browned and the edges are just starting to brown. Meanwhile, place 1 roll bottom, cut-side down, on top of each burger. Place 1 roll top, cut-side down, on top of each roll bottom. When the beef is no longer pink, remove the roll tops and set aside. Slide a spatula under 1 portion of onion, 1 burger, and 1 roll bottom. Flip the stack onto a plate. Place 1 round of pickle on the center of the burger. Cover with the roll top. Repeat with the remaining burgers, pickles, and roll tops.

MAKES 1 SERVING (5 BURGERS)

438 calories, 43 g protein, 41 g carbohydrates, 11 g fat, 4 g sat. fat, 2 g fiber

Original White Castle Slyders (5 burgers): 700 calories, 30 g protein, 65 g carbohydrates, 49 g fat, 15 g sat. fat, fiber (not available)

DRIVE-THRU To make these miniature favorites even faster, you can shape a big batch of the patties to store in the freezer for up to 3 months. Layer them, between sheets of waxed paper, in a plastic container. They'll always be ready to go because there's no need to thaw them before cooking. They'll take only an extra minute or two to steam. In fact, if you also have the rolls in the freezer and dried onion on hand, you can definitely make these in less time than it takes to find your keys and walk to your car, let alone stand in line at **White Castle.**

EVEN BETTER Think about eliminating one or two of the rolls and making a double burger or two. Or skip one of the burgers altogether. For each roll you don't eat, you'll cut **50 calories** and **1 gram of fat.** For each burger you don't eat, you'll save about **32 calories** and **1 gram of fat.**

BEFORE YOU START You'll need an extra-large nonstick skillet to cook all five burgers at once. If you don't have one, simply cook the onions and burgers in two batches, taking care that each batch is a single layer. Transfer the first batch to a plate. Cover to keep warm while the second batch cooks. You'll also need a drinking straw to create the perfect holes.

JACK IN THE BOX: BACON ULTIMATE CHEESEBURGER

SAVE: 507 CALORIES, 54 G FAT, 21 G SAT. FAT

Bacon, bacon, bacon, bacon, bacon, Swiss, American, and plenty of beef . . . now that's a combo. In fact, it's a combo I would never have conjured on my own.

I had an ex-boyfriend who loved (and I mean *loved*) the Jack in the Box commercials. You know, the ones that have "Jack," a man with an ordinary body but a big white globe of a head and the funny yellow cone-shaped hat. Granted, I agree they're clever and probably more memorable than most fast food commercials . . . except, perhaps, the one with a half-naked Paris Hilton, but that's a whole other topic.

Anyway, if you're a person who dreams about bacon, you really can't beat this tower of flavors.

6 ounces 96% lean ground beef (about ¾ cup)

Pinch of salt

5 slices center-cut bacon, halved crosswise

1 restaurant-style sesame seed bun (about 4")

½ tablespoon yellow mustard

1 slice (½ ounce) low-fat Swiss-style cheese

1 slice (½ ounce) 2% milk yellow American cheese

1 teaspoon light mayonnaise

1 teaspoon ketchup

DIVIDE the beef in half. On a sheet of waxed paper, shape each half into a 5" patty. Season both sides lightly with salt. Transfer the waxed paper to a plate. Place, uncovered, in the freezer for 5 minutes.

Lay the bacon slices side by side in a small nonstick skillet set over medium heat. Cook, flipping occasionally, for 4 to 6 minutes, or until cooked but not crisp. Transfer the bacon to a paper towel–lined plate to drain. Cover to keep warm.

Preheat a large nonstick skillet over medium-high heat until drops of water sizzle when splashed on the pan. Place the patties and the bun top and bottom, cut-sides down, in the pan. Cook for 2 to 4 minutes, flipping the burgers halfway through, or until the beef is no longer pink and the buns are toasted.

Place the bun bottom on a plate. Top with half of the reserved bacon, 1 burger, mustard, Swiss-style cheese, the remaining burger, American cheese, and the remaining bacon. Spread the mayonnaise evenly over the toasted side of the top bun. Spread the ketchup over the mayonnaise. Flip onto the sandwich.

MAKES 1 SERVING

587 calories, 56 g protein, 41 g carbohydrates, 23 g fat, 9 g sat. fat, 3 g fiber

Original Jack in the Box Bacon Ultimate Cheeseburger: 1,094 calories, 46 g protein, 53 g carbohydrates, 77 g fat, 30 g sat. fat, 2 g fiber

EVEN BETTER This burger is larger than a single meal should be for anyone. If you love these flavors, try reducing the beef to 4 ounces and the bacon to 2 slices. You'll be left with a sizable burger, and you'll still get bacon in every bite. Also, consider picking your favorite cheese and using only a slice. The result will be a bacon cheeseburger that has 418 calories, 36 g protein, 41 g carbohydrates, 14 g fat, 4 g sat. fat, and 3 g fiber. You'll save 676 calories, 63 g fat, and 26 g sat. fat.

BEFORE YOU START Look in the packaged rolls aisle in the supermarket for restaurant-style sesame seed buns, which are wider than standard buns. They are sometimes called Texas-style sesame seed buns. Also, you'll need a large nonstick skillet to cook the whole sandwich at once. If the patties and buns don't all fit in a single layer in your pan, cook one patty and toast the bun bottom first, then start assembling the sandwich as the others cook.

CARL'S JR.: SIX DOLLAR BURGER

SAVE: 397 CALORIES, 43 G FAT, 18 G SAT. FAT

As if a single burger with close to 960 calories and 62 grams of fat were not enough, the crew at Carl's Jr. followed their Six Dollar Burger with the creation of their Double Six Dollar Burger, guaranteed to contain "a full pound of Angus beef." Perhaps they haven't noticed that you can barely flip channels for 10 minutes or pick up a newspaper in this country without hearing of the growing obesity epidemic facing more and more Americans daily?

Let's stick with the original, shall we?

Olive oil spray (optional)

6 ounces 96% lean ground beef (about ¾ cup)

Garlic salt

1 restaurant-style sesame seed bun (about 4½")

1 slice (½ ounce) 2% milk yellow American cheese

1 tablespoon light mayonnaise, divided

3 rounds crinkle-cut pickle

2 large leaves iceberg lettuce

2 slices tomato (¼" thick)

5 very thinly sliced red onion rings

1 tablespoon ketchup

½ tablespoon yellow mustard

PREHEAT the grill or a nonstick stove-top grill pan. Lightly mist the grill rack or pan with oil spray, if needed.

On a sheet of waxed paper, shape the beef into a 5½" patty. Lightly season both sides with garlic salt to taste. Place the patty on the grill rack or grill pan. Cook for 3 to 5 minutes per side, or until no longer pink.

Meanwhile, place the bun top and bottom, cut-sides down, on the grill rack or grill pan. Cook for about 1 minute, or until toasted. Place the cheese on the patty.

Place the bun bottom on a plate. Spread with ½ tablespoon mayonnaise. Top with the pickles, lettuce, tomato, onion, and the burger. Spread the remaining ½ tablespoon mayonnaise on the toasted side of the bun top. Spread on the ketchup and mustard. Flip onto the sandwich.

MAKES 1 SERVING

563 calories, 47 g protein, 51 g carbohydrates, 19 g fat, 7 g sat. fat, 3 g fiber

Original Carl's Jr. Six Dollar Burger: 960 calories, 38 g protein, 61 g carbohydrates, 62 g fat, 25 g sat. fat, 3 g fiber

HARDEE'S: ⅓-LB WESTERN BACON THICKBURGER

SAVE: 223 CALORIES, 31 G FAT, 16 G SAT. FAT

Okay, so it's not like I'm going to claim that anyone could make this recipe at home quicker than they could get the burger at the drive-thru (unless you live really far from Hardee's, like I do, which is highly possible since it is a regional chain). But I've decided to include it for those onion lovers out there because it truly is an onion-lover's paradise—plus one might argue that no one should be eating an 876-calorie meal that includes 50 grams of fat. But rest assured that if you want a burger and onion rings, you can make any of the onion rings from the book and simply tear some of them to use on this burger.

This is a great one to do with the kids—just be sure you have them share it. This burger is way too big for 1 person, even my version.

ONION STRINGS

Olive oil spray

1 slice small sweet onion (⅓" thick)

2 tablespoons egg substitute

3 tablespoons dry bread crumbs

¼ teaspoon salt

BURGER

2 slices center-cut bacon

½ cup sweet onion strips (sliced ¼" thick and 1" long)

5⅓ ounces (⅓ pound) 96% lean ground beef (about ⅔ cup)

¼ teaspoon salt

Olive oil spray

1 sesame seed sandwich bun (about 5")

2½ tablespoons Hardee's BBQ Sauce (page 35), divided

1 slice (½ ounce) 2% milk yellow American cheese

TO prepare the onion strings: Preheat the oven to 400°F. Lightly mist a nonstick baking sheet with oil spray.

Cut the onion slice in half crosswise. Separate the pieces. Measure about ¼ cup. Save the remainder for another recipe. Place the egg substitute in a small shallow bowl. In a medium resealable plastic bag, combine the bread crumbs and salt. Shake the bag to mix.

(continued)

One at a time, dip each onion piece into the egg-substitute mixture, being sure to coat completely. Allow any excess egg-substitute mixture to drip off. Drop into the bag. Shake the bag to completely coat the onion with the bread crumb mixture. Repeat dipping into the egg-substitute mixture and tossing in the bread crumb mixture. Place the onion pieces on the reserved baking sheet in a single layer so they don't touch. Lightly mist with oil spray.

Bake on the lower oven rack for 6 minutes. Carefully flip the onion pieces. Bake for 7 to 10 minutes, or until the breading is crisp and the onions are tender.

TO prepare the burger: Place the bacon in a small nonstick skillet set over medium heat. Cook for about 1 minute, or until some of the bacon fat melts. Add the onion strips next to the bacon. Cook, flipping the bacon occasionally, for 4 to 6 minutes, or until the bacon is cooked but not crisp and the onion is tender but not browned. Transfer the bacon to a paper towel–lined plate to drain. Cover to keep warm. Move the pan with the onions off the heat. Set aside.

On a sheet of waxed paper, shape the beef into a 6" patty. Season both sides with the salt.

Preheat the grill or a nonstick stove-top grill pan. Lightly mist the grill rack or pan with oil spray, if needed. Place the patty on the grill rack or grill pan. Cook for 2 to 4 minutes per side, or until no longer pink. Meanwhile, place the bun top and bottom, cut-sides down, on the grill rack. Cook for about 1 minute, or until toasted.

Place the bun bottom on a plate, toasted side up. Top with 1 tablespoon barbecue sauce, the Onion Strings, the burger, and the cheese. Lay the bacon slices cross-wise over the cheese. Top with the reserved onions from the bacon pan. Spread the remaining 1½ tablespoons barbecue sauce onto the cut-side of the bun top. Flip onto the sandwich.

MAKES 1 SERVING

653 calories, 52 g protein, 71 g carbohydrates, 19 g fat, 7 g sat. fat, 5 g fiber

Original Hardee's ⅓-Lb Western Bacon Thickburger: 876 calories, 34 g protein, 70 g carbohydrates, 50 g fat, 23 g sat. fat, fiber (not available)

 EVEN BETTER This burger could be just as out-of-this-world without being too big for one. Instead, make 2 servings by using 2 regular hamburger buns instead of an oversize one. Make 2 burgers (4 ounces each) instead of 1 burger weighing 5⅓ ounces, and add another ½-ounce slice of cheese. Divide the bacon, sautéed onion, and Onion Strings between the 2 burgers. Top each burger with 1½ tablespoons of BBQ Sauce. The resulting burger, with all of the same hearty flavors, has **406 calories, 35 g protein, 42 g carbohydrates, 12 g fat, 4 g sat. fat, and 3 g fiber.** You'll save **470 calories, 38 g fat, and 19 g sat. fat.**

BEFORE YOU START If you're a stickler for authenticity like I am, you may want to tuck a tape measure into your pocket before you head to the supermarket. A burger this grand needs a sesame seed sandwich bun bigger than the average—5" to be exact.

HARDEE'S BBQ SAUCE

¼ cup tomato paste

2 tablespoons + 2 teaspoons light brown sugar

2 tablespoons soy sauce

1 tablespoon + 1 teaspoon water

1 tablespoon + 1 teaspoon liquid smoke

2 teaspoons apple cider vinegar

2 teaspoons molasses

½ teaspoon salt

¼ teaspoon ground black pepper

¼ teaspoon garlic powder

¼ teaspoon onion powder

IN a small bowl, combine the tomato paste, sugar, soy sauce, water, liquid smoke, vinegar, molasses, salt, pepper, garlic powder, and onion powder. With a whisk or a spoon, stir until well blended. Cover the bowl with plastic wrap or transfer to a jar. Refrigerate for up to 1 month.

MAKES ½ CUP + 2 TABLESPOONS, ENOUGH FOR 4 SERVINGS

Each serving: 54 calories, 2 g protein, 12 g carbohydrates, trace fat, 0 g sat. fat, 0.5 g fiber

BACK YARD BURGERS: BLACK JACK BURGER

SAVE: 201 CALORIES, 27 G FAT, 10 G SAT. FAT

The adventure of making this burger was probably the most fun of any for me . . . and most embarrassing for my friend Jamie. I arrived in Nashville, where he'd kindly invited me to be his houseguest while working on the recipes from the region—little did he know that I was going to completely take over his bachelor kitchen.

He'd mentioned that the closest Back Yard Burgers was near the airport, so I arrived prepared: food scale tucked into my purse, and ruler and waxed paper sticking out of it. When I explained that we'd need to pull the burger apart and weigh and measure its components in the restaurant, he looked horrified. I gave him a giant grin and then immediately popped out of the car with the energy of an eager student on the first day of school.

After asking the staff way too many questions for Jamie's comfort, I secured my burgers with plenty of extra sauce on the side. We went to the back of the restaurant, and I pulled out my equipment as I began to break the burgers apart, explaining my procedure to Jamie. It was obvious that I wasn't going unnoticed by either the customers or the staff, but we didn't flinch. We finished the measurements, rewrapped the burgers, and escaped without incident . . . phew.

> 1 tablespoon low-fat mayonnaise
>
> ½ teaspoon Creole mustard
>
> 5⅓ ounces (⅓ pound) 96% lean ground beef (about ⅔ cup)
>
> ½ teaspoon Creole or Cajun blackening seasoning
>
> ¼ teaspoon salt
>
> 1 hamburger bun (about 3¾")
>
> 1 slice (½ ounce) 2% milk pepper jack cheese single
>
> 1 slice tomato (¼" thick)
>
> 1 leaf green lettuce

IN a small bowl, combine the mayonnaise and mustard. Stir to mix well. Set aside.

On a sheet of waxed paper, shape the beef into a 4½" somewhat square-shaped patty. Season each side with the Creole or Cajun seasoning and salt.

Preheat a medium nonstick skillet over medium-high heat until drops of water sizzle when splashed on the pan. Place the patty in the pan. Cook for 2 minutes per side, or until no longer pink. Meanwhile, place the bun top and bottom, cut-sides down, in the pan. Cook for 2 to 3 minutes, or until toasted.

Place the bun bottom, toasted side up, on a plate. Spread with ½ teaspoon of the mayonnaise mixture. Top with the burger, cheese, tomato, and lettuce. Spread the remaining 1 tablespoon mayonnaise mixture on the toasted side of the bun top. Flip onto the sandwich.

MAKES 1 SERVING

379 calories, 37 g protein, 31 g carbohydrates, 12 g fat, 4 g sat. fat, 1 g fiber

Original Back Yard Burgers Black Jack Burger: 580 calories, 31 g protein, 36 g carbohydrates, 39 g fat, 14 g sat. fat, 2 g fiber

STOP BEFORE YOU START After learning that **Back Yard Burgers** uses pepper jack singles on its burger, I wondered how I would find a reduced-fat version. As it turns out, reduced-fat pepper jack singles are relatively easy to find in supermarkets in the South. It seems that pepper jack is more in demand because it's widely used in that region. If the singles aren't available in your area, simply buy a block of reduced-fat jack and cut it into thin ½-ounce slices. The finished burger will definitely taste just as great.

ORIGINAL TOMMY'S: BURGER

SAVE: 141 CALORIES, 14 G FAT, 5 G SAT. FAT

Though Original Tommy's is found only in California, it was undeniably worth including, as it has not only been a fixture in Los Angeles since 1946, but it's the only fast food restaurant I've heard of where all burgers are chili burgers of sorts. Yep, their hamburger is served with chili unless you request it without. And their dedication to chili goes even further . . . they'll give you extra without even charging you if you ask for it.

It's also worth noting that Original Tommy's has a disclaimer on their Web site you must click on before you can see the rest of the site. The important part of it states that no one should count on the numbers being correct; they're more of a ballpark estimate. I definitely found this true of Tommy's burgers, as the serving size did vary greatly—though every bite was as delicious as the first.

> 2½ ounces 96% lean ground beef (about ¼ cup + 1 tablespoon)
>
> Pinch of salt
>
> 1 hamburger bun (about 3¾")
>
> ¼ cup Original Tommy's Chili Topping, heated (opposite page)
>
> 1 slice (½ ounce) 2% milk yellow American cheese
>
> 1 tablespoon finely chopped white onion
>
> 3 rounds dill pickle
>
> 1 slice tomato (⅓" thick)
>
> 1 teaspoon yellow mustard

ON a sheet of waxed paper, shape the beef into a 4" patty. Lightly season both sides with salt. Transfer the waxed paper to a plate. Place, uncovered, in the freezer for 5 minutes.

Preheat a medium nonstick skillet over medium-high heat until drops of water sizzle when splashed on the pan. Place the patty in the pan. Cook for 2 minutes per side, or until no longer pink.

Place the bun bottom on a plate. Spoon on the chili topping. Top with the cheese, the burger, onion, pickles, and tomato. Spread the mustard on the bun top. Flip onto the sandwich.

MAKES 1 SERVING

349 calories, 28 g protein, 41 g carbohydrates, 8 g fat, 3 g sat. fat, 3 g fiber

Original Tommy's Burger: 490 calories, 22 g protein, 50 g carbohydrates, 22 g fat, 8 g sat. fat, 3 g fiber

ORIGINAL TOMMY'S CHILI TOPPING

4 ounces 96% lean ground beef (about ½ cup)

4 teaspoons + ¾ cup water

6 teaspoons cornstarch, divided

4 teaspoons chili powder, divided

¼ teaspoon onion powder

¼ teaspoon paprika

Pinch of salt

IN a small bowl, combine the beef, 4 teaspoons water, 2 teaspoons cornstarch, 2 teaspoons chili powder, the onion power, and the paprika. Using a fork, mash the ingredients until they are well blended. Transfer to a small nonstick pan. Place over medium heat. Cook, mashing with a wooden spoon, for 3 to 4 minutes, or until almost mealy and no longer pink.

Meanwhile, in a small bowl, combine ¾ cup water with the remaining 4 teaspoons cornstarch and 2 teaspoons chili powder. Add to the pan. Cook, stirring occasionally, for 3 minutes, or until slightly thickened. Use right away, or allow to cool and then transfer to an airtight container. Refrigerate for up to 2 days.

MAKES ABOUT 1 CUP, ENOUGH FOR 4 SERVINGS

Each serving: 78 calories, 6 g protein, 10 g carbohydrates, 2 g fat, <1 g sat. fat, 1 g fiber

FATBURGER: TURKEYBURGER

SAVE: 151 CALORIES, 20 G FAT

Though this chapter is called "Here's the Beef," I had to include a turkey burger because I know so many people who prefer beef but order turkey burgers, thinking they're eating healthfully. If you, too, are convinced that eating a turkey burger has to be better for your figure than eating a beef burger, take a look at this: Fatburger customarily serves its Turkeyburger on a whole wheat bun without any cheese. However, this innocent-looking burger has more fat than a Big Mac and only 10 calories and 1 gram of fat less than a Fatburger Fatburger (regular beef hamburger).

Uh, one beef burger, please.

> 3 ounces extra-lean ground (99% fat-free) turkey breast (about ¼ cup + 2 tablespoons)
>
> 2 ounces lean (7% fat) ground turkey breast (about ¼ cup)
>
> ½ teaspoon seasoned salt
>
> ¼ teaspoon ground black pepper
>
> 1 whole wheat hamburger bun (about 4¼")
>
> 1 teaspoon yellow mustard
>
> 1 tablespoon sweet pickle relish
>
> 1½ tablespoons chopped white onion
>
> 4 rounds crinkle-cut dill pickle
>
> 1 slice tomato (¼" thick)
>
> ¼ cup shredded iceberg lettuce
>
> 1 tablespoon light mayonnaise

IN a small bowl, combine the extra-lean turkey and lean turkey. With hands, mix until well blended. On a sheet of waxed paper, shape the mixture into a 5" somewhat square-shaped patty. Season each side with seasoned salt and pepper.

Preheat a large nonstick skillet over medium-high heat until drops of water sizzle when splashed on the pan. Place the patty in the pan. Cook for 1 to 2 minutes per side, or until a thermometer inserted sideways in the center registers 165°F and the burger is no longer pink inside.

Meanwhile, place the bun top and bottom, cut-sides down, in the pan. Cook for about 2 to 3 minutes, or until toasted.

Place the bun bottom, toasted-side up, on a plate. Top with the burger, mustard, relish, onion, pickles, tomato, and lettuce. Spread the mayonnaise on the toasted side of the top bun. Flip onto the sandwich.

MAKES 1 SERVING

439 calories, 40 g protein, 47 g carbohydrates, 13 g fat, 2 g sat. fat, 4 g fiber

Original Fatburger Turkeyburger: 590 calories, 32 g protein, 41 g carbohydrates, 33 g fat, sat. fat (not available), fiber (not available)

EVEN BETTER If you want to save even more fat and calories, make the burger with 5 ounces of extra-lean ground turkey, omitting the 7% fat ground turkey. Although the burger is a bit drier, I actually prefer the taste. If you're used to eating really juicy turkey burgers, you may want to stick with the recipe as it's written. If not, definitely try this alternative burger with 15 fewer calories and 3 fewer grams of fat. It's also more convenient because you have to purchase only one package of turkey. You may be surprised how much you love it. The extra-lean burger has **424** calories, **43 g** protein, **47 g** carbohydrates, **10 g** fat, **1 g** sat. fat, and **4 g** fiber. You'll save **166** calories and **23 g** fat.

FINGER LICKIN' GREAT

Crispy breading nestling a plump, juicy piece of chicken . . . this is one food that always hindered my progress during my years of dieting. How on earth would I be able to give up this fried piece of heaven forever and achieve my weight-loss goals? Fortunately, by my early twenties, I figured it out. I wouldn't have to give it up at all, let alone forever. I started making faux-fried chicken—delicious, crispy, breaded chicken that's baked instead of fried. I never turned back. I suspect you won't either.

What Goes Into the Perfect Chicken Dish?

Boneless, Skinless Chicken Breasts

Few things make cooking easier than the convenience of boneless, skinless chicken breasts. To prepare them, begin by rinsing the chicken under cold water. Pat dry with paper towels, and trim any visible fat from the breasts. Next, often at the thicker end of the breast on the underside, you'll notice what appears to be a shiny, white formation of threads. Poke the tip of your knife into the meat just underneath the collection of threads and cut it out. (Nothing worse than a chewy bite of tendon in an otherwise scrumptious sandwich.)

Place the trimmed breast flat on a cutting board with the smooth side up. Lay a sheet of waxed paper over the breast. Using the smooth side of a meat mallet (metal or wooden is fine) or the bottom of a flat-bottomed heavy frying pan, pound the breast until it is as thin as the recipe requires. This will not only help tenderize the meat, but it will also help you achieve pieces that resemble your fast food favorites. Pat dry again, if necessary (moisture will make your seasoning clump). Your chicken is now ready for seasoning.

Bone-In Breasts and Drumsticks

Nothing beats a hot batch of faux-fried chicken for a picnic—the hard part is deciding whether to eat the breasts or the drumsticks. To prepare these pieces, begin by removing the skin and any visible fat. Rinse the chicken under cold water and pat dry with paper towels. Your chicken is now ready for seasoning.

A Perfect Coat of Breading

There are two basic tips that can guarantee your success in mastering the art of faux-fried chicken. First of all, while the ingredient amounts listed in these recipes will be plenty to coat the items you're breading, it will be much easier if you add extra flour mixture and extra bread crumbs, then discard any excess. Ingredients are listed as is for the purpose of determining nutritional analyses, but keep this advice in mind if it makes breading easier for you.

The second thing to bear in mind is that you should carefully select the right bowls for the job. If you are breading small pieces, for instance, it's best to use a small bowl that is not too shallow. That way, you can actually submerge the pieces. If you're breading an entire breast, a larger shallow bowl works better so that the item to be breaded can lie flat.

Step one, the flour: First, combine fine ingredients, such as ground spices, salt, pepper, etc., with the flour (not the bread crumbs) in a resealable plastic bag. This is the best way to ensure that this type of seasoning sticks to the chicken (if you add them with the bread crumbs, they tend to fall to the bottom of the bowl). Also, I've found that it's important to include a little bit of salt, as it reacts with the protein in the chicken and causes it to plump. Without salt, the chicken will not taste nearly as good.

Add the chicken pieces and shake the bag to coat them. Refrigerate the chicken for at least 10 minutes, or as long as 8 hours if you prefer to cook it later. This step also helps the chicken to tenderize. I'd love to claim that I just naturally knew this, but truth be told, I discovered this method by accident. One day, after years of making breaded, baked foods, I was in the middle of breading chicken when I got a phone call, so I threw the bag with the floured, spiced chicken in the refrigerator. After cooking the chicken, it seemed even more tender than usual. It occurred to me that by letting the flour and salt sit on the chicken

BUYING THE BEST CHICKEN

Chicken can be purchased frozen or fresh from the butcher or meat counter. If you purchase it from the freezer, be sure to look at the nutrition label—some frozen varieties are pumped with added fats before they're frozen. A 4-ounce raw, boneless, skinless chicken breast half should have only about 1.5 grams of fat.

If you purchase the chicken from the butcher, don't hesitate to ask him or her to cut it the way you need it, especially if you need a bone-in breast cut to size. Butchers tend to be very helpful—think about it, would you rather talk to a friendly, recognizable face, or stand in a meat locker all day? Like you and me, they enjoy the diversion. Sheila and Roberto at my local chain grocery store are extremely helpful to me. They grind fresh meat (which is particularly important if they are out of the ground varieties of the leanest cuts); they cut meats to size; they trim the meats; they place special orders for me; they have my meat waiting if I call ahead for it; heck, they even split apart large packs of meats at times (so I can buy only what I need). And I'm not talking about a mom-and-pop store. I'm talking about the butchers at the national chain grocery store that is closest to my kitchen. In fact, in the 12 years I've been cooking professionally, I've never frequented a major grocery store where they wouldn't accommodate my requests (and I've had a lot).

during my phone call, I had found the secret to even yummier chicken. I now always give my chicken that extra T.L.C. when I'm breading pieces that are any bigger than bite size.

Step two, the egg: The next step is the egg. Though it's possible to use egg-white substitute or egg substitute, you'll notice that the chicken recipes in this book generally call for egg white mixed with fat-free milk because my personal experience is that this combination produces the best results—a crisp, fluffy breading that's never dry. Now, I know that some people have trouble throwing away the yolks because they feel it's wasting food. True, it is, but in my local stores, it generally costs less to buy eggs and throw away the yolks than it does to buy the equivalent amount of the liquid substitutes, so that's how I justify it.

I should probably also note, however, that there are a few recipes where I do call for egg substitutes. This is because some foods are more delicate than others and are thus tougher to bread. And sometimes it's simply easier to use the substitutes.

Step three, the breading: The final step is the breading. There are many popular options for breading, from crushed corn flakes to seasoned bread crumbs. In this book, however, there are only two that need be called upon: packaged dry bread crumbs (unseasoned) and panko, crispy Japanese bread crumbs that can be found in the international section of most major grocery stores. Dry bread crumbs are much finer than panko, so though these products can be used interchangeably, they will yield very different results. Herbs and other seasonings that are larger than ground spices are best added with the bread crumbs in most cases.

Olive Oil Spray

Many of the recipes in this book suggest spraying food with olive oil to achieve a rich flavor and crisp results with little additional fat. Use an olive oil sprayer filled with a full-flavored extra virgin olive oil that you love, not a store-bought aerosol sprayer that may contain propellants. If you don't have an olive oil sprayer, however, skip the step.

A Great Grilled Flavor

Grilling can be a great, low-fat method for locking in loads of flavor. And in many ways, I find grilling chicken to be similar to cooking ground beef. As when cooking

THAWING FROZEN CHICKEN

It's great to have chicken waiting for you in your freezer. When the craving hits, simply remove as many pieces as you need the night before you plan to cook it. If you forget and need it quickly, it's simple to thaw it. Soak it in or run it under cold water (if you soak it in hot or warm water, it will start to cook the chicken ever so slightly) until it is thawed through, approximately 5 to 10 minutes, then blot any excess moisture with paper towels.

burgers, I always keep my "three Ss" in mind (see "How to Cook the Perfect Burger" on page 21). The main difference with chicken, however, is that once it's seared on high heat, it's important to turn the heat down to low to medium-low to cook the chicken through. Chicken should be cooked until it is just past pink. Though it needs to be white inside, it doesn't need to be white inside and then cooked for another 2 to 10 minutes, which is the biggest mistake people often make. When it's done, it's safe to eat. It doesn't need to be drier than leather to be safe.

Okay, enough reading, time to get cluckin'. . . .

MCDONALD'S: MCCHICKEN SANDWICH

SAVE: 120 CALORIES, 14 G FAT, 3.5 G SAT. FAT

Apparently, the McChicken Sandwich and the Big Mac teamed together and went on diets. Perhaps a New Year's resolution?

I began the nutritional research for this book in July of 2004. At the time, I printed out the nutritional information provided on McDonald's Web site. It listed the McChicken Sandwich as having 23 grams of fat. Then, when I acquired the nutritional analysis pamphlet at McDonald's in early 2005, it listed the McChicken sandwich as having 22 grams of fat. I went back online and realized that much of the nutritional data had changed. In addition to the McChicken Sandwich, the Big Mac also "lost weight": The 2005 Big Mac lost 40 calories and 3 grams of fat over the 2004 Big Mac. But then I realized that the McDonald's Hash Brown, among other items, "gained some weight," so to speak. Bummer.

1 boneless, skinless chicken breast half (4 ounces)

1 teaspoon unbleached or all-purpose flour

$\frac{1}{4}$ teaspoon salt

$\frac{1}{8}$ teaspoon garlic powder

$\frac{1}{8}$ teaspoon paprika

Olive oil spray

1 egg white

1 teaspoon fat-free milk

$2\frac{1}{2}$ tablespoons dry bread crumbs

2 pinches ground black pepper

1 hamburger bun

2 tablespoons shredded iceberg lettuce

2 teaspoons light mayonnaise

PLACE the chicken on a cutting board. Cover with a sheet of waxed paper. With the smooth side of a meat mallet, pound to an even $\frac{1}{3}$" thickness. With a knife, cut a 4" x $3\frac{1}{2}$" piece (about 2 ounces). (Refrigerate or freeze the scraps for another recipe.)

In a small resealable plastic bag, combine the flour, salt, garlic powder, and paprika. Shake to mix well. Add the chicken. Shake to completely coat the chicken with the flour mixture. Place in the refrigerator for at least 10 minutes.

Preheat the oven to 450°F. Lightly mist a small nonstick baking sheet with oil spray.

In a small shallow bowl, combine the egg white and the milk. Beat with a fork until smooth. Place the bread crumbs on a small sheet of waxed paper set next to the egg-white mixture.

Dip the chicken into the egg-white mixture, being sure to coat completely. Allow any excess egg mixture to drip off. Dip into the bread crumbs to coat completely. Repeat dipping into the egg-white mixture and the bread crumbs. Place on the reserved baking sheet. Lightly mist both sides with oil spray. Season both sides with the pepper.

Bake for 4 to 6 minutes per side, or until the breading is crisp and the chicken is no longer pink inside. Meanwhile, preheat a nonstick skillet over medium heat. Place the bun top and bottom, cut-sides down, in the pan. Cook for 2 to 3 minutes, or until toasted.

Place the bun bottom on a plate. Top with the chicken and the lettuce. Spread the mayonnaise over the toasted side of the bun top. Flip onto the sandwich.

MAKES 1 SERVING

310 calories, 21 g protein, 37 g carbohydrates, 8 g fat, 1 g sat. fat, 2 g fiber
Original McDonald's McChicken Sandwich: 430 calories, 15 g protein, 41 g carbohydrates, 22 g fat, 4.5 g sat. fat, 1 g fiber

DRIVE-THRU The chicken can be breaded up to a day in advance. Store it in an airtight plastic container in the refrigerator.

WENDY'S: SPICY CHICKEN FILLET

SAVE: 107 CALORIES, 11 G FAT, 2.5 G SAT. FAT

Outside of the In-N-Out Double-Double, it surfaced during my research that in my particular circle of friends, the Wendy's Spicy Chicken Fillet is purchased about 10 times more than any other fast food sandwich. That's particularly noteworthy to me since Wendy's is not prevalent at all in the Los Angeles area. In fact, in testing these recipes, I had to drive about 7 miles to the closest Wendy's. This may not seem far until you account for LA traffic. Unless my friends are headed out to satisfy their midnight-snack cravings, those who live in my neighborhood are spending a good 35 minutes to an hour (each way) to secure this delicious and addicting sandwich.

1 teaspoon unbleached or all-purpose flour

$\frac{1}{2}$ teaspoon cornstarch

$\frac{1}{4}$ teaspoon paprika

$\frac{1}{4}$ teaspoon cayenne

$\frac{1}{4}$ teaspoon salt

Pinch of garlic powder

Pinch of turmeric

3 ounces boneless, skinless chicken breast, pounded $\frac{1}{3}$" thick

Olive oil spray

1 egg white

1 teaspoon fat-free milk

$3\frac{1}{2}$ tablespoons panko (Japanese bread crumbs)

Ground black pepper

1 kaiser-style hamburger bun (about 4")

1 leaf romaine lettuce

1 slice tomato ($\frac{1}{4}$" thick)

$\frac{1}{2}$ tablespoon light mayonnaise

IN a small resealable plastic bag, combine the flour, cornstarch, paprika, cayenne, salt, garlic powder, and turmeric. Shake to mix well. Add the chicken. Shake to completely coat the chicken with the flour mixture. Place in the refrigerator for at least 10 minutes.

Preheat the oven to 450°F. Lightly mist a small nonstick baking sheet with oil spray. Set aside.

In a small shallow bowl, combine the egg white and the milk. Beat with a fork until smooth. Place the panko on a small sheet of waxed paper set next to the egg-white mixture.

Dip the chicken into the egg-white mixture, being sure to coat completely. Allow any excess egg-white mixture to drip off. Dip into the panko to coat completely. Repeat dipping into the egg-white mixture and the panko. Place on the reserved baking sheet. Lightly mist both sides with oil spray. Season both sides to taste with black pepper.

Bake for 6 to 8 minutes per side, or until the breading is crisp and the chicken is no longer pink inside. Meanwhile, preheat a nonstick skillet over medium heat. Place the bun top and bottom, cut-sides down, in the pan. Cook for 2 to 3 minutes, or until toasted.

Place the bun bottom on a plate. Top with the chicken, lettuce, and tomato. Spread the mayonnaise evenly over the toasted side of the bun top. Flip onto the sandwich.

MAKES 1 SERVING

403 calories, 31 g protein, 53 g carbohydrates, 8 g fat, 1 g sat. fat, 4 g fiber

Original Wendy's Spicy Chicken Fillet: 510 calories, 29 g protein, 57 g carbohydrates, 19 g fat, 3.5 g sat. fat, 2 g fiber

DRIVE-THRU The chicken can be breaded up to a day in advance. Store it in an airtight plastic container in the refrigerator.

ARBY'S: CHICKEN CORDON BLEU SANDWICH

SAVE: 182 CALORIES, 20 G FAT, 5 G SAT. FAT

When I first learned about this sandwich, I thought it might be difficult to make. Traditionally, chicken cordon bleu is made by pounding a chicken breast flat, rolling it up with ham and cheese, and then breading and deep-frying it. Needless to say, I was surprised to learn that Arby's version is simply a perfectly seasoned, breaded, and deep-fried chicken breast fillet placed in a toasted bun with slices of ham and cheese topped off with a touch of mayo. Pretty simple.

$2\frac{1}{2}$ ounces boneless, skinless chicken breast

$\frac{1}{2}$ tablespoon unbleached or all-purpose flour

$\frac{1}{4}$ teaspoon salt

$\frac{1}{4}$ teaspoon sugar

Pinch of garlic powder

Pinch of onion powder

Olive oil spray

1 egg white

1 teaspoon fat-free milk

2 tablespoons dry bread crumbs

$\frac{1}{8}$ teaspoon ground black pepper

1 sesame seed hamburger bun

1 ounce very thinly sliced 97% lean ham

1 slice ($\frac{1}{2}$ ounce) low-fat Swiss-style cheese

$\frac{1}{2}$ tablespoon light mayonnaise

PLACE the chicken on a cutting board. Cover with a sheet of waxed paper. With the smooth side of a meat mallet, pound it to an even $\frac{1}{4}$" thickness.

In a small resealable plastic bag, combine the flour, salt, sugar, garlic powder, and onion powder. Shake to mix well. Add the chicken. Shake to completely coat the chicken with the flour mixture. Place in the refrigerator for at least 10 minutes.

Preheat the oven to 450°F. Lightly mist a small nonstick baking sheet with oil spray. Set aside.

In a small shallow bowl, combine the egg white and the milk. Beat with a fork until smooth. Place the bread crumbs on a small sheet of waxed paper set next to the egg-white mixture.

Dip the chicken into the egg-white mixture, being sure to coat completely. Allow any excess egg-white mixture to drip off. Dip into the bread crumbs to coat completely. Repeat dipping into the egg-white mixture and the bread crumbs. Place on the reserved baking sheet. Lightly mist both sides with oil spray and sprinkle on the black pepper.

Bake for 6 to 8 minutes per side, or until the breading is crisp and the chicken is no longer pink inside. Meanwhile, preheat a nonstick skillet over medium heat. Place the bun top and bottom, cut-sides down, in the pan. Cook for 2 to 3 minutes, or until toasted.

Place the bun bottom on a plate. Top with the chicken, the ham, and the cheese. Spread the mayonnaise over the toasted side of the bun top. Flip onto the sandwich.

MAKES 1 SERVING

388 calories, 32 g protein, 41 g carbohydrates, 9 g fat, 1 g sat. fat, 1 g fiber

Original Arby's Chicken Cordon Bleu Sandwich: 570 calories, 34 g protein, 46 g carbohydrates, 29 g fat, 6 g sat. fat, 2 g fiber

BURGER KING: ORIGINAL CHICKEN SANDWICH

SAVE: 187 CALORIES, 18 G FAT, 5 G SAT. FAT

If there was one dish that I would say was responsible for making me fat as a child, it would definitely be Chicken Parmesan. I couldn't get enough of it. Whether my parents took us for fast food or fine dining, everyone knew what I'd want to order.

At the time, Burger King had a Chicken Parmesan Sandwich on their menu. If I remember correctly, it was basically their Original Chicken Sandwich topped with warm marinara sauce and melted cheese. Mmmm. As far as I was concerned, nothing could be better. I still have fond memories of that sandwich . . . and this one, which, by the way, is excellent with low-fat marinara sauce and a thin slice of low-fat mozzarella (assuming you skip the lettuce and mayo, that is).

1 boneless, skinless chicken breast half (5 ounces)

½ tablespoon unbleached or all-purpose flour

¼ teaspoon salt

Pinch of onion powder

Pinch of garlic powder

Olive oil spray

1 egg white

1 teaspoon fat-free milk

1 tablespoon + 1 teaspoon dry bread crumbs

Ground black pepper

1 sesame seed sandwich roll (about 7" long)

½ teaspoon + ½ tablespoon light mayonnaise

⅓ cup chopped iceberg lettuce

PLACE the chicken on a cutting board. Cover with a sheet of waxed paper. With the smooth side of a meat mallet, pound to an even ⅓" thickness. With a sharp knife, cut into a 6" x 3" piece (about 3 ounces). (Refrigerate the scraps for another recipe.)

In a small resealable plastic bag, combine the flour, salt, onion powder, and garlic powder. Shake to mix well. Add the chicken. Shake to completely coat the chicken with the flour mixture. Place in the refrigerator for at least 10 minutes.

Preheat the oven to 450°F. Lightly mist a small nonstick baking sheet with oil spray. Set aside.

In a small shallow bowl, combine the egg white and the milk. Beat with a fork until smooth. Place the bread crumbs on a small sheet of waxed paper set next to the egg-white mixture.

Dip the chicken into the egg-white mixture, being sure to coat completely. Allow any excess egg-white mixture to drip off. Dip into the bread crumbs to coat completely. Lightly mist both sides with oil spray. Place on the reserved baking sheet. Lightly season both sides with pepper.

Bake for 6 minutes. Carefully flip the chicken. Bake for 5 to 7 minutes, or until the breading is crisp and the chicken is no longer pink inside. Meanwhile, preheat a nonstick skillet over medium heat. Place the roll top and bottom, cut-sides down, in the pan. Cook for 2 to 3 minutes, or until toasted.

Place the roll bottom on a plate. Spread with ½ teaspoon of the mayonnaise. Top with the chicken and the lettuce. Spread the remaining ½ tablespoon of mayonnaise over the toasted side of the roll top. Flip onto the sandwich.

MAKES 1 SERVING

373 calories, 28 g protein, 44 g carbohydrates, 10 g fat, 1 g sat. fat, 2 g fiber

Original Burger King Original Chicken Sandwich: 560 calories, 18 g protein, 52 g carbohydrates, 28 g fat, 6 g sat. fat, 3g fiber

DRIVE-THRU The chicken can be breaded up to a day in advance. Store it in an airtight plastic container in the refrigerator.

HARDEE'S: CHARBROILED CHICKEN SANDWICH

SAVE: 120 CALORIES, 13 G FAT, 4 G SAT. FAT

Before writing this book, if I had been stranded without food on a desert island, and down from the sky dropped a Hardee's menu with a note attached that said, "Pick any item" (I know, I know, this is far-fetched, but please indulge me), I definitely would have ordered the Charbroiled Chicken Sandwich. The carbs in the bun would give me energy, and the chicken breast would be a great source of lean protein. Throw in some lettuce, a couple of tomato slices, maybe even a few pickles and ketchup, mustard, barbecue sauce, or light mayo, and I'd have myself a tasty sandwich. Seems like a cinch, right?

Actually, of all the recipes in this book, this one probably shocked me the most. It has more fat than Hardee's Big Hot Ham 'n Cheese and their Big Roast Beef. Granted, I know that some restaurants rub, or even dip, chicken breasts in oil before grilling them. Some butter the bun before toasting it. Some even heap chicken sandwiches with cheese and/or mayo, so I know to be careful. But even knowing all of that, when I saw the size and composition of this sandwich, I was shocked to learn that it contained 26 grams of fat. Heck, I generally eat between 30 and 40 grams of fat per day, and this sandwich is far from huge. But one taste, and I loved the flavor of the sauce that coats the chicken before it's grilled. So here it is . . . with the fat and calories you'd expect a chicken breast sandwich to have.

> 1 boneless, skinless chicken breast half (5$\frac{1}{2}$ ounces), pounded $\frac{1}{3}$" thick
>
> 1 tablespoon Hardee's Charbroiled Chicken Grilling Sauce (opposite page)
>
> Olive oil spray (optional)
>
> 1 sesame seed sandwich bun (about 5")
>
> 4 teaspoons light mayonnaise, divided
>
> 2 small leaves iceberg lettuce
>
> 2 slices tomato ($\frac{1}{8}$" thick)

IN a small resealable plastic bag, combine the chicken and the sauce. Massage the chicken to coat completely with the sauce. Place in the refrigerator for at least 15 minutes to marinate, but no longer than a few hours.

Preheat the grill to high heat. Lightly mist a grill rack with oil spray, if needed. Place the chicken on the grill rack. On a gas grill, turn the heat to low. On a charcoal grill, place the chicken away from direct heat. Cook for 3 to 5 minutes per side, or until the chicken is no longer pink inside.

Meanwhile, preheat a nonstick skillet over medium heat. Place the bun top and bottom, cut-sides down, in the pan. Cook for 2 to 3 minutes, or until toasted.

Place the bun bottom, toasted side up, on a plate. Spread with 2 teaspoons of the mayonnaise. Top with the lettuce, tomato, and chicken. Spread the remaining 2 teaspoons of mayonnaise over the toasted side of the bun top. Flip onto the sandwich.

MAKES 1 SERVING

470 calories, 44 g protein, 43 g carbohydrates, 13 g fat, 3 g sat. fat, 2 g fiber

Original Hardee's Charbroiled Chicken Sandwich: 590 calories, 36 g protein, 53 g carbohydrates, 26 g fat, 7 g sat. fat, 4 g fiber

(STOP) BEFORE YOU START Sesame seed sandwich buns, the 5" size, are larger than standard hamburger buns (about 3½"). Look for bagged sesame seed sandwich buns in the same supermarket aisle as the hamburger buns. To make sure you have the larger size, grab a package of the hamburger buns for comparison.

HARDEE'S CHARBROILED CHICKEN GRILLING SAUCE

2 tablespoons tomato paste

1 tablespoon + 1 teaspoon brown sugar

2 teaspoons soy sauce

2 teaspoons Worcestershire sauce

1 teaspoon apple cider vinegar

1 teaspoon water

½ teaspoon salt

¼ teaspoon garlic powder

IN a bowl, combine the tomato paste, sugar, soy sauce, Worcestershire sauce, vinegar, water, salt, and garlic powder. Whisk to blend well. Transfer to an airtight plastic container. Refrigerate for up to 3 days.

MAKES ¼ CUP, ENOUGH FOR 4 SERVINGS

Each serving: 24 calories, <1 g protein, 5 g carbohydrates, trace fat, trace sat. fat, 1 g fiber

KFC: ORIGINAL RECIPE CHICKEN BREAST

SAVE: 107 CALORIES, 15 G FAT, 5 G SAT. FAT

When I was in my early twenties, I dated a guy whose mother didn't like me. Every other boyfriend's mother has loved me, because "if nothing else, he'll be well fed." But this particular mother was a proud Southern mother who grew up on fried everything. At the time, I weighed only about 125 pounds, and she, regardless of the fact that I'd just received professional chef certification, was convinced that her "poor son" was going to starve if he was "dating a twig" like me.

I hadn't eaten fried foods in more than 7 years when I started dating him, and I felt good about myself and my body. So, when I'd need to eat at her house, I'd always offer to cook spaghetti to avoid her usual fried-food menu. Convinced that spaghetti was all I ever ate, which was the furthest thing from the truth, she asked one night before dinner, "If that's not all you eat, what else do you eat?" I politely replied, "I eat mostly chicken and fish and lots of salads." She inquired, "So if I order chicken, you'll eat it?" I told her not to go out of her way for me, but she insisted. Less than an hour later, she returned from KFC with two buckets of fried chicken, some biscuits, and some potato wedges. I wanted to cry when she walked in the house. I couldn't eat it. And I had to eat it.

I pulled the breading off an Original Recipe Chicken Breast and ate most of the meat, making it seem as if I'd eaten all of it. I also ate part of a biscuit. Fortunately, though, I was able to feed much of that to their dog when my boyfriend's mother wasn't looking. But I still can't look at a KFC sign without thinking about that meal. At least now I have an alternative, and so do you.

1 bone-in chicken breast half (10–12 ounces)

½ tablespoon unbleached or all-purpose flour

½ teaspoon salt

½ teaspoon sugar

¼ teaspoon ground black pepper

¼ teaspoon onion powder

⅛ teaspoon paprika

Olive oil spray

1 egg white

1 teaspoon fat-free milk

2 tablespoons panko (Japanese bread crumbs)

1 tablespoon dry bread crumbs

PLACE the chicken on a cutting board. Remove and discard the skin and all visible fat. With a sharp knife or kitchen scissors, cut through the chicken and the bone, at the base of the ribs, to detach the bottom third of the breast. (Refrigerate or freeze for another recipe.) The larger piece should weigh about 6½ ounces after trimming.

In a small resealable plastic bag, combine the flour, salt, sugar, pepper, onion powder, and paprika. Shake to mix well. Add the chicken. Shake to completely coat the chicken with the flour mixture. Place in the refrigerator for at least 10 minutes.

Preheat the oven to 450°F. Lightly mist a small nonstick baking sheet with oil spray. Set aside.

In a small shallow bowl, combine the egg white and the milk. Beat with a fork until smooth. Place the panko and the bread crumbs on a small sheet of waxed paper set next to the egg-white mixture. Mix with a fork to blend.

Dip the chicken into the egg-white mixture, being sure to coat completely. Allow any excess egg-white mixture to drip off. Dip into the panko mixture to coat completely. Place, ribs facing up, on the reserved baking sheet. Lightly mist with oil spray.

Bake for 10 minutes. Carefully flip the chicken. Lightly mist again with oil spray. Bake for 12 to 15 minutes, or until the breading is crisp and the chicken is no longer pink inside.

MAKES 1 SERVING

273 calories, 40 g protein, 17 g carbohydrates, 4 g fat, <1 g sat. fat, <1 g fiber

Original KFC Original Recipe Chicken Breast: 380 calories, 40 g protein, 11 g carbohydrates, 19 g fat, 6 g sat. fat, 0 g fiber

DRIVE-THRU The breast can be breaded up to a day in advance. Store it in an airtight plastic container in the refrigerator.

BEFORE YOU START Most butchers are happy to accommodate any special requests from customers. When you buy your chicken breast, ask the butcher to remove the skin and cut the breast to size. That way, you won't have the mess or trouble of cutting through the bone yourself.

CHURCH'S CHICKEN: SOUTHERN FRIED CHICKEN LEGS

SAVE: 28 CALORIES, 11 G FAT

When I set out to write this book, I had no idea that I'd find so much variety among restaurants in the same chains—and so many dishes that didn't quite seem to match their nutritional data. I was also shocked to see how many seemingly basic dishes just disappeared from the menus. Thank goodness these chicken legs seem likely to stay around for a long time—one bite of their crunchy perfection and I was hooked. And though this version is not remarkably lighter in calories, I was able to trim almost two-thirds of the fat from this soul-satisfying combination. Now that's worth singing about.

½ tablespoon unbleached or all-purpose flour

½ teaspoon salt

⅛ teaspoon onion powder

Pinch of garlic powder

2 chicken drumsticks, skin removed

Olive oil spray

1 egg white

½ tablespoon fat-free milk

¼ cup panko (Japanese bread crumbs)

IN a medium resealable plastic bag, combine the flour, salt, onion powder, and garlic powder. Shake to mix well. Add the chicken. Shake to completely coat the chicken with the flour mixture. Place in the refrigerator for at least 10 minutes.

Preheat the oven to 450°F. Lightly mist a nonstick baking sheet with oil spray.

In a small shallow bowl, combine the egg white and the milk. Beat with a fork until smooth. Place the panko on a small sheet of waxed paper set next to the egg-white mixture.

One at a time, dip the chicken drumsticks into the egg-white mixture, being sure to coat completely. Allow any excess egg-white mixture to drip off. Dip into the panko to coat completely. Dip a second time into the egg-white mixture and the panko. Place the chicken drumsticks, not touching, on the reserved baking sheet. Lightly mist with oil spray.

Bake for about 20 minutes, carefully rotating the drumsticks a quarter turn every 5 minutes for even browning, or until the breading is crisp and the drumsticks are no longer pink inside. Lightly mist with oil spray before serving.

MAKES 1 SERVING (2 DRUMSTICKS)

252 calories, 29 g protein, 15 g carbohydrates, 7 g fat, 1 g sat. fat, trace fiber

Original Church's Chicken Southern Fried Chicken Legs (2 drumsticks): 280 calories, 26 g protein, 4 g carbohydrates, 18 g fat, sat. fat (not available), 0 g fiber

DRIVE-THRU The drumsticks can be breaded up to a day in advance. Store them in an airtight plastic container in the refrigerator.

CHICK-FIL-A: CHICK-N-STRIPS

SAVE: 108 CALORIES, 15 G FAT, 3 G SAT. FAT

Did you know that Chick-fil-A celebrates Cow Appreciation Day, "an unofficial, yet nationally recognized, holiday," according to their Web site, by awarding all customers dressed in cow "from head to toe" with a free combo meal?

That's right, on July 15, 2005, they made this offering to save the cow (and to eat the chicken). They set up an entire Web site for interested customers to learn more and even included a link to frequently asked questions. It answers inquiries such as what dressing like a cow "from head to toe" actually means, and offers to those interested in dressing only in part like a cow a free entrée instead of the free combo.

In case you missed Cow Appreciation Day and the chance to receive a free six-piece Chick-n-Strips, medium waffle fries, and medium lemonade (totaling 1,000 calories, 47 g protein, 121 g carbohydrates, 37.5 g fat, 7.5 g sat. fat, and 6 g fiber), you might feel better knowing that you can now make those deliciously sweet strips on your own in the privacy of your own home with only a fraction of the fat and calories—cow suit optional.

> 1 boneless, skinless chicken breast half (5 ounces)
>
> 2 teaspoons unbleached or all-purpose flour
>
> 2 teaspoons sugar
>
> $\frac{1}{2}$ teaspoon salt
>
> $\frac{1}{4}$ teaspoon paprika
>
> $\frac{1}{8}$ teaspoon ground black pepper
>
> $\frac{1}{8}$ teaspoon garlic powder
>
> $\frac{1}{8}$ teaspoon onion powder
>
> $\frac{1}{8}$ teaspoon cayenne
>
> Olive oil spray
>
> 1 egg white
>
> $1\frac{1}{2}$ teaspoons fat-free milk
>
> 3 tablespoons dry bread crumbs

PLACE the chicken on a cutting board. Cover with a sheet of waxed paper. With the smooth side of a meat mallet, pound to an even $\frac{1}{4}$" thickness. Cut diagonally into 6 equal strips (about 4" x $\frac{3}{4}$").

In a small resealable plastic bag, combine the flour, sugar, salt, paprika, black pepper, garlic powder, onion powder, and cayenne. Shake to mix well. Add the chicken. Shake to completely coat the chicken with the flour mixture. Place in the refrigerator for at least 10 minutes.

Preheat the oven to 450°F. Lightly mist a small nonstick baking sheet with oil spray. Set aside.

In a small shallow bowl, combine the egg white and the milk. Beat with a fork until smooth. Place the bread crumbs on a small sheet of waxed paper set next to the egg-white mixture.

One at a time, dip the chicken strips into the egg-white mixture, being sure to coat completely. Allow any excess egg-white mixture to drip off. Dip into the bread crumbs to coat completely. Place, not touching, on the reserved baking sheet.

Lightly mist both sides with oil spray.

Bake for 4 to 6 minutes per side, or until the breading is crisp and the chicken is no longer pink inside.

MAKES 1 SERVING (6 PIECES)

322 calories, 40 g protein, 28 g carbohydrates, 5 g fat, <1 g sat. fat, 1 g fiber

Original Chick-fil-A Chick-n-Strips (6 pieces): 430 calories, 43 g protein, 21 g carbohydrates, 20 g fat, 4 g sat. fat, 1 g fiber

DRIVE-THRU You can bread the strips in batches for storage in the freezer (unbaked) until you need a "fast food" meal. When you want to eat them—no need to thaw—simply follow the recipe directions, baking for 5 to 7 minutes per side. Not only will they be on the table quicker than Chick-fil-A's could be, but you'll know you're taking in a fraction of the fat and far fewer calories. Freeze for up to 2 months.

BURGER KING: CHICKEN TENDERS

SAVE: 101 CALORIES, 14 G FAT, 5 G SAT. FAT

Of all the fast food restaurants we visited in making this book, my assistants and I clearly agreed that Burger King offers the most perfectly uniform foods encountered anywhere.

The topic first surfaced when re-creating the Burger King Onion Rings. Never had we seen so many rings that were exactly the same size, exactly the same shape, and exactly the same weight. Then, in working on the BK Chicken Tenders, the topic resurfaced. These mini-drumstick-looking tenders are just too adorable not to notice, and too fun not to duplicate.

1 boneless, skinless chicken breast half (4 ounces)

2 teaspoons unbleached or all-purpose flour

1/4 teaspoon salt

Pinch of sugar

Pinch of garlic powder

Olive oil spray

1 egg white

1 teaspoon fat-free milk

2 1/2 tablespoons dry bread crumbs

2 pinches of ground black pepper

PLACE the chicken on a cutting board. Cover with a sheet of waxed paper. With the smooth side of a meat mallet, pound to an even 1/4" thickness. Cut the chicken into 8 strips that resemble mini-drumsticks. They should measure about 1" at the wide end and taper to 1/2" at the narrow end.

In a small resealable plastic bag, combine the flour, salt, sugar, and garlic powder. Shake to mix well. Add the chicken. Shake to completely coat the chicken with the flour mixture. Place in the refrigerator for at least 10 minutes.

Preheat the oven to 450°F. Lightly mist a small nonstick baking sheet with oil spray.

In a small shallow bowl, combine the egg white and the milk. Beat with a fork until smooth. Place the bread crumbs on a small sheet of waxed paper set next to the egg-white mixture.

One piece at a time, dip the chicken into the egg-white mixture, being sure to coat completely. Allow any excess egg-white mixture to drip off. Dip into the bread crumbs to coat completely. Repeat a second time dipping into the egg-white mixture and the bread crumbs. Place the pieces, not touching, on the reserved baking sheet. Lightly mist both sides with oil spray and season lightly with pepper.

Bake for 4 to 6 minutes per side, or until the breading is crisp and the chicken is no longer pink inside.

MAKES 1 SERVING (8 PIECES)

239 calories, 30 g protein, 16 g carbohydrates, 5 g fat, trace sat. fat, 1 g fiber

Original Burger King Chicken Tenders (8 pieces): 340 calories, 22 g protein, 20 g carbohydrates, 19 g fat, 5 g sat. fat, <1 g fiber

DRIVE-THRU You can bread the chicken in batches and store it in the freezer (unbaked) for up to 2 months. When you need a "fast food" meal, simply follow the recipe directions, baking the frozen tenders for 5 to 7 minutes per side (no need for thawing first). Not only will they be on the table quicker than Burger King's could be, but you'll know exactly what you're eating.

KFC: POPCORN CHICKEN (LARGE)

SAVE: 306 CALORIES, 39 G FAT, 10 G SAT. FAT

I planned to remake KFC's "Individual"-size Popcorn Chicken. But, alas, when I showed up ready to order, the petite female clerk informed me that they had discontinued it (at least in my local area). I asked her how many people the large version served. With a befuddled look on her angelic face, she said, "Just one." When I got my first container of chicken home, I counted the pieces. There were 38. Twenty of them actually had chicken hiding deep inside the thick layer of breading; 18 didn't—deep-fried bread, anyone?

This is the perfect recipe to make with children. It's fun to make and fun to eat. Plus, all 25 pieces in my version actually contain chicken and share the delicious peppery seasoning of the original.

Olive oil spray

2½ ounces boneless, skinless chicken breast

2 teaspoons unbleached or all-purpose flour

½ teaspoon sugar

¼ teaspoon salt + additional for sprinkling

½ teaspoon ground black pepper + additional for sprinkling

⅛ teaspoon onion powder

2 egg whites

2 tablespoons fat-free milk

¾ cup panko (Japanese bread crumbs)

PREHEAT the oven to 475°F. Lightly mist a nonstick baking sheet with oil spray. Set aside.

Place the chicken on a cutting board. Cover with a sheet of waxed paper. With the smooth side of a meat mallet, pound to an even ¼" thickness. Cut into 25 pieces that are roughly the same size.

In a small resealable plastic bag, combine the flour, sugar, ¼ teaspoon salt, ½ teaspoon pepper, and the onion powder. Shake to mix well. Add the chicken. Shake to completely coat the chicken with the flour mixture. Set aside.

In a small shallow bowl, combine the egg whites and the milk. Beat with a fork until smooth. Place the panko on a small sheet of waxed paper set next to the egg-white mixture.

One at a time, dip the chicken pieces into the egg-white mixture, being sure to coat completely. Allow any excess egg-white mixture to drip off. Dip into the panko to coat completely. Dip a second time into the egg-white mixture and the panko. Drop the pieces on the reserved baking sheet and arrange to make sure they're not touching. Lightly mist with oil spray. Season lightly to taste with salt and pepper.

Bake for 5 minutes. Carefully flip the chicken. Bake for 5 to 7 minutes, or until the breading is crunchy, but not browned, and the chicken is no longer pink inside.

MAKES 1 SERVING (25 PIECES)

354 calories, 30 g protein, 43 g carbohydrates, 5 g fat, trace sat. fat, trace fiber

Original KFC Large Popcorn Chicken (25 pieces): 660 calories, 29 g protein, 37 g carbohydrates, 44 g fat, 10 g sat. fat, <1 g fiber

BEFORE YOU START Like KFC's, this Popcorn Chicken has a strong peppery taste. If you're not a huge pepper fan or you are making this for children, you may want to decrease the pepper to ½ teaspoon or less.

EVEN BETTER Prefer more protein and fewer carbs? Like bigger bites of chicken nestled in the breading? You can satisfy your craving by adding more chicken and using less breading. Follow the recipe, but increase the chicken to 3½ ounces and decrease the panko (Japanese bread crumbs) to ⅔ cup. Increase the flour to 1 tablespoon, the pepper to ¾ teaspoon, and the salt to ½ teaspoon. Bake the chicken for 6 to 8 minutes after it is flipped. The revised version has 375 calories, 36 g protein, 41 g carbohydrates, 5 g fat, trace sat. fat, and <1 g fiber.

DRIVE-THRU The chicken can be breaded up to a day in advance and stored in an airtight plastic container in the refrigerator. Or several batches can be breaded for storage in the freezer, layered between sheets of waxed paper in an airtight plastic container. Freeze for up to 2 months. Pull them out when you want to eat them— no need to thaw—and bake according to the recipe directions for 5 to 7 minutes per side.

FOR THE FISH LOVER IN YOU

A lot of my clients reveal that they find seafood very intimidating to buy and prepare themselves. Perhaps that's one reason it has grown so popular in fast food restaurants. If you love seafood but dread the idea of making it for yourself, this chapter is sure to help!

What Goes Into the Perfect Seafood Dish?

White Fish

Most fast food fish sandwiches are made from hoki or pollock. Hoki is a mild white fish that is imported from New Zealand. It is usually frozen before shipping, is generally inexpensive, has few bones, and flakes easily, thus making it a good fish for breading. Pollock is also a delicate-flavored white fish that is a plentiful member of the cod family. Its abundance makes it more affordable than many other species of fish.

Because hoki and pollock are not easily found in grocery stores across the United States and so are not as consumer friendly as some other species (if you do find them, feel free to use them), I usually use cod, haddock, or even red snapper for fish sandwiches. Not only do they all have mild flavors, but they can be pounded gently with a meat mallet if necessary and will keep shape well when breaded.

For these recipes, you definitely want to buy fillets—boneless, usually skinless pieces cut from one side of the fish. Technically, fillets shouldn't have skin on them, but it's often left on because some people argue that the skin adds great flavor, even if you don't actually eat the skin. Others like skin on the fillets because it can make grilling easier since the fish is then less likely to fall apart. If the fillets at your grocery store have skin on, the butcher or fishmonger is generally happy to remove it at no charge.

Because the tail of a fish moves a lot more than the body does as it swims, the meat found near the tail is often not as tender as the meat near the head or in the body portion. Thus you should always ask for the thickest piece to ensure that it comes from the head-end versus the tail-end.

Once home, always be sure to run your clean fingers along the surface of the fillet before you bread it; because butchers are often in a hurry, they can miss some of the smaller bones, which you must take care to remove. If you're a big fish eater (or aspire to be one), you should invest in a pair of fish tweezers. They're similar to the tweezers you find in your cosmetic bag, but they're larger and a lot sturdier—they allow you to remove the bones with ease without tearing up the meat that surrounds them.

Once the fish is deboned, rinse it under water and then blot it dry with paper towels to remove excess moisture before breading it. If flattening is necessary, place it on a cutting board, cover it with a sheet of waxed paper, and gently pound it with the flat side of a meat mallet. Cut the fish to size according to the recipe specifications, and it's ready to be breaded.

Shrimp

Whether you prefer to buy it cooked or raw, shrimp is always grouped into similar sizes and sold according to the number of shrimp that will be found per pound. For instance, 31- to 40-count shrimp means that there will be 31 to 40 shrimp per pound purchased. Higher counts will be smaller shrimp, and lower counts will be larger. Shrimp is often found in bulk at a fish counter, but if you're the sort of shopper who likes to stock up, I recommend looking for prepacked bags in the freezer section because you can thaw as few or as many as needed. To thaw frozen shrimp, run them under cold (not hot or warm) water. They will thaw within a couple of minutes. Blot them dry with paper towels to remove any excess moisture.

Starting with precooked shrimp also works well in these recipes. Because precooked shrimp generally have a lot of extra water in them, they don't tend to dry out. In fact, I almost always recook precooked shrimp, as I think they taste better.

A Perfect Coat of Breading

The steps required to create perfectly faux-fried fish are similar to those for breading chicken (see page 44), with one exception. It is not necessary to tenderize fish by letting the seasoned flour sit on it for a period of time.

Olive Oil Spray

Many of the recipes in this book suggest spraying food with extra virgin olive oil to achieve a rich flavor and crisp results with little additional fat. Use an olive oil sprayer filled with a full-flavored extra virgin olive oil that you love, not a store-bought aerosol sprayer that may contain propellants. Because it's the first flavor that your tongue senses, the rich flavor will appear more concentrated than it is. If you don't have an olive oil sprayer, however, skip the step.

I should probably mention that although I use extra virgin olive oil in the recipes in this book, fast food restaurants generally do not. I prefer using strongly flavored olive oil because a little goes a long way and because it contains monounsaturated fat. You've probably heard olive oil referred to as good fat because it's been known to lower cholesterol.

COOKING SEAFOOD

To make sure fish is perfectly cooked to its moist and flavorful best, be sure to bake it just to the point that it flakes easily and is no longer translucent. If you bake it beyond that point, the fish will become dry and the breading soggy. In the case of shrimp, they are perfectly done when the shrimp have plumped and lost their translucence (often turning a rosy pink).

POPEYES: POPCORN SHRIMP
PO' BOY

SAVE: 188 CALORIES, 23 G FAT, 7 G SAT. FAT

I love breaded shrimp. If I could have only one breaded food for the rest of my life, it would be breaded jumbo shrimp (though earlier in life, I definitely would have opted for Chicken Parmesan). So I was excited to try this sandwich . . . but imagine my surprise when I realized that the breading was at least three times thicker than the shrimp—Popeyes actually uses salad shrimp. If you're like my friend Steve (see page 126) and like breading more than what's inside, this is the perfect sandwich for you. If you're like me, you might want to try my "Even Better" suggestion that follows or go elsewhere for hearty bites of plump shrimp nestled in a fresh deli roll.

Olive oil spray

1 ounce peeled, cooked salad or bay shrimp (about 20)

1 teaspoon unbleached or all-purpose flour

1/8 teaspoon salt

1/8 teaspoon cayenne

1 egg white

1/2 tablespoon fat-free milk

1/2 cup panko (Japanese bread crumbs)

1 submarine sandwich roll (about 6" long)

1 1/2 tablespoons Popeyes Tartar Sauce (page 75)

3/4 cup shredded iceberg lettuce

4 rounds crinkle-cut dill pickle

PREHEAT the oven to 475°F. Lightly mist a nonstick baking sheet with oil spray. Place the shrimp in a colander to drain excess liquid. Shake gently, then toss lightly in a paper towel to blot dry. Set aside.

In a small bowl, combine the flour, salt, and cayenne. With a fork, mix to blend. In another small bowl, combine the egg white and milk. Beat with a fork until smooth. Place the panko on a sheet of waxed paper set next to the bowl.

A few at a time, dip the shrimp into the flour mixture, making sure to coat them evenly. Shake off any excess flour. Dip into the egg-white mixture, being sure to coat completely. Allow any excess egg-white mixture to drip off. Dip into the panko to coat completely. Dip for a second time in the egg-white mixture and recoat with panko. Place on the reserved baking sheet. Continue until all of the

(continued)

shrimp are breaded. Place in a single layer, not touching, on the baking sheet. Lightly mist with oil spray.

Bake for 4 minutes. Carefully flip the shrimp. Bake for 4 to 6 minutes, or until the breading crisps but isn't completely browned.

Meanwhile, cut partially through the roll lengthwise (so that it opens wide enough to hold the sandwich ingredients). Preheat a small nonstick skillet over medium heat. Place the roll, cut-side down, in the pan. Cook for 2 to 3 minutes, or until toasted.

Place the roll on a plate. Spread the tartar sauce evenly over the top half. Cover with the lettuce. Place the pickles along the roll bottom. Pile the shrimp in the center and close the sandwich.

MAKES 1 SERVING (NUMBER OF PIECES VARIES ACCORDING TO SIZE OF SHRIMP)

442 calories, 18 g protein, 63 g carbohydrates, 9 g fat, 3 g sat. fat, 3 g fiber

Original Popeyes Popcorn Shrimp Po' Boy (20 pieces): 630 calories, 21 g protein, 67 g carbohydrates, 32 g fat, 10 g sat. fat, 1 g fiber

 DRIVE-THRU These shrimp can be made in batches and stored in the freezer before being baked. Simply line an airtight container with waxed paper. Lay the breaded shrimp in single layers, separating each layer with a sheet of waxed paper. When you're ready to eat them, bake the frozen shrimp according to the recipe directions for 5 to 7 minutes per side.

 EVEN BETTER Prefer more protein in your meal? Use larger shrimp. You'll end up with more protein per serving without adding any fat.

BEFORE YOU START Salad shrimp are sometimes also called bay shrimp. They come precooked but have so much water in them that it is okay to cook them again.

POPEYES TARTAR SAUCE

¼ cup low-fat mayonnaise

2 tablespoons dill pickle relish, finely chopped

1 teaspoon dill pickle juice

¼ teaspoon dehydrated finely chopped onion

⅛ teaspoon onion powder

⅛ teaspoon sugar

Pinch of salt

IN a small bowl, combine the mayonnaise, relish, pickle juice, onion, onion powder, sugar, and salt. Stir to blend well. Place in an airtight container. Refrigerate for up to 1 month.

MAKES ABOUT ⅓ CUP, ENOUGH FOR 4 SERVINGS

Each serving: 33 calories, trace protein, 4 g carbohydrates, 2 g fat, trace sat. fat, trace fiber

LONG JOHN SILVER'S: CRUNCHY SHRIMP BASKET (SHRIMP ONLY)

SAVE: 113 CALORIES, 17 G FAT, 5 G SAT. FAT

For me, this recipe was among the trickiest in the book. Not that the dish is hard to make (it's delightfully simple, in fact), but finding the right nutritional data was a real eye-opener. When I arrived at Long John Silver's, I had their nutrition pamphlet from 2003 in tow but soon discovered that few current menu items appeared to be listed. I wasn't sure if the items had changed or if they just called them by different names. Is "Battered Chicken" the same thing as a "Chicken Plank"? Does the nutritional data for the "Crunchy Shrimp (basket)" listed on the pamphlet as having "21 pieces" and displayed with fries in the basket on the menu include the fries?

After asking many questions and realizing that my pamphlet was outdated, I was finally able to secure the most recent one. But the whole experience really reminded me why I prefer to cook for myself. It's the best (and often easiest) way for me to know exactly what is going on my plate and how many calories and grams of fat will stay off my hips. Now you can know, too.

Olive oil spray

2½ ounces raw shrimp (the smallest peel-on shrimp you can find)

½ tablespoon unbleached or all-purpose flour

½ teaspoon sugar

⅛ teaspoon salt

⅛ teaspoon garlic powder

⅛ teaspoon onion powder

1 egg white

2 teaspoons fat-free milk

¼ cup + 1 tablespoon dry bread crumbs

Bottled cocktail sauce (optional)

PREHEAT the oven to 475°F. Lightly mist a nonstick baking sheet with oil spray.

Peel the shrimp, leaving the tail attached. Devein, if necessary. Place in a colander to drain excess liquid. Squeeze gently, then toss lightly in a paper towel. Set aside.

In a small resealable plastic bag, combine the flour, sugar, salt, garlic powder, and onion powder. Shake to blend well. Add the shrimp. Shake to evenly coat with the flour mixture.

In a small bowl, combine the egg white and milk. Beat with a fork until smooth. Place the bread crumbs in a small resealable plastic bag.

Transfer about 4 shrimp at a time from the flour mixture to the egg-white mixture, shaking gently to remove excess flour. Coat with the egg-white mixture and then remove with a fork, one by one, allowing any excess egg-white mixture to drip off. Transfer to the bread-crumb bag. Shake to coat well with the bread crumbs. Transfer back to the egg-white mixture. Repeat the egg-dipping and breading process a second time. Place the twice-breaded shrimp, one at a time, on the reserved baking sheet in a single layer so they do not touch. Continue until all of the shrimp are twice-breaded. Lightly mist with oil spray.

Bake for 5 minutes. Carefully flip the shrimp. Bake for 4 to 6 minutes, or until the breading crisps but is far from completely browned. Serve with cocktail sauce, if desired.

MAKES 1 SERVING (NUMBER VARIES ACCORDING TO SIZE OF SHRIMP)

227 calories, 20 g protein, 31 g carbohydrates, 2 g fat, trace sat. fat, 1 g fiber

Original Long John Silver's Crunchy Shrimp Basket (shrimp only, 21 pieces): 340 calories, 12 g protein, 32 g carbohydrates, 19 g fat, 5 g sat. fat, 2 g fiber

DRIVE-THRU These shrimp can be made in big batches and then stored for up to a month in the freezer before being baked. Simply line an airtight container with waxed paper. Lay the breaded shrimp in single layers, separating each layer with a sheet of waxed paper. When you're ready to eat them, bake the frozen shrimp according to the recipe directions for 5 to 7 minutes per side.

BEFORE YOU START Long John Silver's uses smaller shrimp in their Crunchy Shrimp Basket than are available in most supermarkets (they seemed to be 91 to 120 count at the restaurants I visited). If you are able to find shrimp that small, go ahead and try them out! If not, as long as you remember that 2½ ounces is a little more than ⅛ of a pound, your finished dish will weigh the same—you'll just have bigger pieces to enjoy. Also, if you prefer, you can prepare one of the low-fat tartar sauces (see pages 75, 81, and 83) instead of using bottled cocktail sauce.

LONG JOHN SILVER'S:
LOBSTER CRAB CAKES

SAVE: 66 CALORIES, 12 G FAT, 3 G SAT. FAT

Great TV requires drama . . . real or created. I recently learned that the hard way. I was the guest chef on a show where we threw a surprise party on camera. I was to create a special menu for the guest of honor and then assist his sisters and the show's host in preparing each dish.

When I learned that he loved spicy seafood, I was excited. Immediately, I knew what I wanted to serve: crab cakes. But as we prepared the crab cakes on camera, the host took a bite of the filling and started gagging—it was allegedly "too hot." Though the sisters thought it was pretty mild, every few minutes during the rest of the episode, the crab cakes were referred to as nuclear, or something along those lines. I couldn't believe it when I watched the episode back. Part of me thought it was funny, but another part was a little embarrassed.

Anyway, now I'm especially careful to alert people if the food I'm serving ever strays from mild. Fortunately, unlike my previous version, these crab cakes definitely don't require any such warning.

Olive oil spray

1/2 tablespoon finely chopped Fresno chile or red jalapeño chile

1 teaspoon finely chopped onion

1 1/2 ounces imitation lobster meat, torn into shreds (about 1/2 cup)

1 ounce drained canned crabmeat (about 1/3 cup)

1/2 ounce (about 1/4 cup) finely shredded, reduced-fat Monterey Jack cheese

4 tablespoons dry bread crumbs, divided

3 tablespoons egg substitute, divided

1 tablespoon finely chopped fresh parsley

1 teaspoon light corn syrup

1/4 teaspoon paprika

1/8 teaspoon garlic powder

PREHEAT the oven to 450°F. Lightly mist a small nonstick baking sheet with oil spray.

Preheat a small nonstick skillet over medium heat. Off the heat, mist the skillet with oil spray. Return to medium heat. Add the chile and onion. Cook, stirring occasionally, for about 2 minutes, or until softened.

In a mixing bowl, combine the imitation lobster, crabmeat, cheese, 1 tablespoon bread crumbs, 1 tablespoon egg substitute, parsley, corn syrup, paprika, garlic powder, and the chile-onion mixture. Stir to blend well. Divide the mixture in half. On a sheet of waxed paper, shape each half, packing tightly, into a 3″ patty. Set aside.

Place the remaining 2 tablespoons egg substitute in a small shallow bowl. Place the remaining 3 tablespoons bread crumbs on a small sheet of waxed paper set next to the bowl.

One at a time, carefully place a patty into the bread-crumb mixture (use a spatula if it begins to break apart), then gently turn to coat evenly. If the patty starts to break apart, pack it back together and reshape it. Transfer to the bowl and coat it with egg substitute, then return it to the bread crumbs. Place the patties, not touching, on the reserved baking sheet. Lightly mist with oil spray.

Bake for 5 minutes per side, or until golden brown and heated through.

MAKES 1 SERVING (2 CAKES)

274 calories, 23 g protein, 31 g carbohydrates, 6 g fat, 1 g sat. fat, 2 g fiber

Original Long John Silver's Lobster Crab Cakes (2 cakes): 340 calories, 12 g protein, 32 g carbohydrates, 18 g fat, 4 g sat. fat, 2 g fiber

BEFORE YOU START You can substitute imitation crabmeat for the imitation lobster if you'd prefer. Imitation lobster has a subtle buttery flavor that imitation crabmeat typically does not, but after it's mixed with the seasonings, the buttery flavor becomes practically nonexistent. Plus, imitation crabmeat is often sold in bulk at meat or fish counters, so you often don't have to buy a large package. And the imitation lobster tends to cost more per pound than imitation crabmeat.

Though not many people know Fresno chiles by name, they're very common and you've probably seen them in your local grocery store. They look like jalapeño chiles, but they are red and are sometimes called red jalapeños. Ask your produce person for assistance if you can't find them. If your grocery store does not carry them, you can substitute red bell pepper. If you'd prefer more spice, add a pinch of cayenne along with the red bell pepper.

MCDONALD'S: FILET-O-FISH

SAVE: 117 CALORIES, 10 G FAT, 2 G SAT. FAT

When I was 6, my Girl Scout troop took a field trip to the Baltimore Aquarium, the highlight of which was a lovely lunch at McDonald's on the way home. Just as my friend Erin was about to take a bite out of her Filet-O-Fish sandwich, another girl at the table said, "Hey, wait. That might be one of the fish we saw today." We all started laughing hard—that is, until she accidentally spit her orange soda all over Erin and me.

Even though we were only 6, Erin and I were sure we weren't eating one of the fish we just saw—we knew enough about cooking to know that it would take more time to cook a fish than had passed. But looking back, I wish I had been precocious enough at the time to say, "There's no way. They don't have hoki in Baltimore." Hoki (or pollock), of course, is the fish that McDonald's uses to make the original Filet-O-Fish.

Olive oil spray

1 center-cut cod or other mild white-flesh fish fillet (about 3½ ounces)

1 egg white

1 teaspoon fat-free milk

1 teaspoon unbleached or all-purpose flour

Pinch of paprika

Pinch of salt

1 tablespoon dry bread crumbs

½ teaspoon yellow cornmeal

1 hamburger bun

½ slice (¼ ounce) 2% milk yellow American cheese

1 tablespoon + ½ teaspoon McDonald's Tartar Sauce (opposite page)

PREHEAT the oven to 450°F. Lightly mist a small nonstick baking sheet with oil spray.

Place the fish on a cutting board. Cover with a sheet of waxed paper. With the smooth side of a meat mallet, gently pound to an even ¼" thickness. With a sharp knife, cut into a 3½" x 3" piece (about 2 ounces). (Refrigerate or freeze the scraps for another recipe.)

In a small shallow bowl, combine the egg white and the milk. Beat with a fork until smooth. Place 2 small sheets of waxed paper next to the bowl. On one sheet, combine the flour, paprika, and salt. Mix to blend. On the other sheet, combine the bread crumbs and cornmeal. Mix to blend.

Dip the fish into the flour mixture, making sure to coat it evenly. Shake off any excess flour. Dip into the egg-white mixture, being sure to coat completely. Allow any excess egg-white mixture to drip off. Dip into the bread-crumb mixture to coat completely. Place on the reserved baking sheet. Lightly mist with oil spray.

Bake for 5 minutes. Carefully flip the fish. Bake for 4 to 6 minutes, or until the breading is crisp and the fish flakes easily.

Meanwhile, preheat a small nonstick skillet over medium heat. Place the bun top and bottom, cut-sides down, in the pan. Cook for 2 to 3 minutes, or until toasted.

Place the bottom bun on a plate. Place the cheese on the center (it will not cover the whole bun bottom). Top with the fish, tartar sauce, and bun top.

MAKES 1 SERVING

283 calories, 19 g protein, 34 g carbohydrates, 8 g fat, 2 g sat. fat, 2 g fiber

Original McDonald's Filet-O-Fish: 400 calories, 14 g protein, 42 g carbohydrates, 18 g fat, 4 g sat. fat, 1 g fiber

DRIVE-THRU Don't have time to bread the fish? Buy a baked breaded fish fillet from the freezer section of most major supermarkets. Just be sure they are baked, not fried.

EVEN BETTER For a meal that won't look exactly like the original but will be higher in protein, don't trim the 3½-ounce fish fillet before cooking (increase the cooking time slightly). You'll add **8** grams of protein without adding fat or carbohydrates.

MCDONALD'S TARTAR SAUCE

¼ cup low-fat mayonnaise

1 tablespoon + 2 teaspoons dill pickle relish

¼ teaspoon sugar

Pinch of mustard powder

1 teaspoon chopped capers

IN a small bowl, combine the mayonnaise, relish, sugar, and mustard. Stir to blend well. Cover and refrigerate for up to 1 month.

Stir in the capers just before serving.

MAKES ABOUT ¼ CUP, ENOUGH FOR 4 SERVINGS

Each serving: 32 calories, <1 g protein, 4 g carbohydrates, 2 g fat, <1 g sat. fat, <1 g fiber

BURGER KING: BK FISH FILET

SAVE: 209 CALORIES, 21 G FAT, 6 G SAT. FAT

No longer a fast food follower over the past 12 years, I had my most jarring experience while picking up my BK Fish Filet. The bag containing my first test sandwich read: "Burger King: Running on Fumes: It's not always easy to plan out your next meal. So hold on to this bag. When properly sealed, there are still enough fumes trapped inside—even when empty—to keep a person going until the next visit."

Uh . . . what exactly does this mean?

Olive oil spray

1 center-cut cod or other mild white-flesh fish fillet (about $3\frac{1}{2}$ ounces)

1 egg white

1 teaspoon fat-free milk

1 teaspoon unbleached or all-purpose flour

Pinch of salt

1 tablespoon dry bread crumbs

1 hamburger bun

1 slice ($\frac{1}{2}$ ounce) 2% milk yellow American cheese

$\frac{1}{3}$ cup chopped iceberg lettuce

$1\frac{1}{2}$ tablespoons Burger King Tartar Sauce (opposite page)

PREHEAT the oven to 450°F. Lightly mist a small nonstick baking sheet with oil spray.

Place the fish on a cutting board. Cover with a sheet of waxed paper. With the smooth side of a meat mallet, gently pound to an even $\frac{1}{2}$" thickness. With a sharp knife, cut into a 3" x 3" piece (about $2\frac{1}{2}$ ounces). (Refrigerate the scraps for another recipe.)

In a small shallow bowl, combine the egg white and the milk. Beat with a fork until smooth. Place 2 small sheets of waxed paper next to the bowl. On one sheet, combine the flour and salt. Mix to blend. Place the bread crumbs on the other sheet.

Dip the fish into the flour mixture, making sure to coat it evenly. Shake off any excess flour. Dip into the egg-white mixture, being sure to coat completely. Allow any excess egg-white mixture to drip off. Dip into the bread crumbs to coat completely. Place on the reserved baking sheet. Lightly mist with oil spray.

Bake for 7 minutes. Carefully flip the fish. Bake for 5 to 7 minutes, or until the breading is crisp and the fish flakes easily.

Meanwhile, preheat a small nonstick skillet over medium heat. Place the bun top and bottom, cut-sides down, in the pan. Cook for 2 to 3 minutes, or until toasted.

Place the bun bottom on a plate. Top with the fish, cheese, and lettuce. Spread the Tartar Sauce on the cut-side of the bun top. Flip onto the sandwich.

MAKES 1 SERVING

311 calories, 22 g protein, 36 g carbohydrates, 9 g fat, 2 g sat. fat, 2 g fiber

Original Burger King BK Fish Filet: 520 calories, 18 g protein, 44 g carbohydrates, 30 g fat, 8 g sat. fat, 2 g fiber

 DRIVE-THRU Don't have time to bread the fish? Buy a baked breaded fish fillet. They can be found in the freezer section of most major supermarkets (just be sure they are baked, not fried). Using bagged preshredded lettuce will also save time.

EVEN BETTER For a meal that won't look exactly like the original but will be higher in protein, don't trim the 3½-ounce fish fillet before cooking (increase the cooking time slightly). You'll add 5 grams of protein without increasing carbohydrates or fat.

BURGER KING TARTAR SAUCE

¼ cup low-fat mayonnaise

2 tablespoons dill pickle relish

2 teaspoons light corn syrup

IN a small bowl, combine the mayonnaise, relish, and corn syrup. Stir to blend well. Place in an airtight container. Refrigerate for up to 1 month.

MAKES ABOUT ⅓ CUP, ENOUGH FOR 4 SERVINGS

Each serving: 41 calories, trace protein, 6 g carbohydrates, 2 g fat, trace sat. fat, trace fiber

WHITE CASTLE: FISH NIBBLERS
(SMALL)

SAVE: 72 CALORIES, 13 G FAT, 3.5 G SAT. FAT

While I was in Nashville researching recipes, I happened upon White Castle's Fish Nibblers. They looked tasty. And since I was having trouble selecting the perfect recipes for this chapter, I was excited to give the Nibblers a try . . . and, boy, was I glad I did. I loved them.

When I went to a local grocery store to buy ingredients to re-create them, I happened upon whiting, a fish I'd never seen in my Los Angeles grocery stores. Because it was so inexpensive, I decided to give it a try. I thought it was probably similar to pollock or hoki and figured whiting would be the perfect "white fish" to fill these great little nuggets from the sea. Unfortunately, I was wrong. Whiting was way too fishy for my taste. I immediately rushed back to buy some cod, which worked extremely well. If you find that cod is unavailable, I'd recommend haddock or red snapper to help you re-create this great White Castle experience, too (but skip the whiting).

Olive oil spray

1 center-cut cod or other mild white-fleshed fish fillet (about 4 ounces)

1 tablespoon unbleached or all-purpose flour

$\frac{1}{2}$ teaspoon salt

Pinch of garlic powder

1 egg white

$\frac{1}{2}$ tablespoon fat-free milk

2$\frac{1}{2}$ tablespoons dry bread crumbs

1 teaspoon dried parsley

Bottled low-fat tartar sauce (optional)

PREHEAT the oven to 450°F. Lightly mist a small nonstick baking sheet with oil spray.

Cut the fish into 14 pieces that are about equal in size. Pat dry with paper towels.

In a small resealable plastic bag, combine the flour, salt, and garlic powder. Shake to mix well. Add the fish. Shake to completely coat the fish with the flour mixture. Set aside.

In a small shallow bowl, combine the egg white and milk. Beat with a fork until smooth. Place the bread crumbs and parsley on a small sheet of waxed paper set next to the egg-white mixture. With fingers, mix to blend.

Dip the fish, one piece at a time, into the egg-white mixture, being sure to coat completely. Allow any excess egg-white mixture to drip off. Dip into the bread crumbs to coat completely. Place each piece on the reserved baking sheet. Continue until all of the fish pieces are placed on the baking sheet, not touching, in a single layer. Lightly mist with oil spray.

Bake for 4 minutes. Flip the pieces. Bake for 3 to 5 minutes, or until the breading starts to crisp and the fish flakes easily. Serve with tartar sauce, if desired.

MAKES 1 SERVING (14 NUGGETS)

208 calories, 25 g protein, 18 g carbohydrates, 3 g fat, trace sat. fat, 1 g fiber

Original White Castle Small Fish Nibblers (14 nuggets): 280 calories, 19 g protein, 24 g carbohydrates, 16 g fat, 3.5 g sat. fat, 5 g fiber

DRIVE-THRU These nuggets can be made in big batches and then stored in the freezer for up to 1 month before being baked. Simply line an airtight container with waxed paper. Lay the breaded nuggets in single layers, separating each layer with a sheet of waxed paper. When you're ready to eat them, bake the frozen nuggets according to the recipe directions for **4 to 6 minutes** per side.

BEFORE YOU START If you prefer, you can prepare one of the low-fat tartar sauces (see pages **75, 81,** and **83**) instead of using bottled tartar sauce.

JACK IN THE BOX: FISH AND CHIPS

SAVE: 445 CALORIES, 53 G FAT, 12 G SAT. FAT

If you love Jack in the Box, you're definitely not alone. While doing my research, I learned that their tacos have a huge following. Many friends, in fact, asked specifically if I planned to duplicate the recipe for their Monster Taco. They all said that they're so drippy and delicious.

Intrigued, I went and purchased one. Imagine my surprise when I learned that they stuff the taco and then deep-fry the whole thing. Though that recipe could very well make it into a sequel to this book, there were other taco favorites that better suited the current list.

Jack's Fish and Chips, on the other hand, are a perfect complement to the other recipes in this book. And, like the taco, they're very oily—so oily, in fact, that this is one of the few dishes that after it's fully cooked, I've instructed you to spray it with a light coating of olive oil to make sure it has that distinct glow and flavor. Don't worry, though . . . it still has far less fat than the original.

CHIPS

1¾ teaspoons salt, divided

1 russet potato (about 9 ounces)

1 teaspoon extra virgin olive oil

FISH

Olive oil spray

1 center-cut cod or other mild white-fleshed fish fillet (about 3 ounces)

1 tablespoon + 1 teaspoon unbleached or all-purpose flour

¼ teaspoon salt

1 egg white

1 teaspoon fat-free milk

¼ cup panko (Japanese bread crumbs)

TO prepare the chips: Preheat the oven to 450°F. Bring a large pot of water to a boil over high heat. Add 1 teaspoon salt.

With a knife, cut the potato into ⅓"-thick sticks of varying lengths. When the water boils, place them in the pot. Boil for exactly 3 minutes. Drain and allow to cool for 5 minutes.

Transfer the potato sticks to a medium bowl. Add the oil and ½ teaspoon salt. Carefully toss to coat. Place them in a single layer, not touching, on a large non-stick baking sheet.

Bake for 20 to 25 minutes, turning every 5 minutes, or until crisp and lightly browned. Sprinkle with the remaining 1/4 teaspoon salt, if desired. (Jack's fries are very salty.) While the potatoes are baking, prepare the fish.

TO prepare the fish: Lightly mist a small nonstick baking sheet with oil spray.

Place the fish on a cutting board. Cover with a sheet of waxed paper. With the smooth side of a meat mallet, gently pound to an even thickness just under 1/4". With a sharp knife, cut the fish into 3 strips of slightly different sizes. The strips should be 4" to 5" long and 2" to 2 1/2" wide and should be wider at one end than the other.

In a small resealable plastic bag, combine the flour and salt. Shake to mix well. Place one piece of the fish in the bag. Shake to completely coat the fish with the flour mixture. Remove and set on a piece of waxed paper. Continue flouring the remaining pieces. Set aside.

In a small shallow bowl, combine the egg white and milk. Beat with a fork until smooth. Place the panko on a sheet of waxed paper set next to the bowl.

One piece at a time, dip the fish into the egg-white mixture, being sure to coat completely. Allow any excess egg-white mixture to drip off. Dip into the panko to coat completely. Place on the reserved baking sheet. Continue until all of the fish pieces are placed, not touching, in a single layer on the baking sheet. Lightly mist with oil spray.

Bake for 5 minutes. Carefully flip the fish. Bake for 5 to 7 minutes, or until the breading is crisp and the fish flakes easily. Lightly mist both sides with oil spray. Serve with the chips.

MAKES 1 SERVING (3 PIECES FISH, PLUS CHIPS)

442 calories, 25 g protein, 63 g carbohydrates, 10 g fat, <1 g sat. fat, 6 g fiber

Original Jack in the Box Fish and Chips (3 pieces fish, plus chips): 887 calories, 18 g protein, 62 g carbohydrates, 63 g fat, 13 g sat. fat, 4 g fiber

STOP BEFORE YOU START Organizing your ingredients *before* you start cooking really pays off with this dish—the fish and chips will be ready and piping hot at the same time.

Start by setting out the potato and measuring all of the ingredients for the fish. After the potato is cut, seasoned, and put into the oven, you can quickly and easily dip and bread the fish, then pop them into the oven to bake while the potatoes finish cooking. Make sure both sheets are on the same oven rack or they won't brown properly. Also, since the primary flavor in this dish is oil, be sure to use your favorite full-flavored extra virgin olive oil in a refillable oil spray bottle.

THINK OUTSIDE THE BURGER

As far as I'm concerned, sandwiches and wraps are the ultimate healthy "fast food." Many take only minutes to throw together yet provide tons of nutrition to get you through the day. Some are a bit more time-consuming, but keeping low-fat tortillas, lean deli meats, and fresh produce on hand provides foolproof options for those days and nights that you just plain don't feel like cooking and don't want to rely on the drive-thru.

What Goes Into the Perfect
Sandwiches and Wraps?

The Tortillas

There are tons of burrito-size tortillas to choose from. Some are white, others are whole wheat; some are flavored with sun-dried tomatoes or spinach; others are low-fat, while some are even high in fiber. Always read the packages before purchasing your tortillas. One of my favorite brands is a whole wheat low-carb variety with about 220 calories, while another of my favorites is white but high in fiber; it has only 90 calories but 3 grams of fat. Your selection really depends on your preference. I like the latter a lot, because in addition to it having only 90 calories, I like the fact that I can eat a little less broccoli and still get the fiber my body needs. The 3 grams of fat, which come from extra virgin olive oil, really don't bother me. In this book, I've selected a tortilla that is more middle-of-the-road, so no matter which one you choose (as long as it's relatively low in fat), the nutritional information will be comparably similar.

Veggies

When making wraps, it's best to remember to cut any veggies finely. By doing so, your wrap will be easier to roll, and you'll lessen the chances that the tortilla will tear in the process.

Cheese

Although most available light cheese singles found in grocery stores are $3/4$-ounce each, I've found that most fast food restaurants use $1/2$-ounce cheese slices on their burgers and sandwiches. If you can't find $1/2$-ounce slices, simply purchase $3/4$-ounce slices and then put only two-thirds of the slice on your sandwich or wrap.

SUBWAY: MEATBALL MARINARA

SAVE: 206 CALORIES, 14 G FAT, 8 G SAT. FAT

If you're a true meatball lover, the key thing Subway's sandwich does is make you crave more of their yummy, yummy meatballs. Each 6″ sandwich contains only 4 tiny (1¼″, ¾-ounce) meatballs. Being an East Coast–raised Italian, I take issue with that. We like meat. In fact, we expect meat. So I made my meatballs a bit bigger, while reducing the fat by more than 50 percent.

Another objection I have is that Subway puts American cheese on a Meatball Marinara sandwich. Do they even know what American cheese is in Italy? Though I've kept the recipe true to Subway, I always add mozzarella to mine, and I invite you to do the same. Plus, I've found some amazingly tasty low-fat mozzarella cheeses. If you disagree with me (I'm sure many of you will), feel free to stick with American. I promise not to take it personally.

   Olive oil spray
   1 tablespoon dry bread crumbs
   1 tablespoon fat-free milk
   2½ ounces 96% lean ground beef
   1 tablespoon egg substitute
   ½ teaspoon dried parsley leaves
   ¼ teaspoon garlic powder
   ¼ teaspoon onion powder
   ¼ teaspoon salt
   ½ cup Subway Marinara Sauce (page 93)
   1 submarine sandwich roll (about 6″ long)
   1 slice (½ ounce) 2% milk white American cheese, halved diagonally

PREHEAT the oven to 400°F. Lightly mist a small nonstick baking dish with oil spray. Set aside.

In a small mixing bowl, combine the bread crumbs and the milk. Allow the milk to soak into the bread crumbs. Add the beef, egg substitute, parsley, garlic powder, onion powder, and salt. With hands, mix to blend well. Divide the beef mixture into 4 equal portions. With palms, roll each portion into a ball. Place, not touching, in the reserved baking dish.

Bake for 12 to 15 minutes, or until no longer pink inside. Check by inserting a sharp knife into the center of 1 meatball.

(continued)

Meanwhile, place the sauce in a small nonstick skillet over medium heat. Cook for 3 to 4 minutes, or until heated. Add the meatballs.

Cut partially through the roll lengthwise (so that it opens wide enough to hold the sandwich ingredients). Place the roll on a plate. Place the cheese slices evenly along the length of the roll. Spoon on the meatballs and the remaining sauce. Close the sandwich, allowing the cheese to melt.

MAKES 1 SANDWICH

404 calories, 28 g protein, 53 g carbohydrates, 10 g fat, 3 g sat. fat, 8 g fiber

Original Subway 6" Meatball Marinara: 610 calories, 24 g protein, 63 g carbohydrates, 24 g fat, 11 g sat. fat, 7 g fiber

 EVEN BETTER There is a lot of bread on this sandwich. Instead of using a 6" roll, buy a whole wheat or whole grain hot dog bun. The meatballs will fit perfectly. The revised version will have **382** calories, **26 g** protein, **51 g** carbohydrates, **9 g** fat, **3 g** sat. fat, and **8 g** fiber. You save **228** calories, **15 g** fat, and **8 g** sat. fat.

DRIVE-THRU Long day? Use a low-fat jarred marinara sauce instead of making it homemade. Subway's marinara is very sweet. Try to find a delicious marinara with a subtle but sweet flavor.

If you're really in a hurry, buy low-fat turkey meatballs. Just be sure that they are actually low in fat. Many prepared turkey meatballs derive **50** percent (or more) of their calories from fat.

BEFORE YOU START If you're cooking more than one sandwich at a time, you can multiply the ingredients in the meatballs easily.

SUBWAY MARINARA SAUCE

Olive oil spray

1/4 cup + 2 tablespoons finely chopped onion

2 teaspoons minced garlic

1 1/3 cups canned crushed tomatoes

1/4 cup water

2 teaspoons sugar

2 teaspoons dried oregano

1 teaspoon extra virgin olive oil

LIGHTLY mist a large nonstick skillet with oil spray. Set over medium heat. In the skillet, combine the onion and garlic. Cook, stirring occasionally with a wooden spoon, for 3 to 5 minutes, or until the onion starts to soften but not brown. Reduce the heat to low. Add the tomatoes, water, sugar, oregano, and oil. Stir to blend well. Refrigerate up to 1 week until ready to use.

MAKES 2 CUPS, ENOUGH FOR 4 SANDWICHES

Each serving: 57 calories, 2 g protein, 10 g carbohydrates, 1 g fat, trace sat. fat, 2 g fiber

SUBWAY: CHIPOTLE SOUTHWEST CHEESE STEAK

SAVE: 76 CALORIES, 9 G FAT, 2 G SAT. FAT

Question: How many inches is a 6" sub?

Answer: It varies.

At least in my experience at Subway, it varies. Sometimes a 6" sub was a 6" sub, sometimes it was 5½", and a few times it was 7".

So what does this mean? Well, like many restaurants, from fast food to fine dining, portions can vary. Though it's somewhat harmless, it can of course affect the accuracy of nutritional information . . . often more than you'd think. I've shared more details on my Subway experience beginning on page 13, but here, I've shared the tasty recipe worth going to the extra effort for.

> 5–6 ounces beef top round steak or roast (at least 1½" thick)
>
> Olive oil spray
>
> 1 tablespoon finely chopped white onion
>
> ½ tablespoon finely chopped green bell pepper
>
> ¼ teaspoon salt
>
> 1 submarine sandwich roll (about 6" long)
>
> 1 slice (½ ounce) 2% milk white American cheese, halved diagonally
>
> ½ cup shredded iceberg lettuce
>
> 1 slice large red onion (⅛" thick), separated into rings
>
> 3 slices tomato (⅛" thick)
>
> 3 slices green bell pepper (⅛" thick)
>
> 5 rounds dill pickle
>
> 2 medium black olives, sliced
>
> Red wine vinegar (optional)
>
> 1½ tablespoons Subway Chipotle Southwest Sauce (opposite page)

PLACE the beef in the freezer for 15 to 20 minutes and then transfer to a cutting board. With a sharp knife, cut diagonally across the grain to slice as thinly as possible, almost shaving it. Set aside 3 ounces of beef (a generous ⅓ cup). (Refrigerate the scraps for another recipe.)

Preheat the broiler.

Preheat a small nonstick skillet over medium-high heat until drops of water sizzle when splashed on the pan. Off the heat, lightly mist with oil spray. Return the pan to stove top. Add the white onion, finely chopped pepper, and the beef. Sprinkle with salt. Cook, tossing, for 2 to 4 minutes, or until the beef is no longer pink.

Meanwhile, cut partially through the roll lengthwise (so that it opens wide enough to add the sandwich ingredients). Transfer the beef mixture to the roll. Lay the cheese slices, side by side, over the beef mixture. Place on a broiler pan or sheet of aluminum foil. Broil for about 1 minute, or just until the cheese melts.

Place the lettuce evenly over the cheese. Top with the red onion, tomato, sliced pepper, pickles, and olives. Season to taste with a few splashes of vinegar, if desired. Spoon the sauce evenly over the top. Close the sandwich.

MAKES 1 SERVING

374 calories, 29 g protein, 45 g carbohydrates, 11 g fat, 4 g sat. fat, 5 g fiber

Original Subway Chipotle Southwest Cheese Steak: 450 calories, 24 g protein, 48 g carbohydrates, 20 g fat, 6 g sat. fat, 6 g fiber

(STOP) **BEFORE YOU START** You'll need only **3** ounces of steak for each sandwich, but a larger piece is called for in the recipe because it will make it much easier to slice paper thin. If you're preparing **2** or more sandwiches at the same time, allow about **5** ounces of beef per sandwich.

SUBWAY CHIPOTLE SOUTHWEST SAUCE

¼ cup + 2 tablespoons low-fat mayonnaise

½ tablespoon mild picante sauce

½ tablespoon sugar

½ tablespoon apple cider vinegar

½ teaspoon ground chipotle chile pepper

½ teaspoon dried parsley

IN a small bowl, combine the mayonnaise, picante sauce, sugar, vinegar, chipotle chile pepper, and parsley. Stir to mix well. Cover with plastic wrap. Refrigerate for up to 1 month.

MAKES ABOUT ⅓ CUP, ENOUGH FOR 4 SERVINGS

Each serving: 45 calories, trace protein, 5 g carbohydrates, 3 g fat, 0 g sat. fat, trace fiber

SUBWAY: TURKEY BREAST AND BACON MELT WRAP
(WITH CHIPOTLE SOUTHWEST SAUCE)

SAVE: 108 CALORIES, 14 G FAT, 7 G SAT. FAT

I'm a creature of habit who can eat the same dish meal after meal (assuming it's a dish I love), and it won't bother me. I eat breakfast food for dinner and dinner food for breakfast—even sushi. Yep, I can enjoy sushi for breakfast.

Though I eat wraps frequently—I might even go so far as to say that they are one of my top 5 standby meals (even for breakfast)—I'd never packed one with as many "normal" ingredients as Subway customarily packs (unless you request otherwise) into its Turkey Breast and Bacon Melt Wrap. Now by "normal," I mean that I've loaded wraps with roasted red peppers, fresh basil, chili paste, sprouts, arugula, and other gourmet ingredients, but it never occurred to me that pickles, green peppers, and olives could enhance turkey in such a wonderful way.

Ever since I tried my first bite of this wrap, I've had the combo on my brain (granted, I skip the bacon and cheese and just go for shaved honey turkey breast when eating it often), and I just keep finding myself craving it. That means one thing to me: Not only is this sandwich really tasty, but it's worth going the additional step to chop up a few of the "extras." Those "extras" not only add fiber to my diet, they also make me crave healthy fare.

2 slices center-cut bacon

3 slices (³⁄₄-ounce each) packaged thick-cut oven-roasted turkey breast

¹⁄₃ ounce (about 2¹⁄₂ tablespoons) finely shredded low-fat Cheddar cheese

¹⁄₃ ounce (about 2¹⁄₂ tablespoons) finely shredded reduced-fat Monterey Jack cheese

1 burrito-size (10") low-carbohydrate whole wheat tortilla

¹⁄₂ cup shredded iceberg lettuce

3 slices tomato (¹⁄₈" thick)

1 slice red onion (¹⁄₈" thick), separated into rings

7 strips green bell pepper (¹⁄₈" thick)

7 rounds dill pickle

2 medium black olives, sliced

1¹⁄₂ tablespoons Subway Chipotle Southwest Sauce (page 95)

PLACE the bacon in a small nonstick skillet set over medium heat. Cook, flipping occasionally, for 4 to 6 minutes, or until cooked but not crisp. Transfer to a paper towel–lined plate to drain.

Place a sheet of waxed paper on a work surface. One at a time, fold the turkey slices in half. Place 1 slice on the waxed paper. Place the second slice, folded-side facing in the same direction, overlapping about half of the first slice. Place the third slice, folded-side facing in the same direction, overlapping about half of the second slice. Place the bacon slices crosswise over the turkey. Add the cheeses in an even layer. Transfer the waxed paper to the microwave oven. Cook on low power for 10 seconds. If the cheese has not started to melt, cook in 10-second intervals until the cheese starts to melt and the turkey is heated. Set aside.

Place the tortilla on a plate. Place the lettuce, leaving about 1" bare on both ends, in an even strip (about 3" wide) running across the center. Top the lettuce evenly with the tomato, onion, pepper, pickles, olives, and sauce. Carefully flip the reserved turkey-bacon-and-cheese combo onto the filling ingredients. Fold both bare ends over the filling ingredients. Roll the tortilla tightly, finishing it seam-side down on the plate. Cut in half, if desired.

MAKES 1 SERVING

332 calories, 31 g protein, 32 g carbohydrates, 14 g fat, 3 g sat. fat, 14 g fiber

Original Subway Turkey Breast and Bacon Melt Wrap with Chipotle Southwest Sauce: 440 calories, 34 g protein, 20 g carbohydrates, 28 g fat, 10 g sat. fat, 9 g fiber

KFC: TWISTER

SAVE: 245 CALORIES, 28 G FAT, 6 G SAT. FAT

You may recognize this recipe from the cover of this book. It's interesting to remember that during the photo shoot, when we first saw this wrap through the lens of the camera, I was worried that it was going to look more like a salad with a little bit of chicken in a tortilla. I really wanted it to come across that the chicken pieces are big and juicy and that this dish is not just a lot of rabbit food. The food stylist explained that the tomato slices made the photo "pop," and then he kindly remade it for me. Immediately, I could see that he was right. That gorgeous red tomato outlined the chicken perfectly.

I mentioned in the acknowledgments section of this book that without the help of so many people, I still would not be sleeping and you would not be holding this book in your hands. This is one of the prime examples of behind-the-scenes talent that contributed to this book. And boy am I grateful to every person who contributed.

$\frac{1}{2}$ tablespoon unbleached or all-purpose flour

$\frac{1}{4}$ teaspoon ground black pepper + additional for sprinkling

$\frac{1}{4}$ teaspoon salt + additional for sprinkling

$\frac{1}{8}$ teaspoon onion powder

2 boneless, skinless chicken breast tenders ($1\frac{1}{4}$ ounces each)

Olive oil spray

1 egg white

1 teaspoon fat-free milk

$\frac{1}{4}$ cup + 1 tablespoon panko (Japanese bread crumbs)

1 burrito-size (10") low-fat flour tortilla

1 tablespoon KFC Twister Sauce (opposite page)

$\frac{1}{4}$ cup shredded iceberg lettuce

2 slices tomato ($\frac{1}{8}$" thick)

IN a resealable plastic bag, combine the flour, $\frac{1}{4}$ teaspoon pepper, $\frac{1}{4}$ teaspoon salt, and the onion powder. Shake to mix well. Add the chicken. Shake to completely coat the chicken with the flour mixture. Place in the refrigerator for at least 10 minutes.

Preheat the oven to 475°F. Lightly mist a nonstick baking sheet with oil spray.

In a small bowl, combine the egg white and milk. Beat with a fork until smooth. Place the panko on a small sheet of waxed paper set next to the bowl.

Dip one of the chicken tenders into the egg-white mixture, being sure to coat completely. Allow any excess egg-white mixture to drip off. Dip into the panko to coat completely. Repeat dipping a second time into the egg-white mixture and the panko. Place on the reserved baking sheet. Continue with the second piece of chicken. Place, not touching, on the baking sheet. Lightly mist both sides with oil spray. Season to taste with salt and pepper.

Bake for 5 minutes. Carefully flip the chicken. Bake for 4 to 6 minutes, or until the breading starts to crisp and the chicken is no longer pink inside.

Meanwhile, preheat a large nonstick skillet over medium heat. Place the tortilla in the skillet. Heat for 1 to 2 minutes per side, or until warm.

Starting at the 9 o'clock position on the tortilla, spread the sauce in an even strip (about 3″ wide) running across the tortilla, leaving about 1″ bare at the end of the strip.

Top the sauce-covered area evenly with the lettuce, tomato, and chicken. Fold the bare end over the filling ingredients. Roll the tortilla tightly, finishing it seam-side down on the plate. One end of the wrap will remain open.

MAKES 1 SERVING

425 calories, 29 g protein, 55 g carbohydrates, 10 g fat, <1 g sat. fat, 4 g fiber

Original KFC Twister: 670 calories, 27 g protein, 55 g carbohydrates, 38 g fat, 7 g sat. fat, 3 g fiber

DRIVE-THRU Want a Twister on a whim? Bread a few batches of the chicken and freeze it before baking it. When you're ready for your Twister, pop the frozen chicken into a preheated 475°F oven for 5 to 7 minutes per side.

Keep the Twister Sauce stored in your refrigerator, and you'll be able to assemble the wrap in minutes.

KFC TWISTER SAUCE

¼ cup + ¼ teaspoon light mayonnaise

1 teaspoon sugar

½ teaspoon ground black pepper

IN a small bowl, combine the mayonnaise, sugar, and pepper. Stir to blend well. Cover with plastic wrap. Refrigerate for up to 1 month.

MAKES ¼ CUP, ENOUGH FOR 4 SERVINGS

Each serving: 51 calories, trace protein, 2 g carbohydrates, 5 g fat, <1 g sat. fat, trace fiber

SONIC: COUNTRY-FRIED STEAK SANDWICH

SAVE: 204 CALORIES, 33 G FAT, 10 G SAT. FAT

I fear that this recipe might not be as on-the-money in the flavor department as most of the others in the book, because between the time I was developing it and retesting it, Sonic stopped offering it. I almost decided to cut it completely, but my friend Jessica urged me not to, as it is one of her favorite sandwiches ever and she can no longer get it at all. At least this way, she said, she'll be able to make it at home. I considered her request but feared that perhaps it was discontinued because it just wasn't that popular. Then I remembered that as a kid, my all-time favorite sandwich was the Burger King Chicken Parmesan Sandwich, which has long since been discontinued. Not only did I miss it, but I know a lot of other people did, too.

So here it is. Hopefully, my version was close enough in the original testing stage to have that great flavor and texture that the original had, and it won't really matter that I never had the chance to order it a few more times.

½ tablespoon unbleached or all-purpose flour

¼ teaspoon + ⅛ teaspoon salt

¼ teaspoon ground black pepper + additional for sprinkling

⅛ teaspoon garlic powder

Pinch of turmeric

2¼ ounces 96% lean ground beef (¼ cup + ½ Tbsp.)

4 tablespoons dry bread crumbs, divided

1 tablespoon + 1 teaspoon + 1 tablespoon egg substitute

1 tablespoon fat-free milk

Olive oil spray

1 teaspoon paprika

2 slices Texas toast–style bread

2 teaspoons light butter (softened) or light butter spread

2 teaspoons light mayonnaise

¼ cup chopped iceberg lettuce

2 slices tomato (⅛″ thick)

ON a sheet of waxed paper, combine the flour, ¼ teaspoon salt, ¼ teaspoon pepper, garlic powder, and turmeric. Mix to blend. Set aside.

In a small bowl, combine the beef with 2 tablespoons bread crumbs, 1 tablespoon + 1 teaspoon egg substitute, milk, and the remaining ⅛ teaspoon salt. Mix to blend.

On a sheet of waxed paper, shape the mixture into a patty that is roughly 5" x 4". It shouldn't be a perfect rectangle. Very carefully, dip both sides into the flour mixture, making sure to coat it evenly. (If it breaks slightly, just reshape it.) Cover loosely with plastic wrap. Place in the freezer for 15 minutes.

Preheat the oven to 450°F. Lightly mist a small nonstick baking sheet with oil spray.

In a shallow bowl, combine the remaining 1 tablespoon egg substitute and paprika. Beat with a fork to blend. Place the remaining 2 tablespoons bread crumbs on a sheet of waxed paper set next to the bowl.

With a spatula, dip the patty into the egg-substitute mixture, being sure to coat completely. Allow any excess egg-substitute mixture to drip off. Dip into the bread crumbs to coat completely. If it breaks slightly, just reshape it. Season both sides with pepper to taste. Lightly mist both sides with oil spray. Place on the reserved baking sheet.

Bake for 4 minutes. Carefully flip the patty. Bake for 4 to 6 minutes, or until it is crisp and no longer pink inside. Check by inserting a sharp knife into the center.

Meanwhile, preheat a medium nonstick skillet over medium heat. Spread 1 side of each bread slice with 1 teaspoon of butter or butter spread. Place, buttered-sides down, in the skillet. Cook for 2 to 3 minutes, or until toasted. Place 1 slice of bread, toasted-side down, on a plate. Spread evenly with the mayonnaise. Top with the lettuce, tomato, steak, and the remaining bread slice, toasted-side up.

MAKES 1 SERVING

544 calories, 25 g protein, 51 g carbohydrates, 14 g fat, 2 g sat. fat, 3 g fiber

Original Sonic Country-Fried Steak Sandwich: 748 calories, 24 g protein, 56 g carbohydrates, 47 g fat, 12 g sat. fat, 2 g fiber

SONIC: GRILLED CHICKEN WRAP

SAVE: 205 CALORIES, 19 G FAT, 4 G SAT. FAT

We all know that grilled chicken is much better for us than fried chicken . . . right? Most of the time, this rule of thumb is definitely true. So imagine my surprise when I learned that the Sonic Grilled Chicken Wrap has only 35 calories and 2 grams of fat less than their Chicken Strip Wrap, which features breaded and fried chicken strips. According to their Web site, the Grilled Chicken and the Chicken Strip Wraps both include a flour tortilla, lettuce, tomato, and "Lite Ranch Dressing," yet there is little difference in their nutritional value. And even though they use "Lite Ranch" as standard, both wraps still have about 27 to 29 grams of fat per wrap before any add-ons such as crispy bacon, cheese, etc. Because I wanted to provide the widest possible variety of dishes in this chapter, that bit of information sealed my decision to create a lighter version of this delicious wrap.

> 1 boneless, skinless chicken breast half (about 3 ounces)
>
> 1 teaspoon unbleached or all-purpose flour
>
> $\frac{1}{4}$ teaspoon salt
>
> $\frac{1}{8}$ teaspoon paprika
>
> Pinch of onion powder
>
> Olive oil spray
>
> 1 burrito-size (10") low-fat flour tortilla
>
> 2 tablespoons Sonic Ranch Sauce (opposite page)
>
> $\frac{1}{2}$ cup chopped iceberg lettuce
>
> 2 slices tomato ($\frac{1}{8}$" thick)

PLACE the chicken on a cutting board. Cover with a sheet of waxed paper. With the smooth side of a meat mallet, pound to an even $\frac{1}{3}$" thickness. Set aside.

In a small resealable plastic bag, combine the flour, salt, paprika, and onion powder. Shake to mix well. Add the chicken. Shake to completely coat the chicken with the flour mixture. Place in the refrigerator for at least 10 minutes.

Preheat the grill to high heat. Lightly mist the chicken with oil spray. Place it on the grill rack. Grill for 3 to 5 minutes per side, or until both sides are seared with grill marks and the chicken is no longer pink inside. If the chicken is browning too fast, reduce the heat to medium on a gas grill or move away from direct heat on a charcoal grill. Allow the chicken to rest about 5 minutes on a clean cutting board and then cut it into 4 crosswise strips. Set aside.

Meanwhile, preheat a large nonstick skillet over medium heat. Place the tortilla in the skillet. Heat for 1 to 2 minutes per side, or until warm.

Place the tortilla on a plate. Spread the sauce, leaving about 1″ bare on both ends, in an even strip (about 3″ wide) running across the center. Top the sauce evenly with the lettuce, tomato, and chicken. Fold both bare ends over the filling ingredients. Roll the tortilla tightly, finishing it seam-side down on the plate.

MAKES 1 SERVING

334 calories, 25 g protein, 40 g carbohydrates, 8 g fat, 1 g sat. fat, 4 g fiber

Original Sonic Grilled Chicken Wrap: 539 calories, 29 g protein, 40 g carbohydrates, 27 g fat, 5 g sat. fat, 2 g fiber

(STOP) **BEFORE YOU START** To get the fullest flavor, grill the chicken on a charcoal grill, gas grill, or stove-top grill pan. I don't recommend a contact grill, however. Contact grills steam more than grill, so the chicken won't develop the wonderful flavor that searing gives it.

SONIC RANCH SAUCE

¼ cup low-fat buttermilk

¼ cup light mayonnaise

1 teaspoon ranch dressing mix

1 teaspoon sugar

Pinch of salt

IN a small bowl, combine the buttermilk and mayonnaise. Whisk to blend. Add the dressing mix, sugar, and salt. Whisk to blend. Cover with plastic wrap. Refrigerate for up to 3 days.

MAKES ABOUT ½ CUP, ENOUGH FOR 4 SERVINGS

Each serving: 63 calories, <1 g protein, 3 g carbohydrates, 5 g fat, <1 g sat. fat, 0 g fiber

STEAK 'N SHAKE: FRISCO MELT

SAVE: 729 CALORIES, 75 G FAT, 22.5 G SAT. FAT

I have to hand it to the folks at Steak 'n Shake. Their nutritional data breaks out each individual ingredient—I actually get to know when cutting a component is worth it.

After studying the numbers, if I were to custom-order a Steak 'n Shake Frisco Melt, I'd definitely skip the "grilling oil for bread." Apparently, the oil used on the exterior of the sandwich accounts for 30 grams of fat. That's right, 30 grams. That's practically what I eat in a day, and it's on the outside of the sandwich.

One of the other things I really appreciate about Steak 'n Shake is that I was able to watch the cook make my sandwich. I watched him slather 30 grams of "grilling oil for bread" onto my bread in one steady motion by grabbing a slice from the bag and running it over something that looked like a drum rotating in warm oil. From there, my bread practically fell right onto the grill. How amazing is that? Fully 270 calories in one fell swoop.

> 5 ounces 96% lean ground beef
>
> 1 tablespoon light butter spread, divided
>
> 2 slices sourdough sandwich bread
>
> 1 slice ($\frac{1}{2}$ ounce) light Swiss cheese
>
> 2 slices ($\frac{1}{2}$ ounce each) 2% milk yellow American cheese, halved diagonally
>
> 1 tablespoon + $\frac{1}{2}$ teaspoon Steak 'n Shake Frisco Sauce (opposite page)
>
> $\frac{1}{2}$ leaf romaine lettuce
>
> 1 slice tomato ($\frac{1}{4}$" thick)

DIVIDE the beef in half. On a sheet of waxed paper, shape each half into a $4\frac{1}{2}$" squarish patty. Set aside.

Meanwhile, preheat a large nonstick skillet over medium-high heat until drops of water sizzle when splashed on the pan. Spread 1 side of each bread slice with half of the butter spread. Place, buttered-sides down, in the skillet. Place the patties next to the bread. Cook the bread for 2 to 3 minutes, or until toasted. Cook the patties for 1 to 2 minutes per side, or until the beef is no longer pink.

Place 1 slice of bread, toasted-side down, on a plate. Top with the Swiss cheese, 1 burger, the American cheese, and the second burger. On the nontoasted side of the second bread slice, spread the sauce evenly to within $\frac{1}{4}$" of the edge. Place, sauce-side down, onto the sandwich. On top of the finished sandwich, place the lettuce and then the tomato.

MAKES 1 SERVING

444 calories, 40 g protein, 31 g carbohydrates, 18 g fat, 6 g sat. fat, 1 g fiber

Original Steak 'n Shake Frisco Melt: 1,173 calories, 40 g protein, 44 g carbohydrates, 93 g fat, 28.5 g sat. fat, 1 g fiber

STEAK 'N SHAKE FRISCO SAUCE

¼ cup low-fat mayonnaise

1 tablespoon + 1 teaspoon ketchup

1 teaspoon sugar

½ teaspoon sweet pickle relish

IN a small bowl, combine the mayonnaise, ketchup, sugar, and relish. Stir to mix. Cover with plastic wrap. Refrigerate for up to 1 month.

MAKES ABOUT ¼ CUP, ENOUGH FOR 4 SERVINGS

Each serving: 35 calories, trace protein, 5 g carbohydrates, 2 g fat, 0 g sat. fat, trace fiber

ARBY'S: BIG MONTANA

SAVE: 230 CALORIES, 22 G FAT, 10 G SAT. FAT

This sandwich gets the "Fast Food Fix" Award for easiest and quickest recipe of the book. There's no way (unless you literally live right next door to an Arby's, and even then it's probably not possible) to buy this delicious sandwich quicker than you can make it if you stock the tiny list of ingredients in your refrigerator. It's simple; it's fast; you really don't even need to know how to cook to make it; yet the fat is reduced by more than 75 percent.

> 1 restaurant-style sesame seed bun (about 3¾")
>
> 7 ounces packaged 97% fat-free shaved delicatessen roast beef

PREHEAT a nonstick skillet over medium heat. Place the bun top and bottom, cut-sides down, in the pan. Cook for 2 to 3 minutes, or until toasted.

Meanwhile, lay a sheet of waxed paper on a microwavable plate. Pile the roast beef on the waxed paper. Place in the microwave oven. Cook on low power for 10 seconds. If the roast beef is not warm in the center, rotate it, then cook in 10-second intervals until the center is heated. Place the bun bottom on a plate. Pile the roast beef onto the bun. Cover with the bun top.

MAKES 1 SERVING

360 calories, 41 g protein, 31 g carbohydrates, 7 g fat, 4 g sat. fat, <1 g fiber

Original Arby's Big Montana: 590 calories, 47 g protein, 41 g carbohydrates, 29 g fat, 14 g sat. fat, 3 g fiber

(STOP) BEFORE YOU START Restaurant-style sesame seed buns, sometimes labeled Texas-style buns, are larger than standard hamburger buns, which are about 3½". Look for bagged sesame seed buns in the same supermarket aisle as the hamburger buns. To make sure you have the larger size, grab a package of the hamburger buns for comparison.

HARDEE'S: BIG HOT HAM 'N' CHEESE

SAVE: 73 CALORIES, 11 G FAT, 7 G SAT. FAT

There was a time I thought that ham was so fattening, I'd have to say good-bye to it forever. This was particularly daunting because, as a kid, one of my favorite things to do with my mother was make homemade Spam. She'd put my sister and me on the kitchen counter, then pull the leftover ham from the refrigerator. She'd let us help grind it—watching it emerge from the grinder was just about the coolest thing for a little kid. We'd then add mayo and relish, and voilà. It was so good. And although not even my mom would eat homemade Spam today, the thought of ham always makes me smile.

Fortunately, we've come a long way nutritionally, and some ham is actually pretty lean. After losing weight, I never thought I'd consider eating a big meaty ham and cheese sandwich, but now I can and you can too, as inspired by Hardee's.

> 1 sesame seed sandwich bun (about 5")
>
> 4 ounces packaged 97% fat-free shaved delicatessen honey ham
>
> 3 slices (½ ounce each) 2% milk Swiss-style cheese

PREHEAT a nonstick skillet over medium heat. Place the bun top and bottom, cut-sides down, in the pan. Cook for 2 to 3 minutes, or until toasted.

Meanwhile, lay a sheet of waxed paper on a microwavable plate. Pile half of the ham on the waxed paper. Top with 1 slice cheese. Pile on the remaining ham and then the second slice of cheese. Place in the microwave oven. Cook on low power for 10 seconds. If the center cheese has not started to melt, cook in 10-second intervals until the center cheese starts to melt and the ham is heated.

Place the bun bottom on a plate. Flip the ham and cheese stack onto the bun. Remove the waxed paper. Top with the remaining 1 slice cheese and the bun top.

MAKES 1 SERVING

447 calories, 35 g protein, 45 g carbohydrates, 13 g fat, 6 g sat. fat, 2 g fiber

Original Hardee's Big Hot Ham 'N' Cheese: 520 calories, 40 g protein, 40 g carbohydrates, 24 g fat, 13 g sat. fat, 2 g fiber

STOP **BEFORE YOU START** Sesame seed sandwich buns, the 5" size, are larger than standard hamburger buns, which are about 3½". Look for bagged sesame seed sandwich buns in the same supermarket aisle as the hamburger buns. To make sure you have the larger size, grab a package of the hamburger buns for comparison.

BLIMPIE: BEEF AND CHEDDAR WRAP

SAVE: 321 CALORIES, 29 G FAT, 8 G SAT. FAT

When I picked up my first Blimpie wrap, I was surprised to learn that Blimpie serves its wraps on extra-large tortillas—the 12" size that isn't easy to find outside of Mexican markets and specialty stores. Personally, being a meat lover and a person who doesn't want to totally overdo it on carbs, I prefer to have this sandwich on a standard low-fat 10" burrito-size wrap, which is plenty big enough to hold the beef, Cheddar, and trimmings. Since I've never seen a low-fat 12" tortilla (most have 10 grams of fat or more!), I've made over the sandwich using a low-fat 10" burrito-size tortilla. Although the size and weight of the tortilla are only slightly less than the original, the calories and fat are dramatically reduced. Plus, the weight of the important stuff—all of the scrumptious fillings—is the same as the original.

> 1 burrito-size (10") low-fat flour tortilla
>
> 4 ounces packaged 97% fat-free shaved roast beef
>
> 3 slices (about 1/3 ounce each; 1 ounce total) low-fat Cheddar cheese, diagonally cut
>
> 1/2 cup shredded iceberg lettuce
>
> 2 slices tomato (1/8" thick)
>
> 1 slice large red onion (1/8" thick), separated into rings
>
> 1 1/2 tablespoons Blimpie Peppercorn Sauce (opposite page)

PLACE the tortilla on a plate. Place the beef, leaving about 1" bare on both ends, in an even strip (about 3" wide) running across the center. Top the beef evenly with the cheese, lettuce, tomato, onion, and sauce. Fold both bare ends over the filling ingredients. Roll the tortilla tightly, finishing it seam-side down on the plate.

MAKES 1 SERVING (PREPARED WITH A 10" LOW-FAT TORTILLA)

389 calories, 35 g protein, 43 g carbohydrates, 8 g fat, 3 g sat. fat, 4 g fiber

Original Blimpie Beef and Cheddar Wrap (prepared with a 12" regular tortilla): 710 calories, 34 g protein, 57 g carbohydrates, 37 g fat, 11 g sat. fat, fiber (not available)

BLIMPIE PEPPERCORN SAUCE

¼ cup low-fat mayonnaise

1 tablespoon fat-free milk

2 teaspoons low-fat buttermilk

2 teaspoons reduced-fat grated Parmesan cheese

1 teaspoon white vinegar

⅛ teaspoon ground black pepper

IN a small bowl, combine the mayonnaise, fat-free milk, buttermilk, cheese, vinegar, and pepper. Whisk to blend well. Cover with plastic wrap. Refrigerate for up to 3 days.

MAKES ABOUT ⅓ CUP, ENOUGH FOR 4 SERVINGS

Each serving: 33 calories, <1 g protein, 3 g carbohydrates, 2 g fat, trace sat. fat, trace fiber

CHAPTER
6

WOULD YOU LIKE FRIES WITH THAT?

A burger isn't a burger without the fries or onion rings. But the sides don't have to be deep-fried. If you've never had fries or rings baked from scratch, you'll most likely be shocked by the fresh taste and incredible texture of these creations. And in my opinion, if these don't stop your cravings, nothing will.

What Goes Into the Perfect Fries?

Russet Potatoes

Also known as baking potatoes, these spuds are the best variety to use for all of the french fries recipes in this book, not only because their large, uniform size makes for easier cutting, but also because they contain just the right amount of starch to yield a nice, fluffy fry every time. Waxy or creamy potatoes (like Yukon Gold and Red Bliss) are delicious in their own right but better used in mashed potatoes and potato salad.

A Perfectly Crisp Exterior

Personally, I love soft fries. But I know many people don't think fries are fries unless they're crisp. Restaurants often double-fry them: The first frying releases the moisture from the potatoes, and the second frying makes them nice and crisp just before serving. (That's also the secret behind many of the frozen fries available at the grocery store—even if you bake them at home, they're not likely to be as low in fat as the recipes in this chapter, because they've been fried before freezing.)

However, I'm pleased to report that it is possible to re-create the crispness of a perfectly fried fry (with far less fat) by boiling them for a few minutes before baking them. Just like that first frying step that restaurants use, boiling gives the potatoes a head start in the cooking process and releases some of the water, which helps them crisp during baking. Just be careful you don't boil them too long, or they'll break before you ever have a chance to get them on the baking sheet. If you, like me, prefer soft fries, you can skip the boiling altogether and simply bake them.

BAKING "FAUX-FRIED" FRIES

If you find that your fries burn before they're crisp, the problem could be one of two things.

1. You may be using a dark baking sheet. If you use one with a black surface, you'll need to reduce the oven temperature by 25°F.

2. Your oven temperature might be off. Try reducing the temperature by 50°F if your fries are burning before crisping or increasing it by 50°F if they're never crisping. With a little bit of experimentation, you're bound to find the equation for creating the perfect fries at home time after time.

Olive Oil

The key to baked fries (fries without a lot of spices, anyway) is the olive oil. It's important to use a high-quality extra virgin olive oil with a strong flavor in these recipes. If you do, you'll be surprised that even the small amounts used here will mimic a subtle oil taste on the finished fries. Because good oils are relatively expensive, it's often worthwhile to visit a specialty cooking store or health food store that serves samples—it's a great way to find one you love.

What Goes Into the Perfect Onion Rings?

A Perfect Coat of Breading

Unlike chicken, fish, etc., onions are relatively dry and nonporous, making them one of the toughest items to bread . . . unless you're aware of the pitfalls. To ensure that the breading sticks, it's best to dip the rings directly into the egg, skipping the flour step that's called for in most of the chicken and fish recipes in this book. Also, it's best to put the egg in a bowl that is just larger in diameter than the biggest ring you need to coat. This way, you'll be able to dunk it without using a ton of egg, which will help in keeping it coated.

I've found through plenty of trial and error that after shaking the onion rings in a bag of crumbs, the best way to remove them is with a clean, dry fork (if you touch them with your fingers or a fork that already has a lot of egg and bread crumbs stuck to it, it will cause the bread crumbs to fall off). And keep in mind that though the recipes call for specific amounts of egg and bread crumbs, you may find breading easier if you use more.

ARBY'S: CURLY FRIES
(SMALL)

SAVE: 105 CALORIES, 16 G FAT, 2.5 G SAT. FAT

When I was a kid, I would have eaten any food that was curly—curly fries, chocolate curls, curled carrots, even green onion curls and fusilli (spiral pasta). Maybe the appeal had something to do with the fact that I would have done anything for naturally curly hair. Perhaps I had curl envy and acted it out with food?

By junior high, I'd found Arby's Curly Fries to satisfy my curl craving. But based on my weight gain, I probably should have gotten a perm instead.

Anyhow, now that I can make them with only a few more calories and fat than I'd get from a baked potato, I indulge in them all the time. My guess is that once you try them, you'll be hooked, too.

1¾ teaspoons salt, divided

4 russet potatoes (8 ounces each; 2 pounds total), peeled

Olive oil spray

2½ tablespoons egg substitute

1½ tablespoons unbleached or all-purpose flour

2 teaspoons paprika

¼ teaspoon cayenne

⅛ teaspoon garlic powder

⅛ teaspoon onion powder

BRING a large pot of water to a boil over high heat. Add 1 teaspoon salt.

Meanwhile, with a twin curl cutter, cut 7 ounces of potato curls, about 2 cups. (Cover with water and refrigerate the scraps for another recipe.) Preheat the oven to 450°F. Lightly mist a small nonstick baking sheet with oil spray. Set aside.

Transfer the potato curls to the boiling water. Cook for exactly 3 minutes but no longer or they will break. Drain in a colander. Set aside for about 5 minutes to cool.

Meanwhile, in a large mixing bowl, combine the egg substitute, flour, paprika, cayenne, garlic powder, onion powder, and the remaining ¾ teaspoon salt. With a fork, mix until well blended. Add the potatoes. Toss them with your fingers until they are coated with the seasoning mixture. Transfer, allowing any excess seasoning mixture to drip off, to the reserved baking sheet. Arrange the potatoes, not touching, in a single layer. Lightly mist with oil spray. Bake for 18 to 24 minutes, turning them about halfway through, until crisp and cooked through.

MAKES 1 SERVING

235 calories, 9 g protein, 47 g carbohydrates, 2 g fat, trace sat. fat, 4 g fiber

Original Arby's Small Curly Fries: 340 calories, 4g protein, 39 g carbohydrates, 18 g fat, 2.5 g sat. fat, 4 g fiber

BEFORE YOU START If you don't own a twin curl cutter for creating curly strips of potatoes, sample the recipe using the seasonings on the same amount of straight-cut fries. It'll work fine. But if you love fun cooking projects, especially with kids, pick up an inexpensive (less than $5) twin curl cutter in a cookware shop or on a Web site that sells kitchen equipment. The twin curl cutter, which looks a bit like a knitting needle with a turn key attachment, is often packaged as part of a garnishing kit. Once you get the hang of making these whimsical spuds, you'll never go straight again!

DRIVE-THRU Don't have the time (or patience) to curl the fries? Simply cut 7 ounces (about 2 cups) of $\frac{1}{4}$"-thick potato sticks using a regular chef's knife. Prepare according to recipe directions.

CARL'S JR.: CHILI CHEESE FRENCH FRIES

SAVE: 380 CALORIES, 43 G FAT, 13 G SAT. FAT

Carl's Jr. serves a huge serving of soft (not crisp) fries in their Chili Cheese French Fries. Imagine my surprise when I realized that the "chili" that tops them is more akin to seasoned taco beef than to any chili I've ever tasted. It actually makes the whole process much simpler.

2 russet potatoes (1 pound total), peeled

1/2 teaspoon extra virgin olive oil

1/8 teaspoon salt

2 tablespoons Carl's Jr. Chili Seasoning Mix (opposite page)

1/4 cup water

2 1/2 ounces 4% lean ground beef (1/4 cup + 1 tablespoon)

1/2 ounce (about 1/4 cup) finely shredded low-fat orange Cheddar cheese

1/2 ounce (about 1/4 cup) finely shredded low-fat yellow Cheddar cheese

PREHEAT the oven to 400°F.

Place the potatoes on a cutting board. With a knife, cut into 1/4"-thick sticks. Transfer to a mixing bowl. Add the oil and salt. Carefully toss to coat well. Place the potatoes, not touching, in a single layer on a large nonstick baking sheet.

Bake for 8 to 10 minutes per side, or until cooked through but not browned.

Meanwhile, in a small cup or bowl, combine the chili seasoning and water. Stir to blend well. Set aside.

Place the beef in a small nonstick skillet set over medium-high heat. Cook, crumbling with a wooden spoon, until all chunks are gone. Stir in the chili-seasoning mixture. Cook, stirring, for 1 to 3 minutes, or until all of the water is gone. Sprinkle with the orange Cheddar and the yellow Cheddar. Remove from the heat. Cover to keep warm.

When the fries are cooked, transfer them to a medium bowl. Spoon the beef mixture on top.

MAKES 1 SERVING

540 calories, 31 g protein, 89 g carbohydrates, 8 g fat, 3 g sat. fat, 8 g fiber

Original Carl's Jr. Chili Cheese French Fries: 920 calories, 29 g protein, 89 g carbohydrates, 51 g fat, 16 g sat. fat, 9 g fiber

DRIVE-THRU Too harried to gather a lot of spices? Simply replace the chili seasoning mix with 2 teaspoons of store-bought taco seasoning mix whisked with 2 tablespoons of water.

EVEN BETTER A full order of Carl's Jr. Chili Cheese French Fries contains 2 whole baked potatoes along with the beef and cheese. For a much more balanced meal, follow the recipe, but use only $\frac{1}{2}$ pound of potatoes tossed in $\frac{1}{4}$ teaspoon of oil and increase the beef to 4 ounces. The revised version contains 399 calories, 34 g protein, 48 g carbohydrates, 9 g fat, 3 g sat. fat, and 5 g fiber.

CARL'S JR. CHILI SEASONING MIX

1 tablespoon + 2 teaspoons cornstarch

1 tablespoon + 1 teaspoon chili powder

2 teaspoons paprika

2 teaspoons onion powder

$1\frac{1}{4}$ teaspoons garlic powder

$1\frac{1}{4}$ teaspoons salt

$\frac{1}{2}$ teaspoon cayenne

IN a small bowl, combine the cornstarch, chili powder, paprika, onion powder, garlic powder, salt, and cayenne. Mix to blend. Place in an airtight container. Store in a dry, dark spot for up to 1 month.

MAKES ABOUT $\frac{1}{3}$ CUP, ENOUGH FOR 4 SERVINGS

Each serving: 31 calories, <1 g protein, 7 g carbohydrates, <1 g fat, trace sat. fat, 1 g fiber

POPEYES: CAJUN BATTERED FRIES
(REGULAR)

SAVE: 109 CALORIES, 10 G FAT, 5 G SAT. FAT

If you go online and print out Popeyes nutritional data, you'll find the following statement at the bottom of the listings: "Serving sizes may vary from the quantity analyzed for the nutritional data listed at this site . . ."

To do a fair comparison, this recipe was reconstructed based on an 88-gram serving—the serving size according to the company's Web site, which I found to be true at 1 out of 3 Popeyes restaurants in my area (more details on that experience on page 15). I'm pointing this out because I promised in the front of the book that each serving size would be at least as big as the original. And if you happen to do your own side-by-side comparison and find that the one you made looks smaller than the one you've purchased, it's because they've given you more for free. Well, free to your bank account . . . not free to your body.

1¾ teaspoons salt, divided

Olive oil spray

1 russet potato (7 to 8 ounces)

1 tablespoon egg substitute

½ tablespoon unbleached or all-purpose flour

½ teaspoon paprika

¼ teaspoon ground black pepper

⅛ teaspoon cayenne

Pinch of garlic powder

BRING a large pot of water to a boil over high heat. Add 1 teaspoon salt.

Preheat the oven to 400°F. Lightly mist a large nonstick baking sheet with oil spray. Set aside.

Place the potato on a cutting board. Make straight cuts on the 4 long sides of the potato to remove some of the peel. Discard the trimmed pieces. Some skin will remain on the sides and the ends. With a knife, cut the potato lengthwise into ⅓"-thick sticks. These can vary in length. On a scale, weigh 5¼ ounces of potatoes or measure 1½ cups.Transfer the potato strips to the boiling water. Cook for exactly 3 minutes but no longer or they will break. Drain in a colander. Set aside for about 5 minutes to cool.

Meanwhile, in a mixing bowl, combine the egg substitute, flour, paprika, black pepper, cayenne, garlic powder, and the remaining ¾ teaspoon salt. With a fork, beat to mix. Add the potato strips. With hands, toss to coat well. Allow any excess egg-substitute mixture to drip off. Transfer to the reserved baking sheet. Arrange, not touching, in a single layer.

Bake for 20 minutes, turning about every 5 minutes, or until crisp and golden.

MAKES 1 SERVING

152 calories, 5 g protein, 31 g carbohydrates, 2 g fat, trace sat. fat, 3 g fiber

Original Popeyes Regular Cajun Battered Fries: 261 calories, 3 g protein, 34 g carbohydrates, 12 g fat, 5 g sat. fat, 3 g fiber

SONIC: TATER TOTS (REGULAR)

SAVE: 115 CALORIES, 14 G FAT, 3 G SAT. FAT

Green potatoes and ham, anyone? Oh, no, that was green eggs and ham. Green potatoes don't have the same ring. And that was the challenge with this recipe.

When I first attempted to remake these delicious nuggets, I shredded fresh potatoes. Not only was it a process because I had to be careful to squeeze out as much water from the shreds as possible or they wouldn't stay together, but I also had to chop the potatoes after shredding them because the shreds were too long. The long shreds wanted to poke from the sides of the nuggets.

Next, I tried using a food processor. Oddly, the finished nuggets had a bit of a green tone to them. Very strange. I considered that maybe the potatoes weren't as fresh as I'd thought? So I made them again with the freshest potatoes I could find, only to see the slightest hint of green.

Then all of a sudden, it hit me. Preshredded potatoes! They're already parboiled so they won't turn green, and they won't take long to prepare. Chop them a bit more . . . leisurely . . . and you're all set for the perfect tots.

> Olive oil spray
> 1¼ cups bagged refrigerated preshredded potatoes
> 1½ tablespoons egg substitute
> ½ teaspoon salt

PREHEAT the oven to 450°F. Lightly mist a large nonstick baking sheet with oil spray.

Place the potatoes on a cutting board. With a knife, chop them finely. Transfer to a mixing bowl. Add the egg substitute and salt. Stir to mix well.

Using a measuring spoon, scoop out a level tablespoon of the mixture. Shape into a nugget and place on the reserved baking sheet. Continue until all of the mixture is scooped, shaped, and placed, not touching, in a single layer on the baking sheet. There should be about 13 nuggets.

Lightly mist with oil spray. Bake for about 20 minutes, flipping the nuggets a quarter turn every 5 minutes, or until crisp and lightly colored.

MAKES 1 SERVING (13 NUGGETS)

144 calories, 4 g protein, 30 g carbohydrates, 2 g fat, 0 g sat. fat, 1 g fiber

Original Sonic Regular Tater Tots (13 nuggets): 259 calories, 0 g protein, 27 g carbohydrates, 16 g fat, 3 g sat. fat, 3 g fiber

(STOP) **BEFORE YOU START** Preshredded potatoes can be found in the produce or refrigerated sections of most major supermarkets. They are prepared from fresh potatoes and have no added fat. If you cannot locate them, check the freezer section for preshredded potatoes. Just be sure they don't have any added fat.

If you use the frozen ones (a second choice), thaw them and then squeeze out as much moisture as possible. This is very important. If you don't get the excess liquid out, the potato mixture will not stay together.

MCDONALD'S: FRENCH FRIES
(MEDIUM)

SAVE: 106 CALORIES, 12 G FAT, 2 G SAT. FAT

According to my friends who are true fast food followers, the thing that sets McDonald's fries above most all other fries is that they're extra salty and they're crisp. I knew the salt would be no problem . . . simply add more. But how do you get fries to bake to perfect crispness? During my research, I tried to reproduce the double-fried technique by double-baking them. Unfortunately, it didn't work. Slightly frustrated, I tried coating them in egg whites and egg substitute. I tried tossing them in a small amount of various oils before baking. I tried baking them on a cooling rack to see if the air would circulate and crisp them. I even tried baking them on a pizza stone. But nothing was working. All I could think was, "How can I write a fast food cookbook and not include a recipe for McDonald's-style french fries?" The idea haunted me.

Then one day during a midafternoon jog, the answer suddenly occurred to me . . . because there's too much moisture in the potatoes for them to crisp during baking, I needed to release some of the water first. I ran home at record speed (for me), went directly to the kitchen, and tried parboiling the fries before baking them—the result was a virtually perfect batch of McDonald's-style fries. Phew.

1¾ teaspoons salt, divided

2 russet potatoes (1 pound)

1 teaspoon extra virgin olive oil

BRING a large pot of water to a boil over high heat. Add 1 teaspoon salt.

Meanwhile, preheat the oven to 400°F.

Set the potatoes on a cutting board. Make straight cuts on the 4 long sides of the potatoes to remove the peel. With a vegetable peeler or small knife, peel the ends of the potatoes. Discard the peels. With a knife, cut the remaining potatoes lengthwise into ¼"-thick sticks. These can vary in length. On a scale, weigh 9 ounces of potatoes or measure 2 cups. Transfer the potatoes to the boiling water. Cook for exactly 2½ minutes but no longer or they will break. Drain in a colander. Set aside for about 5 minutes to cool.

Transfer the potatoes to a mixing bowl. Add the oil and ½ teaspoon salt. Carefully toss to coat well. Place the potatoes, not touching, in a single layer on a large nonstick baking sheet.

Bake for 20 to 25 minutes, turning the potatoes about every 5 minutes, or until crisp and golden. Sprinkle, if desired, with the remaining ¼ teaspoon salt. (McDonald's fries are very salty.)

MAKES 1 SERVING

244 calories, 5 g protein, 46 g carbohydrates, 5 g fat, <1 g sat. fat, 4 g fiber

Original McDonald's Medium French Fries: 350 calories, 5 g protein, 47 g carbohydrates, 17 g fat, 3 g sat. fat, 4 g fiber

DEL TACO: CRINKLE-CUT FRIES
(LARGE)

SAVE: 224 CALORIES, 27 G FAT, 4 G SAT. FAT

I went to a small public school in Pennsylvania where everyone shared one cafeteria and we enjoyed three main options for lunch: the meal of the day, a slice (or 2) of pizza, or a bowl of crinkle-cut fries. One of my best friends, Melinda, who was probably the thinnest girl in our class, ate a bowl of the crinkle-cut fries every day.

I can't look at a bowl of crinkle-cut fries without thinking of Melinda, who is still thin, and wonder how on earth she was able to do that . . . well, before she knew that this revised rendition existed, that is. Now, even I can eat them.

> 1¼ teaspoons salt, divided
>
> 3 russet potatoes (1¼ to 1½ pounds total)
>
> 1 teaspoon extra virgin olive oil

BRING a large pot of water to a boil over high heat. Add 1 teaspoon salt.

Place the potatoes on a cutting board. Using a handheld crinkle cutter, make cuts on all sides of the potatoes to remove the peel and shape the potatoes into cubes. Discard the peels. Using the crinkle cutter, cut the cubes lengthwise into ⅓"-thick sticks. These can vary in length. On a scale, weigh 10 ounces of potatoes or measure 2 cups.

Preheat the oven to 450°F.

Transfer the potatoes to the boiling water. Cook for exactly 3 minutes but no longer or they will break. Drain in a colander. Set aside for about 5 minutes.

Transfer the potatoes to a mixing bowl. Add the oil and the remaining ¼ teaspoon salt. Carefully toss to coat well. Place the potatoes, not touching, in a single layer on a large nonstick baking sheet.

Bake for 7 to 10 minutes per side, or until they are crisp and golden.

MAKES 1 SERVING

266 calories, 6 g protein, 51 g carbohydrates, 5 g fat, <1 g sat. fat, 4 g fiber

Original Del Taco Large Crinkle-Cut Fries: 490 calories, 5 g protein, 47 g carbohydrates, 32 g fat, 5 g sat. fat, 5 g fiber

 BEFORE YOU START You'll need a crinkle cutter for this recipe. Inexpensive handheld types are sold online and in cookware shops.

BURGER KING: ONION RINGS
(MEDIUM)

SAVE: 77 CALORIES, 12 G FAT, 4 G SAT. FAT

Along with my Burger King Chicken Parmesan sandwich that I ate and ate and ate and ate (I could continue, but you get the point) as I kid, I always had a large (ugh!) serving of these onion rings, which I considered to be like no other. They were perfect. The perfect size, the perfect shape, and the perfect accompaniment. I rarely eat these (even my own version) as a side these days. I do, however, love them on my grilled chicken sandwiches and torn up in my salads—particularly a barbecued chicken ranch salad. Yum. Truthfully, I can't get enough of them.

I'm sure that after one bite, you'll have your own creative ideas for them.

Olive oil spray

3 medium white onions

¼ cup egg substitute

⅓ cup + 1 tablespoon dry bread crumbs

½ teaspoon salt

PREHEAT the oven to 400°F. Lightly mist a large nonstick baking sheet with oil spray.

Cut the onions into ⅓"-thick slices. Separate into rings. Select 15 rings that are all as close as possible to 2" in diameter. Set aside. (Refrigerate the remaining onion for another recipe.)

Pour the egg substitute into a small shallow bowl. In a resealable plastic bag, combine the bread crumbs and salt. Shake to mix well.

One at a time, dip the onion rings into the egg substitute, being sure to coat completely. Allow any excess egg substitute to drip off. Place in the bread-crumb bag. Shake to coat completely. Repeat dipping a second time into the egg substitute and the bread crumbs. Place on the reserved baking sheet. Continue until all of the onion rings are placed, not touching, on the baking sheet. Lightly mist with oil spray.

Bake for 8 minutes. Carefully flip the rings. Bake for 8 to 12 minutes, or until the breading is crisp and the onions are tender.

MAKES 1 SERVING

243 calories, 13 g protein, 38 g carbohydrates, 4 g fat, trace sat. fat, 3 g fiber

Original Burger King Medium Onion Rings: 320 calories, 4 g protein, 40 g carbohydrates, 16 g fat, 4 g sat. fat, 3 g fiber

JACK IN THE BOX: ONION RINGS

SAVE: 275 CALORIES, 26 G FAT, 6 G SAT. FAT

My friend Steve loves fried foods so much, he regularly jokes (or maybe he's actually serious?) that there should be a restaurant in which all menu items are breaded. When I mentioned to him that I had created the Burger King Onion Rings for this book, he said, "Oh, those are good, but Jack in the Box's are better. With Jack in the Box's, you can take the onion out and just eat the breading." Now that's true dedication . . . to breading.

Olive oil spray

1 medium-large sweet onion (3½"–4" diameter)

1 egg white

1 tablespoon low-fat buttermilk

⅓ cup dry bread crumbs

1 tablespoon yellow cornmeal

½ teaspoon salt

PREHEAT the oven to 400°F. Lightly mist a large nonstick baking sheet with oil spray.

Cut a ½"-thick slice from the middle of the onion. Separate into rings. If there are fewer than 8 rings, cut a second ½"-thick slice. Separate the rings to collect 8 individual rings. Set aside. (Refrigerate the remaining onion for another recipe.)

In a small shallow bowl, combine the egg white and buttermilk. Beat with a fork until smooth. In a resealable plastic bag, combine the bread crumbs, cornmeal, and salt. Shake to mix well.

One at a time, dip the onion rings into the egg-white mixture, being sure to coat completely. Allow any excess egg-white mixture to drip off. Transfer to the bread-crumb bag. Shake gently to coat. Repeat dipping into the egg-white mixture and coating with the crumb mixture. Place on the reserved baking sheet. Continue until all of the rings are breaded and placed, not touching, on the baking sheet. Lightly mist with oil spray.

Bake for 10 minutes. Carefully flip the rings. Bake for 8 to 12 minutes, or until the breading is crisp and the onions are tender.

MAKES 1 SERVING

225 calories, 11 g protein, 37 g carbohydrates, 4 g fat, trace sat. fat, 3 g fiber

Original Jack in the Box Onion Rings: 500 calories, 6 g protein, 51 g carbohydrates, 30 g fat, 6 g sat. fat, 3 g fiber

EL POLLO LOCO:
MACARONI AND CHEESE

SAVE: 168 CALORIES, 22 G FAT, 14 G SAT. FAT

This recipe is, surprisingly even to me, by far one of my favorite recipes in the book . . . and I'm not even the hugest fan of macaroni and cheese. I made it using Cabot's 75% light Cheddar and couldn't believe what an amazing buttery taste it had even though it had no butter in it. I was instantly hooked. When I remade it for friends to sample, the comments were consistent: "I can't believe that's low-fat. It tastes so buttery and so cheesy."

One thing to point out, though—make sure the pasta is cooked until soft (the way pasta was served perhaps in your elementary school cafeteria) if you really want your finished dish to resemble the restaurant original. I, however, prefer pasta a little less done.

> ¼ cup uncooked elbow macaroni
>
> 1 teaspoon unbleached or all-purpose flour
>
> 3 tablespoons fat-free milk, divided
>
> 1¾ ounces (about ¾ cup + 2 tablespoons) finely shredded low-fat yellow Cheddar cheese
>
> ⅛ teaspoon salt

COOK the macaroni according to the package directions for about 7 minutes. It should be soft. Drain the macaroni. Set aside.

Meanwhile, in a small nonstick saucepan, combine the flour with 1 tablespoon milk. With a Teflon whisk, whisk until smooth. Tip the pan slightly, if needed, to pool the mixture. Slowly add the remaining 2 tablespoons milk, whisking constantly, until no lumps remain.

Place over medium heat. Add the cheese and salt. Cook, stirring constantly with a wooden spoon, for 2 to 3 minutes or until the cheese melts and the mixture starts to thicken. It may appear lumpy at first. Add the reserved macaroni. Stir to blend well.

MAKES 1 SERVING

213 calories, 18 g protein, 26 g carbohydrates, 4 g fat, 2 g sat. fat, 1 g fiber

Original El Pollo Loco Macaroni and Cheese: 381 calories, 11 g protein, 25 g carbohydrates, 26 g fat, 16 g sat. fat, 2 g fiber

(STOP) **BEFORE YOU START** If you want the macaroni and cheese to look exactly like El Pollo Loco's, you'll need to use yellow Cheddar. But white Cheddar also works fine and tastes just as great.

BEST INGREDIENTS, BEST PIZZA

Ah, pizza. Gooey cheese, drippy sauce, lots of meaty toppings, and greasy crusts. No matter how you slice it (literally), it seems like pizza shouldn't be good for you. But in moderation, anything is fine—especially when you follow these recipes that remove so much of the unnecessary oils.

What Goes Into the Perfect Pizza?

The Crust

Whether you like crusts that are thick and chewy or thin and crispy, I've found that it's easy to eliminate a lot of fat and calories by using little or no oil in the dough. If you want to taste the flavor of oil in your finished crust, simply rub a small amount of a full-bodied extra virgin olive oil in the pan before putting the crust in it. The oil will soak into the crust, providing a crunchy, rich taste like Pizza Hut's, without excess oil or fat. If you prefer a buttery crust, like Domino's, simply substitute a bit of light butter for the oil.

The Sauce

Time after time, the people who helped me test all of the dishes in this book raved that the sauces in this chapter are probably some of the most dead-on recipes in the book. Whether we happened to use exactly the same ingredients, we'll never know, but we do know that batch after batch and pizza after pizza, the sauces tasted extremely similar to the restaurant originals . . . without adding any oils.

The Cheese

It's important to use a low-fat mozzarella that tastes good to you. Remember, not all low-fat cheeses taste the same. Some are rubbery, while others closely resemble their full-fat counterparts (see Sources on page 213 for more information). I've tried so-called mozzarella cheeses that taste like a bad American cheese at best; others, however, are delicious. Also, it is critical that you always shred low-fat cheeses finely. Not only will you be able to cover more area of the pizza with less cheese, it will melt better. This means that you'll need less to be guaranteed plenty of cheese in every bite. If I'm shredding more than a few ounces of cheese, I use the shredder attachment on my food processor, which saves a ton of time. If I'm throwing together a quick pizza and need only a bit, I'll use a box grater to avoid pulling out the food processor. If you don't have a scale, use the conversion chart on page 9 to measure your cheese.

The Toppings

You may have noticed that this chapter has a lot of pizzas with plenty of meat toppings and not so many with veggies. That's because meats more frequently push the calories and fats over the top on pizzas. Too many pieces of broccoli, spinach, and mushrooms have sent few people (if any) to the doctor. So I wanted to show you that you can actually enjoy a version of Pizza Hut Meat Lover's pizza, though I would recommend serving it with a salad or some steamed broccoli on the side.

When making meat toppings, I always use the leanest cuts of meat (96% lean ground beef and pork) because I want the toppings to taste as close to the originals as possible. You could save even more calories and fat by instead using extra-lean ground turkey, which is 99 percent fat-free. It tastes slightly different, but I promise the finished product will still be delicious.

Because there are so many great herbs and spices in these toppings, I've found it nearly impossible to taste a difference between the original topping and my leaner versions. Texture, on the other hand, is another matter. That's why I've added egg white or egg substitute and bread crumbs to the meats. This strategy adds moisture without adding unnecessary fat, making the consistency similar to that of the full-fat counterparts.

HOW TO FORM A PERFECT CRUST

Horrified by the thought of tossing your pizza dough into the air and watching it stick to your ceiling? You're not alone. But you don't have to toss your dough to get a perfectly shaped pie. To get foolproof results every time, keep these five easy steps in mind.

1. Start with a ball. You'll never achieve a perfectly flat circle shape if you don't start off with a round ball first, so toss it back and forth in your hands a few times to reshape it before placing it on a lightly floured surface.

2. Flatten the dough into a disk. Use the palm of your hand to press down gently and evenly on the dough, making sure to press and reshape the outer edge so the dough remains circular.

3. Start in the center and press outward. Using either lightly floured hands or a rolling pin, gently stretch the dough with long, firm strokes.

4. Turn the dough regularly as you work. To avoid stretching the dough into an oblong shape, make sure to work opposite sides evenly.

5. Use a pan. To put the finishing touches on your masterpiece, transfer it to your pan for final shaping. Press it flat with your hands to ensure that it's as even as possible.

As for veggie toppings, my advice is to go crazy with whatever you like. Throw on plenty of bell peppers, broccoli, mushrooms, spinach, fresh tomatoes, zucchini, etc. Just be aware that many veggies expel moisture as they are cooked, which could, if you're not careful, turn your pizza into a soggy mess. If you're using a small amount, this is not an issue. However, if you want to place a significant amount of bell peppers, mushrooms, or zucchini on your pizza, be sure to partially cook them before adding them to your pizza. You can either place the cut veggies in a single layer on a nonstick baking sheet that has been sprayed with olive oil spray and bake them at 400°F until they seem to be about halfway cooked (the time will vary depending on the vegetable and the thickness of it, but you'll notice liquid on the baking sheet); or you can cook them over medium heat in a nonstick skillet misted with olive oil spray. Again, the time will vary, but they should be about halfway between cooked and raw. The idea is simply to release some of the liquid so that it won't puddle on your pizza.

PIZZA HUT: SUPREME PERSONAL PAN PIZZA

SAVE: 217 CALORIES, 25 G FAT, 12 G SAT. FAT

"**A**sk and you shall receive." These are definitely words to live by . . . you just may be surprised at *what* you receive.

When I picked up my first Supreme Personal Pan Pizza sample, I was intrigued by the pans used to bake them, since the crisp yet chewy crust is such a signature feature of this particular pizza. I knew the pans were probably custom-made for Pizza Hut, but I was determined to gather as much information as I could so that I could provide a viable alternative in this recipe. Apparently, I asked a few too many questions (or in my opinion, the right number of them), because the friendly man behind the counter eventually grew tired of my inquiries. I asked, "Is the pan metal or . . . ," and before I was even able to finish my sentence, he looked at me like I was nuts, and kindly offered, "Do you want one?" Without hesitation, I said, "Sure." He scurried to the back, then returned and handed me my very own Pizza Hut Personal Pan Pizza Pan.

Based on the fact that the restaurant logo is imprinted on the bottom of the pan, I was correct that the pans are custom-made. But don't get me wrong: I'm not suggesting that you, too, hound a clerk until he makes you go away by giving you your very own pan. There are plenty of alternatives. You'll find them listed on page 134 under "Before You Start."

> ¼ recipe Pizza Hut Pizza Dough (page 135)
>
> 1 teaspoon extra-virgin olive oil
>
> Olive oil spray
>
> ¼ cup red onion strips (about 1½" long x ¼" wide)
>
> ¼ cup green bell pepper strips (about 1½" long x ¼" wide)
>
> 1 mushroom, sliced
>
> Flour for work surface
>
> ¼ recipe (scant ¼ cup) Pizza Hut Pizza Sauce (page 136)
>
> 1 ounce (¼ cup + 1 tablespoon) finely shredded low-fat mozzarella cheese, divided
>
> ¼ recipe (about ⅛ cup) Pizza Hut Beef Topping (page 136), divided
>
> ½ recipe (about ⅛ cup) Pizza Hut Pork Topping (page 137), divided
>
> 0.4 ounce (6 slices) packaged turkey pepperoni, divided

PREPARE the dough. Set aside to rise.

Meanwhile, preheat the oven to 400°F. Coat a 6" round nonstick individual pizza pan or other round nonstick baking pan with 1 teaspoon oil. Set aside. Lightly mist a nonstick baking sheet with oil spray.

(continued)

Place the onion, pepper, and mushroom, not touching, on the baking sheet. Bake for about 4 minutes, or until partially cooked. Set aside.

Meanwhile, when the dough has doubled, gently punch it down and place it on a lightly floured surface. Pat into a 6″ circle. Transfer to the reserved 6″ pan. Press into the bottom and about ½″ up the sides of the pan. Spoon on the sauce, leaving a bare ½″ border. Sprinkle half of the cheese over the sauce. Top evenly with three-quarters of each of these toppings: the beef, pork, pepperoni, and the onion-pepper-mushroom mixture. Sprinkle on the remaining cheese. Top evenly with the remaining one-quarter of the beef, pork, pepperoni, and onion-pepper-mushroom mixture.

Bake for 12 to 16 minutes, or until the cheese is melted and the crust starts to crisp. If baking with a terra-cotta saucer (see "Before You Start" note below), adjust time to 20 minutes. Allow to sit in the pan on a rack for 3 to 5 minutes. Cut into quarters.

MAKES 1 SERVING (6″ PIZZA)

533 calories, 28 g protein, 81 g carbohydrates, 11 g fat, 3 g sat. fat, 6 g fiber

Original Pizza Hut Supreme Personal Pan Pizza (6″): 750 calories, 32 g protein, 73 g carbohydrates, 36 g fat, 15 g sat. fat, 6 g fiber

 EVEN BETTER The crust on this pizza is rich and oily. If you don't mind it without the oily flavor, just skip oiling the pizza pan. You'll save an additional **42 calories, 5 g fat, and 0.5 g sat. fat.**

 BEFORE YOU START Specialty cookware shops and Web sites sell individual-size pizza pans, but you can use any 6″ round nonstick baking or cake pan for this recipe. A dark metal pan will crisp and color the crust better than a shiny pan will. If you don't have one, you can purchase an inexpensive 6″ round unglazed terra-cotta flowerpot saucer at a hardware or plant store. In fact, if you use the terra-cotta saucer, your pizza will come out the perfect shape since Pizza Hut's pans also have flared sides. If you opt for the saucer, season it by rubbing it with any vegetable oil. Use a paper towel to soak up any excess. Bake the saucer in a **400°F** oven for **15** minutes. Allow it to cool completely before using. (You need to do this only once, not every time you want to use it.)

DRIVE-THRU To make these personal pizzas pronto, you can shape one or more batches of the meat toppings to store in the freezer for up to 2 months. Spending some time making the toppings is a particularly fun project to do with children. Layer the prepared uncooked topping in a waxed paper–lined airtight plastic container between sheets of waxed paper.

If you don't care if the toppings look perfectly uniform, simply use your fingers to break the prepared meat mixtures into roughly ¼″ pieces. Spread out on a waxed paper–lined freezer-proof tray. Cover loosely with a sheet of waxed paper. Place in the freezer for about 2 hours, or until frozen solid. Transfer the pieces to a resealable plastic freezer bag. Return to the freezer for up to 2 months.

Also, the 3 extra dough balls (punched down after rising) can be frozen individually in resealable plastic freezer bags. To use, thaw for several hours at room temperature. Or, for even greater convenience, after the initial rising, the dough balls can be punched down and shaped into 6" round pizza pans (if you have extra). Set in the freezer for about 2 hours, or until frozen solid. With a butter knife, pop the dough out of the pan. Wrap tightly in plastic wrap and then in aluminum foil before placing back into the freezer. When you're ready to make a pizza, just pop the frozen dough back into the pan.

When you want the pizza, it will come together really quickly because the crust and meat toppings need no thawing. Bake for about 25 minutes. You can definitely whip out these pizzas in less time than a trip to Pizza Hut. You'll save money on gasoline, too!

PIZZA HUT PIZZA DOUGH

Olive oil spray

1 cup warm water (105°–115°F)

1 package (¼ ounce) active dry yeast

2 teaspoons sugar

1½ cups + 4 tablespoons unbleached flour + additional for work surface

¾ cup bread flour

2 teaspoons salt

LIGHTLY mist a mixing bowl with oil spray. Set aside.

In a small bowl, combine the water, yeast, and sugar. Whisk until the yeast is dissolved.

In the bowl of a food processor fitted with the dough blade, or in a mixing bowl, combine 1½ cups unbleached flour, the bread flour, and salt. Pulse several times or stir with a wooden spoon to mix. When the yeast mixture starts to bubble, add it to the bowl. Process or stir for about 1 minute, or until a sticky ball forms. If the mixture is too sticky, add up to 4 tablespoons unbleached flour, 1 tablespoon at a time. Process or stir until a smooth ball forms. Turn onto a lightly floured work surface. Knead by hand several times, until the dough is smooth and elastic. Place the dough in the reserved bowl. Lightly mist the dough with oil spray. Cover the bowl tightly with plastic wrap. Set aside in a warm place. Allow it to rise for about 1 hour, or until doubled in size.

MAKES DOUGH FOR 4 PERSONAL PAN PIZZAS OR 1 MEAT LOVER'S HAND-TOSSED STYLE PIZZA

Each serving (based on ¼ of the recipe): 270 calories, 9 g protein, 56 g carbohydrates, <1 g fat, trace sat. fat, 2 g fiber

PIZZA HUT PIZZA SAUCE

$^3/_4$ cup canned crushed tomatoes

$1^1/_2$ tablespoons tomato paste

1 tablespoon + 1 teaspoon sugar

1 teaspoon dried oregano leaves

$^1/_2$ teaspoon garlic powder

Pinch of ground black pepper

IN a bowl, combine the crushed tomatoes and tomato paste. Whisk until smooth. Add the sugar, oregano, garlic powder, and pepper. Stir to blend well. Store in an airtight plastic container for up to 5 days.

MAKES ABOUT 1 SCANT CUP, ENOUGH FOR 4 PERSONAL PAN PIZZAS OR 1 LARGE MEAT LOVER'S HAND-TOSSED STYLE PIZZA

Entire recipe: 157 calories, 5 g protein, 35 g carbohydrates, trace fat, 0 g sat. fat, 5 g fiber

PIZZA HUT BEEF TOPPING

3 ounces 96% lean ground beef (about $^1/_4$ cup + 2 tablespoons)

1 tablespoon + 1 teaspoon egg substitute

2 teaspoons dry bread crumbs

$^1/_2$ teaspoon salt

IN a small bowl, combine the beef, egg substitute, bread crumbs, and salt. With a fork, mix to blend. At this point, the mixture can be crumbled into small pieces directly onto the pizza. If making ahead, scoop out balls with a $^1/_4$ teaspoon measure and place, not touching, in a waxed paper–lined rectangular airtight plastic container. Continue layering between sheets of waxed paper. Refrigerate for up to 3 days.

MAKES $^2/_3$ CUP, ENOUGH FOR 4 PERSONAL PAN PIZZAS OR 1 LARGE MEAT LOVER'S HAND-TOSSED STYLE PIZZA

Entire recipe: 124 calories, 19 g protein, 3 g carbohydrates, 4 g fat, 1 g sat. fat, trace fiber

PIZZA HUT PORK TOPPING

$1\frac{1}{2}$ ounces extra-lean ground pork (3 tablespoons)

2 teaspoons egg substitute

$1\frac{1}{2}$ teaspoons dry bread crumbs

1 teaspoon pure maple syrup

$\frac{1}{8}$ teaspoon ground black pepper

$\frac{1}{8}$ teaspoon salt

$\frac{1}{8}$ teaspoon garlic powder

$\frac{1}{8}$ teaspoon ground sage

Pinch of cayenne

IN a small bowl, combine the pork, egg substitute, bread crumbs, maple syrup, pepper, salt, garlic powder, sage, and cayenne. With a fork, mix to blend. At this point, the mixture can be crumbled into small pieces directly onto the pizza. If making ahead, scoop out balls with a $\frac{1}{4}$ teaspoon measure and place, not touching, in a waxed paper–lined rectangular airtight plastic container. Continue layering between sheets of waxed paper. Refrigerate for up to 3 days.

MAKES $\frac{1}{3}$ CUP, ENOUGH FOR 2 PERSONAL PAN PIZZAS OR 1 LARGE MEAT LOVER'S HAND-TOSSED STYLE PIZZA

Entire recipe: 89 calories, 10 g protein, 8 g carbohydrates, 2 g fat, <1 g sat. fat, trace fiber

PIZZA HUT: MEAT LOVER'S HAND-TOSSED STYLE PIZZA

SAVE: 168 CALORIES, 16 G FAT, 9 G SAT. FAT

When I was a kid, we would often order pizza. Even though Pizza Hut was my favorite because I loved the crust, my mother would rarely order it because she found the crust too greasy for her taste. Any time I had an opportunity to get pizza with friends, I would suggest, without hesitation, Pizza Hut. As far as I was concerned, there was nothing like that crunchy crust with its rich, oily flavor.

Since I'd always been such a huge fan, I suspected that the crust might be virtually impossible to duplicate to my standards without using an immense amount of oil. Imagine my surprise when I needed only a tablespoon of my favorite full-bodied, extra virgin olive oil to create the same mouth feel and to simulate the taste. True, mine is actually pretty light; and if you put it on a napkin and then pick it up, there won't be any visible oil seeped into the napkin . . . but I'm okay with that, and I think you will be, too.

1 recipe Pizza Hut Pizza Dough (page 135)

6 slices center-cut bacon, cut into 1½" pieces

1 tablespoon + 1 teaspoon extra virgin olive oil, divided

Flour for work surface

1 recipe Pizza Hut Pizza Sauce (page 136)

5 ounces (1½ cups + 3 tablespoons) finely shredded low-fat mozzarella, divided

1¾ ounces packaged extra-lean ham steak, sliced into 1" x ½" x ⅛" strips (½ cup), divided

2 ounces (34 slices) packaged turkey pepperoni, divided

1 recipe Pizza Hut Beef Topping (page 136), divided

1 recipe Pizza Hut Pork Topping (page 137), divided

1 recipe Pizza Hut Sausage (page 140), divided

PREPARE the dough. Set aside to rise.

Place the bacon pieces in a small nonstick skillet over medium heat. Cook, flipping occasionally, for about 3 to 4 minutes, or until barely cooked and not crisp. Transfer to a paper towel–lined plate to drain. Cover with a lid to keep warm.

Preheat the oven to 450°F. Coat the bottom and sides of a 14" round nonstick deep-dish pizza pan with 1 tablespoon oil. Set aside.

When the dough has doubled, gently punch it down and place on a lightly floured surface. With a lightly floured rolling pin or hands, roll or pat into a 14″ circle (if you're new to making pizza, see page 131 for more advice on how to do this). Transfer to the reserved pizza pan. Starting from the center, pat and stretch the dough to the edges of the pan so that a ½″ border is about twice as thick as the rest of the dough. Allow to stand for 30 seconds. If the dough contracts, restretch it gently. With a finger, rub the remaining 1 teaspoon oil over the outer 1″ border of the dough. With a fork, poke about 20 times to evenly perforate the dough.

Spread evenly with the sauce, leaving a bare ½″ border. Sprinkle half of the cheese evenly over the sauce. Top with about three-quarters of each of these toppings: the ham, pepperoni, beef, pork, sausage, and the reserved bacon. Sprinkle on the remaining cheese and the remaining one-quarter of the ham, pepperoni, beef, pork, sausage, and bacon.

Bake for 12 to 16 minutes, or until the cheese melts and the crust is golden. Let it rest for 5 minutes, then cut into 12 slices.

MAKES 6 SERVINGS (2 SLICES PER SERVING)

Each serving: 392 calories, 24 g protein, 51 g carbohydrates, 10 g fat, 3 g sat. fat, 3 g fiber

Original Pizza Hut Meat Lover's Hand-Tossed Style Pizza (2 large slices): 560 calories, 28 g protein, 54 g carbohydrates, 26 g fat, 12 g sat. fat, 4 g fiber

DRIVE-THRU If you crave a spur-of-the-moment pizza but think you don't have the time, think again. All of the prepared toppings can be waiting in the freezer (see page 134).Using your favorite canned or jarred pizza sauce is another time-saving option. Be sure you like the taste of the sauce on its own, because it's a major flavor component of the dish.

Alternatively, you can buy prepared pizza dough at many supermarkets. Look for brands that have no more than 1 to 2 grams of fat per slice.

Though reheating pizza in a microwave will warm it, reheating it in an oven is well worth the time to get that just-baked crispness. Simply place a slice on a sheet of aluminum foil. Bake in a preheated 400°F oven for about 10 minutes, or until the cheese in the center of the slice is just melting.

PIZZA HUT SAUSAGE

3 ounces extra-lean ground pork or pork tenderloin, ground (about ¼ cup + 2 tablespoons)

1 tablespoon + 1 teaspoon egg substitute

2 teaspoons dry bread crumbs

¼ teaspoon crushed fennel seeds

¼ teaspoon onion powder

¼ teaspoon salt

⅛ teaspoon sugar

⅛ teaspoon garlic powder

⅛ teaspoon Italian seasoning

⅛ teaspoon ground black pepper

⅛ teaspoon cayenne

IN a small bowl, combine the pork, egg substitute, bread crumbs, fennel seeds, onion powder, salt, sugar, garlic powder, Italian seasoning, black pepper, and cayenne. With fork or hands, mix to blend. At this point, the mixture can be crumbled into small pieces directly onto the pizza. If making ahead, scoop out balls with a ¼ teaspoon measure and place, not touching, in a waxed paper–lined rectangular airtight plastic container. Continue layering between sheets of waxed paper. Refrigerate for up to 3 days.

MAKES ⅔ CUP SAUSAGE, ENOUGH FOR 1 LARGE MEAT LOVER'S HAND-TOSSED STYLE PIZZA

Entire recipe: 138 calories, 21 g protein, 5 g carbohydrates, 3 g fat, 1 g sat. fat, <1 g fiber

DOMINO'S: CRUNCHY THIN CRUST CHEESE PIZZA

SAVE: 159 CALORIES, 17 G FAT, 6 G SAT. FAT

As a kid, we celebrated many of our birthdays at a pizza place called Showbiz Pizza. It was very much like Chuck E. Cheese's. They had video games and animated cartoon characters who sang birthday songs and entertained. They would give the birthday girl (or guy) plenty of video game tokens, and we'd eat plenty of pizza that was like no other we ever ate—they cut it into squares instead of wedges. Though I always loved Pizza Hut pizza crusts, I definitely don't consider myself a "crust person." In fact, the reason I most loved to go to Showbiz was that I thought it was so cool that some of the pizza slices were crustless. They cut their pizza into 16 almost-square pieces instead of wedges, so all of the center slices were really gooey with cheese. I can't even look at Domino's Crunchy Thin Crust Cheese Pizza without thinking about those fun days. And, of course, I still can't wait to get my hands on a center slice.

> 1 recipe Domino's Crunchy Thin Crust Pizza Dough (page 142)
>
> Flour for work surface
>
> 1 recipe Domino's Pizza Sauce (page 143)
>
> 5 ounces (about 1½ cups + 3 tablespoons) finely shredded low-fat mozzarella cheese

PREPARE the dough. Set aside to rise.

Meanwhile, preheat the oven to 450°F. When the dough has doubled, gently punch it down and place it on a lightly floured surface.

With a lightly floured rolling pin or hands, roll or pat into a 14" round (if you're new to making pizza, see page 131 for more advice on how to do this). Transfer to a 14" nonstick round deep-dish or flat pizza pan. With a fork, poke about 20 times to evenly perforate the dough.

Bake for 5 minutes. Check for any air bubbles. Press gently with a fork to deflate them. Bake for 3 to 5 minutes, or until crisp. Remove the pan and set it on a heat-proof surface. Spread the sauce evenly over the surface of the crust. Top with the cheese. Bake for 5 minutes, or until the cheese melts.

Allow the pizza to sit for 5 minutes. Cut into 16 rectangular pieces.

MAKES 4 SERVINGS (¼ PIZZA)

Each serving: 217 calories, 9 g protein, 38 g carbohydrates, 3 g fat, 1 g sat. fat, 3 g fiber

Original Domino's Crunchy Thin Crust Cheese Pizza (¼ pizza): 376 calories, 14 g protein, 38 g carbohydrates, 20 g fat, 7 g sat. fat, 2 g fiber

DRIVE-THRU Need dinner in minutes? This pizza crust is similar to a crisped tortilla. So when you're on the run, make this pizza using four 7" low-fat flour tortillas. Follow the instructions for crisping the tortillas in the recipe for Taco Bell Mexican Pizza (see page 164). Then add the sauce and cheese to taste.

Also, you can use a low-fat, jarred pizza sauce. Just make sure you choose one that you like, because it's a major flavor component of the dish.

BEFORE YOU START For the crispiest crust, select a pizza pan that is black or dark gray or has small holes in the bottom.

DOMINO'S CRUNCHY THIN CRUST PIZZA DOUGH

Olive oil spray

$\frac{1}{3}$ cup warm water (105°–115°F)

1 teaspoon active dry yeast

1 teaspoon sugar

$\frac{3}{4}$ cup + 4 tablespoons unbleached flour + additional for work surface

$\frac{1}{4}$ cup bread flour

$\frac{1}{2}$ teaspoon salt

LIGHTLY mist a large bowl with oil spray. Set aside.

In a small bowl, combine the water, yeast, and sugar. Stir until the yeast is dissolved. Set aside.

In the bowl of a food processor fitted with a dough blade or in a mixing bowl, combine $\frac{3}{4}$ cup unbleached flour, the bread flour, and salt. Pulse several times or stir with a wooden spoon to mix. When the yeast mixture starts to bubble, add it to the bowl. Process or stir for about 1 minute, or until a sticky ball forms. If the mixture is too sticky, add up to 4 tablespoons unbleached flour, 1 tablespoon at a time. Process or stir until a smooth ball forms. Turn onto a lightly floured work surface. Knead by hand several times, until the dough is smooth and elastic. Place the dough in the reserved bowl. Lightly mist the dough with oil spray. Cover the bowl tightly with plastic wrap. Set aside in a warm place. Allow it to rise for about 1 hour, or until doubled in size.

MAKES DOUGH FOR 1 THIN CRUST CHEESE PIZZA

Each serving: 134 calories, 4 g protein, 28 g carbohydrates, <1 g fat, trace sat. fat, 1 g fiber

DOMINO'S PIZZA SAUCE

    2 tablespoons tomato paste

    ½ cup tomato sauce

    1 teaspoon sugar

    ½ teaspoon salt

    ½ teaspoon dried oregano

    Pinch of ground black pepper

PLACE the tomato paste in a small bowl. Gradually add the tomato sauce while whisking. Whisk until smooth. Add the sugar, salt, oregano, and pepper. Whisk to blend. Transfer to an airtight plastic container. Refrigerate for up to 5 days.

MAKES ABOUT ⅔ CUP, ENOUGH FOR 1 PIZZA

    Each serving: 20 calories, 1 g protein, 4 g carbohydrates, trace fat, 0 g sat. fat,
    <1 g fiber

DOMINO'S: ULTIMATE DEEP DISH AMERICA'S FAVORITE FEAST PIZZA

SAVE: 275 CALORIES, 39 G FAT, 13 G SAT. FAT

When I saw that Domino's calls their pepperoni, sausage, and mushroom pizza "America's Favorite Feast," I was surprised. How on earth did mushrooms get included on "America's Favorite" list? Not being a huge mushroom fan myself, I figured there are plenty of toppings that beat out mushrooms.

Much to my surprise, there aren't. Mushrooms are, in fact, loved by more Americans than I'd realized. According to surveys done by the pizza industry, mushrooms rank number 3 behind only pepperoni and sausage. I was so shocked the night I realized this that I mentioned it to my friend Michelle, who is also not a mushroom fan. I couldn't believe how impassioned she was, immediately exclaiming, "I can totally believe it; every time I order a pizza with anyone, they want mushrooms. What's up with that?"

Well, so, this isn't my favorite pizza, but it's obviously the favorite for a lot of people, so I'm officially outnumbered. And I'm okay with that. Enjoy.

> 1 recipe Domino's Ultimate Deep Dish Pizza Dough (page 146)
>
> 1 tablespoon light butter, melted
>
> Olive oil spray
>
> 1½ cups sliced button mushrooms
>
> Flour for work surface
>
> 1 recipe Domino's Pizza Sauce (page 143)
>
> 6 ounces (2 cups – 2 tablespoons) finely shredded low-fat mozzarella cheese, divided
>
> 2 ounces (34 slices) packaged turkey pepperoni, divided
>
> 1 recipe Domino's Sausage (page 147), divided
>
> ¼ teaspoon garlic powder

PREPARE the dough. Set aside to rise.

Meanwhile, preheat the oven to 400°F. Coat the bottom and sides of a 14" non-stick round deep-dish pizza pan with the butter. Set aside.

Lightly mist a nonstick baking sheet with oil spray. Place the mushrooms, not touching, on the baking sheet. Bake for 2 minutes, or until the mushrooms start to release liquid.

When the dough has doubled, gently punch it down and place on a lightly floured surface. With a lightly floured rolling pin or hands, roll or pat into a 14" circle (if you're new to making pizza, see page 131 for more advice on how to do this). Transfer to the reserved pizza pan. Starting from the center, pat and stretch the dough to the edges of the pan to form a $\frac{1}{2}$" border that's about twice as thick as the rest of the dough. Allow to stand for 30 seconds. If the dough contracts, restretch it gently. With a fork, poke about 20 times to evenly perforate the dough.

Spread evenly with the sauce, leaving a bare $\frac{1}{2}$" border. Sprinkle half of the cheese evenly over the sauce. Top with about half of the pepperoni, sausage, and mushrooms. Sprinkle on the remaining cheese and the remaining half of the pepperoni, sausage, and mushrooms. Sprinkle on the garlic powder.

Bake for 15 to 20 minutes, or until the cheese melts and the crust is golden. Allow to sit for 5 minutes. Cut into 8 wedges.

MAKES 4 SERVINGS (2 SLICES PER SERVING)

Each serving: 591 calories, 30 g protein, 98 g carbohydrates, 8 g fat, 3 g sat. fat, 6 g fiber

Original Domino's Ultimate Deep Dish America's Favorite Feast Pizza (2 large slices): 866 calories, 34 g protein, 84 g carbohydrates, 47 g fat, 16 g sat. fat, 6 g fiber

DRIVE-THRU To save time when you want this pizza right now, prepare one or more batches of the sausage in advance for the freezer. Pack in a waxed paper–lined plastic container, in layers separated by waxed paper. Freeze for up to 2 months. No need to thaw before placing on the pizza.

DOMINO'S ULTIMATE DEEP DISH PIZZA DOUGH

Olive oil spray

1¼ cups warm water (105°–115°F)

1 tablespoon active dry yeast

1 tablespoon sugar

2¾ cups + 4 tablespoons unbleached flour + additional for work surface

¾ cup bread flour

½ tablespoon salt

LIGHTLY mist a large bowl with oil spray. Set aside.

In a small bowl, combine the water, yeast, and sugar. Stir until the yeast is dissolved.

In the bowl of a food processor fitted with the dough blade, or in a large mixing bowl, combine 2¾ cups unbleached flour, the bread flour, and salt. Pulse several times or stir with a wooden spoon to mix. When the yeast mixture starts to bubble, add it to the bowl. Process or stir for about 1 minute, or until a sticky ball forms. If the mixture is too sticky, add up to 4 tablespoons unbleached flour, 1 tablespoon at a time. Process or stir until a smooth ball forms. Turn onto a lightly floured work surface. Knead by hand several times, until the dough is smooth and elastic. Place the dough in the reserved bowl. Lightly mist with oil spray. Cover the bowl tightly with plastic wrap. Set aside in a warm place. Allow it to rise for about 1 hour, or until doubled in size.

MAKES DOUGH FOR 1 DEEP-DISH PIZZA

Each serving: 397 calories, 13 g protein, 84 g carbohydrates, trace fat, trace sat. fat, 3 g fiber

(STOP) **BEFORE YOU START** You'll need 2 packages (¼ ounce or about 2¼ teaspoons each) of active dry yeast to get the 1 tablespoon needed to make this dough. You can tightly seal the remaining yeast and refrigerate it for use in another recipe.

2½ ounces extra-lean ground pork or pork tenderloin, ground (about ¼ cup + 1 tablespoon)

1 tablespoon + 1 teaspoon egg substitute

2 teaspoons dry bread crumbs

½ teaspoon whole fennel seeds

¼ teaspoon garlic powder

¼ teaspoon salt

¼ teaspoon Italian seasoning

¼ teaspoon ground black pepper

⅛ teaspoon cayenne

IN a small bowl, combine the pork, egg substitute, bread crumbs, fennel seeds, garlic powder, salt, Italian seasoning, black pepper, and cayenne. With fork or hands, mix to blend. At this point, the mixture can be crumbled into small pieces directly onto the pizza. If making ahead, use a ¼ teaspoon measure to scoop out balls and place, not touching, in a waxed paper–lined rectangular airtight plastic container. Continue layering between sheets of waxed paper. Refrigerate for up to 3 days.

MAKES ABOUT ⅓ CUP, ENOUGH FOR 1 PIZZA

Each serving: 42 calories, 6 g protein, 1 g carbohydrates, 1 g fat, <1 g sat. fat, trace fiber

SBARRO: STUFFED PEPPERONI PIZZA

SAVE: 391 CALORIES, 27 G FAT

I can't eat this pizza without thinking of my early catering days. Because I come from an East Coast Italian family, stromboli to me was like a hot dog to a baseball fan. I had no idea that some people might not know what it was (in case you don't know, it's pizza dough shaped flat into a rectangle and spread with toppings—my family always favored pepperoni and provolone—then rolled up jelly roll–style, baked, and served in slices).

Anyway, I used to serve stromboli at all of my catering jobs because it was so easy, relatively inexpensive, and always so popular. I was shocked at how many people would come in the kitchen after parties to ask what I called "my creation" (if only I had created it). Like Sbarro Pizza, the combo of pepperoni and melted cheese goo-ing among sauceless dough made the flavors so strong and wonderful. Though I've chosen to keep more oil in this recipe than in any other in the book, you still save an immense amount of fat and calories. After all, this is a family favorite, so I can't make it too low-fat.

It's also worth pointing out that Sbarro makes their pizza in a much larger pan than the ones most people would have on hand, so I've scaled down the recipe to use a standard 14" pan. The serving sizes stay the same, but you won't be able to serve as many people with my version, which is probably a shame, becauce this is a surefire crowd-pleaser.

> 1 recipe Sbarro Stuffed Crust Pizza Dough (page 150)
>
> 3 slices center-cut bacon, cut into ½" pieces
>
> 2 tablespoons extra virgin olive oil, divided
>
> 1 egg
>
> 1 tablespoon water
>
> Flour for work surface
>
> 2½ tablespoons (about ½ ounce) grated reduced-fat Parmesan cheese
>
> 1 recipe Sbarro Sausage (page 151)
>
> 9 ounces (about 2¾ cups) finely shredded low-fat mozzarella cheese, divided
>
> 6 ounces (100 slices) packaged turkey pepperoni
>
> 1 tablespoon finely chopped fresh parsley

PREPARE the dough. Set aside to rise.

Place the bacon pieces in a small nonstick skillet over medium heat. Cook, flipping occasionally, for 2 to 3 minutes, or until partially cooked. Transfer to a paper towel–lined plate to drain.

Preheat the oven to 425°F. Coat a 14″ nonstick round deep-dish pizza pan with 2 teaspoons oil. Set aside.

In a small bowl, combine the egg and water. Beat until smooth. Set aside.

Meanwhile, when the dough has doubled, gently punch it down. Cut into 2 portions. Return 1 portion to the bowl and cover with plastic wrap. Shape the other portion into a ball and place on a lightly floured surface. With a lightly floured rolling pin or hands, roll or stretch into a 14″ circle (if you're new to making pizza, see page 131 for more advice on how to do this). Repeat with remaining dough. (Work slowly to avoid tearing the dough; if the dough should tear, patch it with dough from another area and use that piece on the bottom since patched tears on the top crust may open up during baking.)

Transfer one piece of dough to the reserved pan. Press the dough about ¼″ up the pan sides. Drizzle with 2 teaspoons oil, leaving a bare ½″ border. With a pastry brush or fingertip, paint the border with some of the reserved egg mixture. Set the egg mixture aside.

Leaving the ½″ border bare, evenly sprinkle on the Parmesan. Crumble the sausage in ½″ pieces over the Parmesan. Top evenly with half of the mozzarella and all of the pepperoni slices, slightly overlapping. Sprinkle the remaining mozzarella over that. Set aside.

Place the remaining piece of dough on top of the pizza. Using your fingers, press the dough borders together to seal the bottom and top crusts. With a butter knife, mark 4 parallel lines in the dough top, being careful not to cut through the dough. Create a crisscross pattern by marking 4 parallel lines perpendicular to the first four.

With a pastry brush or fingers, paint the dough top with some of the reserved egg mixture. Drizzle the remaining 2 teaspoons oil over the top. With the pastry brush or fingers, paint the crust evenly with the oil. Sprinkle the reserved bacon and the parsley evenly over the top.

Bake for 20 to 25 minutes, or until the crust is golden and the pizza is hot. Check by inserting a sharp knife into the center. Let it rest 10 minutes, then cut into 6 slices.

MAKES 6 SERVINGS (1 SLICE PER SERVING)

Each serving: 569 calories, 37 g protein, 68 g carbohydrates, 15 g fat, 4 g sat. fat, 4 g fiber

Original Sbarro Stuffed Pepperoni Pizza (1 slice): 960 calories, 52 g protein, 89 g carbohydrates, 42 g fat, sat. fat (not available), 4g fiber

SBARRO STUFFED CRUST PIZZA DOUGH

Olive oil spray

1¼ cups warm water (105°–115°F)

1 package active dry yeast

1 tablespoon sugar

3¾ cups flour + additional for work surface

1¼ teaspoons salt

LIGHTLY mist a large bowl with oil spray. Set aside.

In a small bowl, combine the water, yeast, and sugar. Stir until the yeast is dissolved.

In the bowl of a large food processor fitted with the dough blade, or in a large mixing bowl, combine 3¾ cups flour and the salt. Pulse several times, or stir with a wooden spoon to blend. When the yeast mixture starts to bubble, add it to the bowl. Process, or stir for about 1 minute, or until a sticky ball forms. If the mixture is too sticky, add more flour, 1 tablespoon at a time. Process, or stir until a smooth ball forms. Turn onto a lightly floured work surface. Knead by hand several times, until the dough is smooth and elastic. Place in the reserved bowl. Lightly mist with oil spray. Cover the bowl tightly with plastic wrap. Set aside in a warm place. Allow it to rise for about 1 hour, or until doubled in size.

MAKES DOUGH FOR 1 STUFFED PIZZA

Each serving: 264 calories, 8 g protein, 55 g carbohydrates, trace fat, trace sat. fat, 2 g fiber

SBARRO SAUSAGE

$^3/_4$ pound extra-lean ground pork or pork tenderloin, ground (1 $^1/_2$ cups)

$^1/_3$ cup egg substitute

3 tablespoons dry bread crumbs

$^3/_4$ teaspoon crushed fennel seeds

$^3/_4$ teaspoon onion powder

$^1/_2$ teaspoon salt

$^3/_4$ teaspoon garlic powder

$^1/_2$ teaspoon cayenne

IN a mixing bowl, combine the pork, egg substitute, bread crumbs, fennel seeds, onion powder, salt, garlic powder, and cayenne. With fork or hands, mix to blend. At this point, the mixture can be crumbled into small pieces directly onto the pizza. If making ahead, transfer the mixture to a resealable plastic bag. Refrigerate for up to 3 days.

MAKES ABOUT 1 POUND, ENOUGH FOR 1 STUFFED PIZZA

Each serving: 91 calories, 14 g protein, 3 g carbohydrates, 2 g fat, <1 g sat. fat, trace fiber

PAPA JOHN'S: HAWAIIAN BBQ CHICKEN ORIGINAL CRUST PIZZA

SAVE: 180 CALORIES, 13 G FAT, 3 G SAT. FAT

As I did when creating the other sauce recipes in this book, I ordered my first Hawaiian pizza from Papa John's and asked for "extra sauce on the side" (it's my way of making sure I'm not tasting another component of the dish before I try to re-create the sauce). When I tried the pizza, I thought it was tasty, yet I really didn't care for the sauce by itself . . . at all. How could this be? I elected to ignore the fact that I didn't love the flavor and duplicated the sauce faithfully.

Later, during the testing phase, we bought another pizza. One bite and I remembered my initial reaction. My tester and I were convinced that the sauce on the pizza was much sweeter. Stumped, we decided to go ahead and make our version and see what happened. We did, and we were pleasantly surprised; ours was really good. Just like the Papa John's original, our sauce tasted great blended with the other ingredients.

Perhaps, we figured, it had something to do with the sweetness of the pineapple? Or maybe once it got spread out, it was much less concentrated and thus tasted sweeter? Regardless, don't be alarmed by the taste of the sauce on its own. It takes on a whole new life once nestled under the cheese in this masterpiece from Papa John's.

1 recipe Papa John's Pizza Dough (page 154)

1 recipe Papa John's BBQ Sauce (page 155)

6 slices center-cut bacon, cut into 1" pieces

½ pound boneless, skinless chicken breast

½ teaspoon extra virgin olive oil

2 pinches of salt

Flour for work surface

5 ounces (1½ cups + 3 tablespoons) finely shredded low-fat mozzarella cheese, divided

½ cup drained pineapple tidbits packed in juice, divided

½ cup white onion strips (¼" thick of varying lengths), divided

TO prepare the pizza:

Prepare the dough. Set aside to rise.

Prepare the sauce. Set aside.

Preheat a grill or stove-top grill pan to high heat.

Place the bacon pieces in a small nonstick skillet over medium heat. Cook, flipping occasionally, for about 3 to 4 minutes, or until barely cooked and not crisp. Transfer to a paper towel–lined plate to drain.

Place the chicken on a cutting board. Cover with a sheet of waxed paper. With the smooth side of a meat mallet, pound to an even 1/3" thickness. Rub both sides of the breast with oil and season with salt.

Place the chicken on the grill rack or grill pan. Grill for about 2 minutes per side, or until barely pink inside. Allow the chicken to sit for 5 minutes. Cut the breast in half lengthwise and then cut each half into 1/4"-thick crosswise strips. Set aside.

Meanwhile, preheat the oven to 500°F.

When the dough has doubled, gently punch it down. Place it on a lightly floured surface. With a lightly floured rolling pin or hands, roll or pat into a 14" circle (if you're new to making pizza, see page 131 for more advice on how to do this). Transfer to a 14" nonstick round deep-dish or flat pizza pan.

Bake for 5 minutes. Remove and set on a heat-proof surface. Spread evenly with the sauce, leaving a bare 1/2" border. Sprinkle one-quarter of the cheese evenly over the sauce. Top evenly with three-quarters of the chicken and three-quarters of the bacon. Next, top evenly with one-quarter of the pineapple and one-quarter of the onion. Top evenly with the remaining cheese, chicken, bacon, pineapple, and onion.

Bake for 8 to 12 minutes, or until the crust is golden. Allow the pizza to stand for 5 minutes on a rack. Cut into 8 slices.

MAKES 4 SERVINGS (2 SLICES EACH)

Each serving: 500 calories, 29 g protein, 74 g carbohydrates, 9 g fat, 3 g sat. fat, 4 g fiber

Original Papa John's Hawaiian BBQ Chicken Original Crust Pizza (2 large slices): 680 calories, 32 g protein, 92 g carbohydrates, 22 g fat, 6 g sat. fat, 4 g fiber

PAPA JOHN'S PIZZA DOUGH

Olive oil spray

$3/4$ cup warm water (105°–115°F)

1 $1/2$ teaspoons active dry yeast

2 teaspoons sugar

1$3/4$ cups + 4 tablespoons unbleached flour + additional for work surface

$1/2$ cup bread flour

$1/2$ teaspoon salt

2 teaspoons extra virgin olive oil

LIGHTLY mist a mixing bowl with oil spray. Set aside.

In a small bowl, combine the water, yeast, and sugar. Stir until the yeast is dissolved. Set aside.

In the bowl of a food processor fitted with a dough blade, or in a mixing bowl, combine 1$3/4$ cups unbleached flour, the bread flour, and salt. Pulse several times or stir with a wooden spoon to mix. When the yeast mixture starts to bubble, add it to the bowl. Add the oil to the bowl. Process or stir for about 1 minute, or until a sticky ball forms. If the mixture is too sticky, add up to 4 tablespoons unbleached flour, 1 tablespoon at a time. Process or stir until a smooth ball forms. Turn onto a lightly floured work surface. Knead by hand several times, until the dough is smooth and elastic. Place the dough in the reserved bowl. Lightly mist with oil spray. Cover the bowl tightly with plastic wrap. Set aside in a warm place. Allow it to rise for about 1 hour, or until doubled in size.

MAKES DOUGH FOR 1 ORIGINAL CRUST PIZZA

Each serving: 289 calories, 9 g protein, 56 g carbohydrates, 3 g fat, trace sat. fat, 2 g fiber

PAPA JOHN'S BBQ SAUCE

1 tablespoon + 1 teaspoon tomato paste

1 tablespoon + 1 teaspoon molasses

1 teaspoon liquid smoke

1 teaspoon white vinegar

½ teaspoon salt

½ teaspoon garlic powder

¼ teaspoon onion powder

TO prepare the sauce:

In a small bowl, combine the tomato paste, molasses, liquid smoke, vinegar, salt, garlic powder, and onion powder. Stir to mix well. Set aside.

Each serving: 25 calories, <1 g protein, 6 g carbohydrates, trace fat, 0 g sat. fat, trace fiber

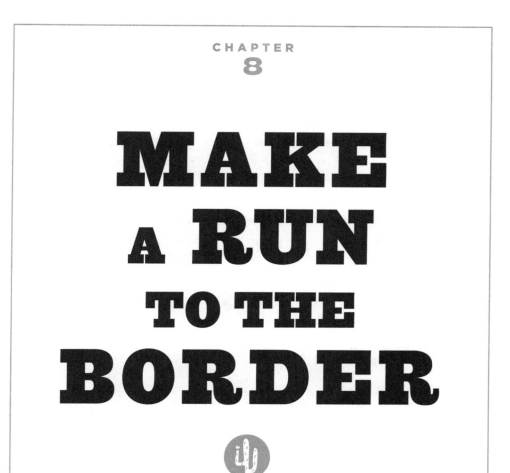

MAKE A RUN TO THE BORDER

While all of the recipes in this chapter are quite easy, timing is key. If you make sure that the lettuce and tomatoes are chopped and the sauces are sitting in front of you first, you're destined for perfectly prepared Mexican favorites. If you heat the tortillas and cook the beef, then realize the tomatoes need to be chopped, it's likely that your cheeses won't melt and the finished dish will be lukewarm at best. So be prepared for the simple but numerous steps, grab a margarita, and enjoy.

What Goes Into the Perfect Mexican Dish?

Tortillas

No matter what size tortilla you seek, look for tortillas that are labeled "low-fat." Though it's okay to substitute low-carb tortillas for low-fat ones in wraps or burritos where the tortillas are warmed but don't actually get cooked, it's not okay to do that when making most Mexican favorites. For example, if you attempt to make a Mexican pizza or crispy taco shell with a low-carb tortilla, it will burn well before it crisps and will likely give off a foul odor (unfortunately, I know because I tried).

Lettuce and Tomatoes

Make sure you start with really fresh ingredients. If the produce doesn't look great at your grocery store when you arrive, ask the produce guy (or gal) if he (or she) has more in the back. Often they hide the freshest produce because what is already sitting out will of course go bad quickly—and who would buy it if something fresher were sitting nearby? But, again, ask and (often) you shall receive. After all, you deserve the freshest and the best.

Beef

Because these recipes call for 96% lean ground beef, it is unnecessary to drain any residual liquid from the pan before adding seasonings, as you would with higher-fat cuts. There will be very little fat at most.

To stay true to the recipes, particularly those of Taco Bell. the beef should be cooked to a very uniform consistency, not chunky as it would be in chili. I prefer my taco beef to be chunkier, so I often "cheat" and make it how I like it. You should, too.

Cheese

Always shred fat-free or low-fat cheeses finely. Not only do they melt better, but you need less to get some in every bite. The good news is that there are great low-fat Cheddar cheeses available. Just make sure you taste-test them before you start to cook with them—some brands are not nearly as good as others.

Sauces

Though all of these recipes call for mild sauces (because those are the ones most commonly served at your favorite Mexican fast food restaurants), use whatever you like. The restaurants don't want to deter anyone from eating their food because the food is "too hot," but if you're like me and you prefer your food to have a bit more of a kick, go for it. Whether spicy or mild, low-fat taco sauce is a great flavor booster for very few calories.

EL POLLO LOCO: CHEESE QUESADILLA

SAVE: 159 CALORIES, 15 G FAT, 8 G SAT. FAT

Though I found some conflicting sets of nutritional information for this particular dish on El Pollo Loco's Web site (see page 13 for more on that ordeal), I am confident that this version of their hugely popular favorite offers far less fat and fewer calories, no matter how you look at it.

I do, however, know that this recipe is definitely worth including. First, I was so excited to find that my reduced-fat version has all the gooey richness of a decadent quesadilla—actually, it's way better than I would have expected—as well as a nice balance of protein and carbohydrates, which many experts claim can make weight loss a little easier. Combine that with the fact that it takes only minutes to make, and it's definitely a keeper.

> 1 burrito-size (10") low-fat flour tortilla
>
> 2 ounces (about 1 cup) finely shredded low-fat yellow Cheddar cheese
>
> 1½ ounces (about ¾ cup) finely shredded reduced-fat Monterey Jack cheese
>
> Olive oil spray

PREHEAT a large nonstick skillet over medium heat. Lay the tortilla flat on a plate and evenly sprinkle the Cheddar and Monterey Jack cheeses over half. Fold the bare side over the cheese side. Mist lightly with oil spray and place sprayed-side down in the heated pan.

Cook for 2 to 5 minutes, or until some brown spots appear on the bottom. Lightly mist the top with oil spray. Flip and cook for 2 to 5 minutes, or until brown spots appear on the bottom and the cheese is melted through.

Place the quesadilla on a plate. Cut into 4 equal wedges.

MAKES 1 SERVING

384 calories, 33 g protein, 34 g carbohydrates, 11 g fat, 6 g sat. fat, 3 g fiber

Original El Pollo Loco Cheese Quesadilla: 543 calories, 22 g protein, 51 g carbohydrates, 26 g fat, 14 g sat. fat, 2 g fiber

TACO BELL: SOFT TACO SUPREME
(BEEF)

SAVE: 31 CALORIES, 10 G FAT, 5 G SAT. FAT

It seems I hear ads for "99-cent" tacos a lot. Working as a caterer and knowing the cost of food, it always makes me wonder how in the world restaurants can make money with that sales strategy. Granted, anything that draws a crowd and makes them thirsty enough to purchase a $2 soft drink is likely to help profits, but I know a lot of budget-conscious consumers who go and buy just the tacos.

After some careful research, I can see why they are so popular—and how they are likely quite profitable after all. In looking at the company's nutritional data, I found out that there are only 11 grams of protein in an entire taco. When you consider that 1 ounce of lean beef has about 5 or 6 grams of protein and 1 ounce of low-fat cheese has about 6 or 7 grams of protein, it's clear that each taco contains only a tiny amount of beef—which explains why I want to eat so many to feel satisfied!

> 1 flour tortilla (7"), 98% fat-free
>
> 1½ teaspoons Taco Bell Seasoning Mix (opposite page)
>
> 2 teaspoons water
>
> 1½ ounces 96% lean ground beef (about 3 tablespoons)
>
> 1 tablespoon light sour cream
>
> ¼ cup shredded iceberg lettuce
>
> 2 tablespoons chopped tomatoes
>
> ½ ounce (about ¼ cup) shredded low-fat yellow Cheddar cheese
>
> Mild or hot red taco sauce (optional)

PREHEAT the oven to 400°F.

Wrap the tortilla in aluminum foil so it remains flat. Place directly on the oven rack. Heat for about 5 minutes, or until warm.

Meanwhile, in a small bowl, combine the seasoning mix and water. Stir until smooth. Set aside.

Preheat a small nonstick skillet over medium-high heat until drops of water sizzle when splashed on the pan. Crumble the beef into the pan. Cook, stirring with a wooden spoon, for 2 to 3 minutes, or until no longer pink. Stir in the reserved seasoning mixture. Cook, stirring, for 1 to 2 minutes, or until no liquid remains.

In one hand, hold the tortilla as you would hold a finished taco. Spoon the beef mixture in a strip along the bottom. Top evenly with the sour cream, lettuce, tomatoes, and cheese. Season with taco sauce, if desired.

MAKES 1 SERVING

229 calories, 17 g protein, 30 g carbohydrates, 4 g fat, 2 g sat. fat, 3 g fiber

Original Taco Bell Soft Taco Supreme (beef): 260 calories, 11 g protein, 22 g carbohydrates, 14 g fat, 7 g sat. fat, 3 g fiber

DRIVE-THRU Need dinner in a jiffy? Substitute 1½ teaspoons packaged low-sodium taco seasoning for the homemade mixture. Also, you can heat the tortilla in the microwave instead of in the oven. Simply place it between 2 damp paper towels on a microwavable plate. Then microwave it on low power in 10-second intervals until it is just warm.

TACO BELL SEASONING MIX

2 teaspoons cornstarch

1 teaspoon chili powder

1 teaspoon sweet paprika

1 teaspoon dried minced onion

⅛ teaspoon garlic powder

½ teaspoon salt

Pinch of ground cumin

IN a small bowl, combine the cornstarch, chili powder, paprika, onion, garlic powder, salt, and cumin. Stir to mix well. Transfer to a jar or other airtight container. Store in a cool, dark spot for up to 1 month.

MAKES 2 TABLESPOONS, ENOUGH FOR 4 SERVINGS OF SOFT TACO SUPREME BEEF, DOUBLE DECKER TACO SUPREME, MEXICAN PIZZA, OR NACHOS SUPREME

TACO BELL: DOUBLE DECKER TACO SUPREME

SAVE: 53 CALORIES, 13 G FAT, 6 G SAT. FAT

The most challenging part of this entire chapter was figuring out a way to transform a soft corn tortilla into a perfectly crisp baked taco shell. I didn't want to rely on a taco mold—they are way too difficult to locate—so instead I tried making my own contraptions out of aluminum foil, wrapping the tortillas around metal cans and inside cookie cutters before baking them, and using string to tie them in place. I even tried skewering tortillas and then hanging them inside loaf pans, but with every technique I used, they always broke at the bend after a few minutes of baking.

Then I did a little research and learned that deep-fried corn tortillas are first softened with a quick dip in some water so they don't break when they are placed in molds. Once fried, they become crispy and golden, the way taco shells should be.

I was pretty sure that same technique would not translate from frying to baking, but then an idea dawned on me. If I wrap them completely in foil and bake them for a few minutes, they will soften slightly. I would then be able to mold them and bake them until they start to take shape. I could then remove the mold so they would fully crisp, and they might stay together. I was right . . . and I can't even tell you how relieved and happy I was to finally find an answer to this dilemma that had been a mystery to me for months.

1½ teaspoons Taco Bell Seasoning Mix (page 161)

2 teaspoons water

1 soft yellow corn tortilla (6")

1 flour tortilla (7"), 98% fat-free

Pinch of salt

1½ ounces 96% lean ground beef (about 3 tablespoons)

2 tablespoons canned fat-free refried beans

1 tablespoon light sour cream

¼ cup shredded iceberg lettuce

2 tablespoons chopped tomatoes

½ ounce (about ¼ cup) finely shredded low-fat yellow Cheddar cheese

Mild or hot red taco sauce (optional)

PREHEAT the oven to 400°F. Cut a piece of aluminum foil that is about 12" x 12". Fold it in half and then scrunch it into a log shape, about 5" long x 1" thick. Set aside.

In a small bowl, combine the seasoning mix and water. Stir until smooth. Set aside.

Wrap each tortilla in separate pieces of aluminum foil so they remain flat. Set the flour tortilla aside. Place the corn tortilla directly on the oven rack. Heat for about 5 minutes, or until warm.

Remove the corn tortilla. With your fingers, sprinkle one side of the corn tortilla very lightly with water. Season lightly with salt. Flip the tortilla, salted side down, onto a small nonstick baking sheet. Place the aluminum foil log down the center of the tortilla. Fold the tortilla to form a half-moon. Fasten by inserting a toothpick about 1/2" from the rounded edges. Push the toothpick straight through both rounded edges, allowing a 1" space between the 2 halves.

Bake for 5 minutes. Carefully, leaving the toothpick in place, flip the tortilla and remove the log. Meanwhile, bake the corn tortilla for 4 to 8 minutes longer, or until the folded part is crisp. Watch carefully that the tortilla doesn't burn. Remove the toothpick after you take the tortilla out of the oven. Place the reserved flour tortilla directly on the oven rack and bake for 5 minutes, or until warm.

Meanwhile, preheat a small nonstick skillet over medium-high heat until drops of water sizzle when splashed on the pan. Crumble the beef into the pan. Cook, stirring with a wooden spoon, for 2 to 3 minutes, or until no longer pink. Stir in the reserved seasoning mixture. Cook, stirring, for 1 to 2 minutes, or until no liquid remains.

Place the beans in a microwavable dish. Microwave on low power in 10-second intervals until warm. Cover and set aside.

Remove the flour tortilla and place on a plate. Spread evenly with the beans, leaving a bare 1/2" border. Place the corn taco in the center of the flour tortilla. Fold the sides of the flour tortilla so the beans are sandwiched between the 2 tortillas. In one hand, hold the tortillas as you would hold a finished taco. Spoon the beef mixture in a strip along the bottom of the corn taco. Top evenly with the sour cream, lettuce, tomatoes, and cheese. Season to taste with taco sauce, if desired.

MAKES 1 SERVING

327 calories, 20 g protein, 49 g carbohydrates, 5 g fat, 2 g sat. fat, 5 g fiber

Original Taco Bell Double Decker Taco Supreme: 380 calories, 15 g protein, 40 g carbohydrates, 18 g fat, 8 g sat. fat, 6 g fiber

DRIVE-THRU If you're in a hurry, you can substitute 1 1/2 teaspoons of store-bought low-sodium taco seasoning for the homemade seasoning mix. Or, if you're a big fan of this recipe, mix up a batch of the seasoning mix and keep it in your spice drawer so you'll always have it on hand.

STOP BEFORE YOU START Make sure you have aluminum foil on hand before you begin this recipe. Otherwise, it might be tough to crisp the corn tortilla in the right shape.

TACO BELL: MEXICAN PIZZA

SAVE: 105 CALORIES, 25 G FAT, 9 G SAT. FAT

My friend Jim has a son who may just be the cutest little boy I've ever seen. Thus I refer to him as WCLB, short for "World's Cutest Little Boy."

When I ran into Jim at a recent culinary convention, he asked how I was progressing on this book. I mentioned that I was so excited to learn during my attempts to re-create Taco Bell's Mexican Pizza that I could turn a flour tortilla into a wonderfully thin and crispy pizza crust by simply baking it. Jim thought it was an interesting idea, so he went home and tried it for himself. He called me a couple of weeks later to tell me that he liked it so much that he served pizzas at WCLB's second birthday party using the tortilla crusts.

Whether or not you're a fan of Mexican Pizza (I am!), it's worth making the "crusts." Top them with your favorite pizza sauce, low-fat cheese, and toppings—meals really don't get much easier than that.

1½ teaspoons Taco Bell Seasoning Mix (page 161)

¼ teaspoon chili powder

¼ teaspoon paprika

2 teaspoons water

2 ounces 96% lean ground beef (about ¼ cup)

2 flour tortillas (7"), 98% fat-free

3½ tablespoons canned fat-free refried beans

2 tablespoons mild picante sauce

¼ ounce (about 2 tablespoons) finely shredded fat-free pepper jack cheese

½ ounce (about 2½ tablespoons) finely shredded low-fat mozzarella cheese

½ ounce (about ¼ cup) finely shredded low-fat yellow Cheddar cheese

2 tablespoons chopped tomatoes

1½ tablespoons chopped green onion tops

PREHEAT the oven to 400°F.

In a small bowl, combine the seasoning mix, chili powder, paprika, and water. Stir until smooth. Set aside.

Preheat a small nonstick skillet over medium-high heat until drops of water sizzle when splashed on the pan. Crumble the beef into the pan. Cook, stirring with a wooden spoon, for 2 to 3 minutes, or until no longer pink. Stir in the reserved seasoning mixture. Cook, stirring, for 1 to 2 minutes, or until no liquid remains. Remove from the heat. Cover to keep warm.

Place the tortillas in a single layer on a nonstick baking sheet. Bake for 3 to 5 minutes per side, or until just crisp and starting to brown. If air pockets form during baking, carefully pierce with a fork and press down to deflate.

Leave the tortillas on the baking sheet. Spread 1 tortilla evenly with the beans, leaving a bare ½" border. Evenly spoon the beef mixture over the beans. Top with the remaining tortilla. Spread evenly with picante sauce, leaving a bare ½" border. Sprinkle on the cheeses in layers, first the jack cheese, then the mozzarella cheese, and last the Cheddar cheese. Top with the tomatoes and onions.

Bake for 5 to 7 minutes, or until the cheeses melt. Cut into 4 wedges.

MAKES 1 SERVING

445 calories, 30 g protein, 67 g carbohydrates, 6 g fat, 2 g sat. fat, 9 g fiber

Original Taco Bell Mexican Pizza: 550 calories, 21 g protein, 46 g carbohydrates, 31 g fat, 11 g sat. fat, 7 g fiber

(STOP) **BEFORE YOU START** Do not attempt to substitute low-carb tortillas for the low-fat ones in this recipe. They will not crisp properly.

Also, take note of the specific order in which to add the cheeses. When using a fat-free cheese, it is always best to layer it below other cheeses with some fat or even under sauce. This strategy prevents the fat-free cheese from drying out, which it otherwise will tend to do. The resulting texture and feel will be more similar to that of full-fat cheese.

DEL TACO: MACHO BEEF BURRITO

SAVE: 469 CALORIES, 40 G FAT, 19 G SAT. FAT

When the clerk at Del Taco handed me my nicely wrapped burrito, I thought, "That's not a meal, it's a carry-on bag!" I then proceeded directly to a Mexican market—the only place I knew to secure a "Burrito Grande" flour tortilla (at 12 inches, it was still an inch smaller than the one I was served at Del Taco).

Though I personally don't think it wise to eat 1,170 calories and 62 grams of fat in one sitting (that's pretty much my calorie budget for a whole day, and my fat budget for 2 days), I do think the folks at Del Taco gave their burrito a good name. A *macho* guy with a labor-intensive job where his muscles get *beef*ed up all day (i.e., a construction worker) could justify eating the 700-plus calories and 22 grams of fat in my made-over version. The rest of us might want to stick to eating half of it or trying my "Even Better" version (see opposite page).

1 flour tortilla (12")

1 tablespoon packaged low-sodium taco seasoning

¼ cup water

6 ounces 96% lean ground beef (about ¾ cup)

2 tablespoons light sour cream

2 ounces (about 1 cup) finely shredded low-fat yellow Cheddar cheese

1 cup shredded iceberg lettuce

¾ cup chopped tomatoes

2 tablespoons mild green taco sauce

1 tablespoon mild red taco sauce

PREHEAT the oven to 300°F. Wrap the tortilla completely in aluminum foil so it remains flat. Set aside.

In a small bowl, combine the taco seasoning and water. Stir until smooth. Set aside.

Preheat a small nonstick skillet over medium-high heat until drops of water sizzle when splashed on the pan. Crumble the beef into the pan. Cook, stirring with a wooden spoon, for 2 to 3 minutes, or until no longer pink. Stir in the reserved seasoning mixture. Cook, stirring, for about 5 minutes, or until no liquid remains.

Meanwhile, place the wrapped tortilla in the oven. Bake for about 5 minutes, or until warmed.

Place the tortilla on a plate (the sides may drape over the edges). Spread the sour cream, leaving about 1" bare on both ends, in an even strip (about 4" wide) running across the center. Top the sour cream evenly with the cheese, the ground beef mixture, lettuce, and tomatoes. Drizzle on the green and red taco sauces. Fold both bare ends over the filling ingredients. Roll the tortilla tightly, finishing it seam-side down on the plate.

MAKES 1 SERVING

701 calories, 54 g protein, 64 g carbohydrates, 22 g fat, 10 g saturated fat, 4 g fiber

Original Del Taco Macho Beef Burrito: 1,170 calories, 60 g protein, 89 g carbohydrates, 62 g fat, 29 g sat. fat, 7 g fiber

EVEN BETTER Replace the 12" regular full-fat tortilla with a 98% fat-free 10" (standard burrito size) flour tortilla. Reduce the amount of beef to 4 ounces and use only 2 teaspoons taco seasoning. Reduce the cheese to ½ cup, the sour cream to 1 tablespoon, the red taco sauce to 2 teaspoons, and the tomatoes to ¼ cup. When you roll this one, it will be too full to tuck in the sides.

You'll still be left with a hearty burrito—one that's much more balanced: 405 calories, 37 g protein, 45 g carbohydrates, 8 g fat, 4 g sat. fat, 5 g fiber. You'll save 765 calories, 54 g fat, and 25 g sat. fat.

TACO BELL: NACHOS SUPREME (BEEF)

SAVE: 69 CALORIES, 18 G FAT, 7 G SAT. FAT

To me, the most important element in getting this dish right is the cheese sauce. I thought that it would be a challenge to remake the sauce, but then I realized that I didn't need to . . . and neither do you.

You may be pleasantly surprised to find, like I was, that nacho cheese sauce containing only 50 calories and 3.5 grams of fat per 2 tablespoons is readily available in jars at most major grocery stores. Those 3.5 grams of fat are virtually insignificant in light of the great, authentic flavor they have to offer. Plus, by the time you factor in baked chips, lean beef, and light sour cream, you can afford a few extra grams that will, without a doubt, quell even the strongest nacho cravings.

1½ teaspoons Taco Bell Seasoning Mix (page 161)

2 teaspoons water

1½ ounces 96% lean ground beef (about 3 tablespoons)

3 tablespoons canned fat-free refried beans

2 tablespoons jarred mild nacho cheese sauce (salsa con queso)

25 baked yellow corn tortilla chips with salt

1 tablespoon light sour cream

2 tablespoons chopped plum tomatoes

1 tablespoon chopped green onion tops

IN a small bowl, combine the seasoning mix and water. Stir until smooth. Set aside.

Preheat a small nonstick skillet over medium-high heat until drops of water sizzle when splashed on the pan. Crumble the beef into the pan. Cook, stirring with a wooden spoon, for 2 to 3 minutes, or until no longer pink. Stir in the reserved seasoning mixture. Cook, stirring, for 1 to 2 minutes, or until no liquid remains. Stir in the beans and let them cook until the mixture is heated through.

Remove from the heat. Cover to keep warm.

Meanwhile, place the cheese sauce in a small microwavable bowl. Microwave on low power for 5 to 10 seconds, or until warm. Set aside.

Pile the tortilla chips in a medium shallow bowl. Spoon on the beef mixture and then the cheese sauce. Dollop the sour cream on the center. Sprinkle the tomatoes and onions evenly over the top.

MAKES 1 SERVING

381 calories, 16 g protein, 62 g carbohydrates, 8 g fat, 2 g sat. fat, 8 g fiber

Original Taco Bell Nachos Supreme (beef): 450 calories, 13 g protein, 42 g carbohydrates, 26 g fat, 9 g sat. fat, 7 g fiber

STOP **BEFORE YOU START** To present these supremely delicious nachos in true Taco Bell style, try to find a shallow 7½" x 5½" oval serving dish, such as a porcelain au gratin dish.

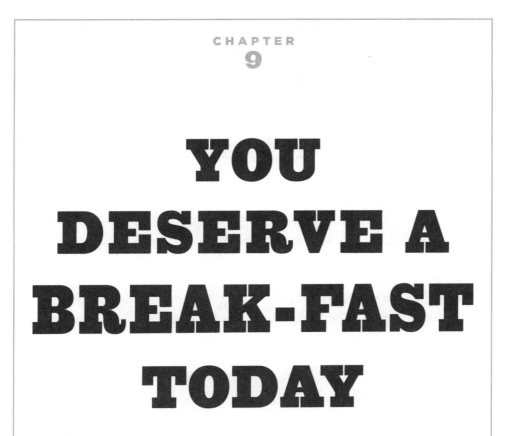

YOU DESERVE A BREAK-FAST TODAY

In my opinion, there's only one way to start your day—by nourishing your body, giving it some fuel to get started on the right path. Whether your idea of breakfast is an apple you grab before heading out the door or a hearty meal you've whipped up from scratch, breakfast truly is the most important meal of the day. Follow these recipes, and you may find it's the most enjoyable meal of the day, too.

What Goes Into the Perfect Breakfast?

Bacon

I always buy center-cut bacon because it's easy to cook it to crispy bacon perfection. For one thing, it's meatier, so it contains less fat than standard or thick-cut bacon. Plus, it doesn't have what I consider to be a rubbery consistency, like many brands of turkey bacon.

Most fast food restaurants cook their bacon far less than I prefer. The recipes in this book are written to mimic the original dishes as closely as possible. However, if you, like me, prefer your bacon to be cooked more, I encourage you to do so.

Sausage

I always make sausage out of extra-lean ground pork, turkey breast, or chicken breast. I've used pork in these recipes, however, because that's what fast food restaurants do. But go ahead and substitute chicken or turkey if you prefer.

When buying ground pork, be sure to buy extra-lean. It should have approximately 4.5 grams of fat per 4-ounce serving. If you can't find extra-lean ground pork, select a pork tenderloin and use this as another opportunity to befriend your butcher. Simply ask him or her to trim and grind it for you. Butchers generally oblige at no extra charge.

Egg vs. Egg Substitute vs. Egg White Substitute

As I explained in the chicken chapter (see page 46), I usually prefer to use egg whites over egg substitute or egg-white substitute when breading. I don't always feel the same way when making egg dishes. Granted, if I'm making an omelet, I prefer actual egg whites (again, it's a consistency issue). But if I'm re-creating a dish that used whole eggs, I like to use egg substitute because I can achieve the same yellow color of the original without adding any fat. Plus, pouring liquid egg substitute from a carton is simply easier than cracking fresh eggs. Overall, I recommend you go with whatever ingredient you prefer.

Cheese

Although most available light-cheese singles found in grocery stores are ³⁄₄ ounce each, it seems to me that most fast food restaurants use ¹⁄₂-ounce cheese slices on their breakfast sandwiches. In cases where the recipes call for ¹⁄₂-ounce slices, if you don't find them readily available, simply purchase ³⁄₄-ounce slices and then put only two-thirds of the slice on your breakfast sandwich. It will still cover most of the surface area of the sandwich, and you won't have to go on a wild-goose chase.

MCDONALD'S: EGG MCMUFFIN

SAVE: 73 CALORIES, 7 G FAT, 3 G SAT. FAT

One of the first fast food makeovers I ever developed was the McDonald's Sausage McMuffin. Because I'm such a huge fan of sausage, I just couldn't resist the combo of a fresh muffin with its perfectly crisped nooks and crannies housing a delicious sausage patty. Among my friends, however, the McDonald's Egg McMuffin is a bit more popular.

I've chosen to include the Egg McMuffin for you in case you, too, are a bigger fan of it. However, if you're like me and you're taunted by the sausage–English muffin combo, feel free to satisfy the craving by borrowing the sausage patty from the Burger King Enormous Omelet Sandwich (see page 174) or the Jack in the Box Extreme Sausage Sandwich (see page 176). You'll have a sandwich that's pretty close to the unforgettable Sausage McMuffin.

Olive oil spray

2 egg whites or ¼ cup egg-white substitute

1 English muffin, split

1 slice (½ ounce) 2% milk yellow American cheese

1 slice (½ ounce) Canadian bacon (2" wide)

PREHEAT the oven to 400°F.

Lightly mist a 4" ramekin or ovenproof glass bowl with oil spray. Add the egg whites or egg-white substitute. Place the ramekin in a medium baking dish filled with about 1½" of warm water. Carefully place the dish in the oven.

Bake for 20 minutes, or until no longer runny.

Just before the egg whites are cooked, toast the English muffin. Place on a plate. Place the cheese on the muffin bottom. Using a knife to loosen, carefully remove the egg whites from the ramekin. Place on top of the cheese. Top with the bacon and the muffin top.

MAKES 1 SERVING

217 calories, 18 g protein, 27 g carbohydrates, 4 g fat, 2 g sat. fat, 2 g fiber
Original McDonald's Egg McMuffin: 290 calories, 17 g protein, 30 g carbohydrates
11 g fat, 5 g sat. fat, 2 g fiber

DRIVE-THRU Don't have 20 minutes to cook the egg? Instead, pour the egg whites or egg-white substitute in a ramekin lightly misted with oil spray and microwave on low heat for 30-second intervals until no longer runny.

BURGER KING: ENORMOUS OMELET SANDWICH

SAVE: 303 CALORIES, 34 G FAT, 10 G SAT. FAT

After hearing the controversy that surrounded this sandwich when it was first released, I was surprised to see how enormous it really wasn't. Put it on a scale, and it's really only a couple of ounces larger than the Burger King Original Chicken Sandwiches we ordered.

So why all the hype? Perhaps it has something to do with reports that the sausage patty was deep-fried. Add that to the 2 large omelet-style egg patties, 2 strips of bacon, and 2 slices of cheese, and it sounded like it would be enormous.

So what's the good news, now that the dust has settled? It's easy to eliminate more than two-thirds of the fat and more than one-third of the calories and still enjoy the same flavors found in Burger King's creative and delicious sandwich.

> Olive oil spray
>
> $2/3$ cup egg substitute
>
> 2 slices center-cut bacon
>
> 1 Burger King Breakfast Sausage Patty (opposite page)
>
> 1 oval sesame seed sandwich roll (about 7" long)
>
> 2 slices ($1/2$ ounce each) 2% milk yellow American cheese

PREHEAT the oven to 350°F.

Lightly mist 2 nonstick mini loaf pans (6" x 3" x 2") with oil spray. Pour half of the egg substitute into each pan. Bake for 10 to 12 minutes, or until set.

Place a nonstick skillet over medium-high heat. Lay the bacon slices and the sausage patty in the pan. Cook the sausage for 2 to 3 minutes per side, or until lightly browned and no longer pink inside. Cook the bacon, flipping occasionally, for 4 to 6 minutes, or until cooked but not crisp. Transfer the sausage and bacon to a paper towel–lined plate to drain. Cover with a lid to keep warm.

Meanwhile, set a small nonstick skillet over medium heat. Place the bun top and bottom, cut-sides down, in the pan. Cook for 1 to 3 minutes, or until toasted.

Place the bun bottom, toasted-side up, on a plate. Carefully, using a knife to loosen, remove one omelet from the pan and place on the bun bottom. Cut the sausage patty in half. Place the halves over the omelet, running the length of the bun. They will overlap slightly. Top with the bacon and the remaining omelet. Top with the cheese running the length of the bun. Cover with the bun top.

MAKES 1 SERVING

437 calories, 41 g protein, 40 g carbohydrates, 12 g fat, 6 g sat. fat, 3 g fiber
Original Burger King Enormous Omelet Sandwich: 740 calories, 37 g protein, 45 g carbohydrates, 46 g fat, 16 g sat. fat, 3 g fiber

(STOP) BEFORE YOU START In order to produce omelets that are similar to those of Burger King, you'll need 2 nonstick mini loaf pans (6" x 3" x 2"). If you don't have them, use a large nonstick loaf pan (about 10" x 5" x 3") and cut the omelet in half after baking.

DRIVE-THRU Mornings are hectic? Mix a few batches of the sausage beforehand. Layer the uncooked patties between sheets of waxed paper in an airtight plastic container. Store in your freezer for up to 2 months, so you can pull one out whenever you want. No need to thaw. Add 1 to 2 minutes per side when cooking. Cook the egg substitute, folding it into an omelet, in a nonstick pan on the stove top instead of baking it in a pan. You'll be able to assemble the whole sandwich in minutes.

BURGER KING BREAKFAST SAUSAGE PATTIES

7 ounces extra-lean ground pork or pork tenderloin, ground (about 1 cup – 2 tablespoons)

1 tablespoon + 1 teaspoon pure maple syrup

1 teaspoon onion powder

½ teaspoon salt

½ teaspoon ground sage

¼ teaspoon ground black pepper

¼ teaspoon red-pepper flakes

⅛ teaspoon ground nutmeg

IN a small bowl, combine the pork, maple syrup, onion powder, salt, sage, black pepper, red-pepper flakes, and nutmeg. With hands or a fork, mix to blend well. On a sheet of waxed paper, divide the mixture into 4 equal portions. Shape each portion into a 4" patty. Place in a plastic container lined with waxed paper. Cover and refrigerate for up to 3 days.

MAKES 4.

Each patty: 81 calories, 11 g protein, 5 g carbohydrates, 2 g fat, <1 g sat. fat, trace fiber

JACK IN THE BOX: EXTREME SAUSAGE SANDWICH

SAVE: 316 CALORIES, 37 G FAT, 12 G SAT. FAT

Extreme isn't as drastic as I would have thought with this amazingly scrumptious breakfast treat from Jack. In fact, I found that each patty weighs only 1½ ounces, making the sandwich relatively small. Though Jack's sandwich is extra generous on fat, this classic combination of flavors doesn't lose much at all when made lighter. In fact, it quickly became my favorite breakfast item in this book.

> Olive oil spray
>
> 1 egg white
>
> 2 Jack in the Box Breakfast Sausage Patties (opposite page)
>
> 2 slices (½ ounce each) 2% milk yellow American cheese
>
> 1 hamburger bun

SET a spatula, butter knife, and oven mitt by the stove top. Lightly mist a small nonstick pan and the inside edge of a 3½" round metal cookie cutter with oil spray. Preheat the pan over medium-high heat until drops of water sizzle when splashed on the pan. Pour the egg white into the cookie cutter (hold it in place until the egg is set), and place the sausage patties next to it. Cook both for 1 to 2 minutes, or until the egg white is set on the bottom and starting to brown. With the butter knife, loosen the egg white from the cutter. Wearing the oven mitt, remove the cutter. Flip the egg white and the sausage patties. Cook for 1 to 2 minutes, or until the egg white is no longer runny and is just starting to brown on the bottom. Transfer the egg and sausage to a clean plate and place 1 slice of cheese on each sausage patty. Cover loosely with a lid to keep warm.

Place the bun top and bottom, cut-sides down, in the pan. Cook for 1 to 2 minutes, or until toasted.

Place the bun bottom on a plate. Top with 1 sausage patty (cheese-side up), the egg white, the remaining patty (cheese-side down), and the bun top.

MAKES 1 SERVING

> 357 calories, 38 g protein, 25 g carbohydrates, 11 g fat, 5 g sat. fat, 2 g fiber
>
> Original Jack in the Box Extreme Sausage Sandwich: 673 calories, 29 g protein, 32 g carbohydrates, 48 g fat, 17 g sat. fat, 2 g fiber

DRIVE-THRU Mornings are crunched?

You can cook the sausage patties the night before. In the morning, reheat the patties in a **400°F** oven while the cheese melts over them. Quickly fry the egg white (skip the cookie cutter) and throw them together. The whole process will take less than **5 minutes.**

You can also make the patties in bulk and freeze them, uncooked, for up to **2 months.** The recipe doubles, triples, even quadruples.

BEFORE YOU START To make this sandwich look exactly like Jack's, you'll need a round 3½"-diameter cookie cutter. Or you can use a silver dollar pancake pan or the inside of any 3¼"-diameter tuna fish can with both ends removed to fry the egg. But even if you don't have any of the above, don't despair. As long as you have a good nonstick skillet and make sure it is hot, the egg white will fry well without running too much. The finished sandwich won't have the perfectly processed look of the original, but it will taste just as yummy.

JACK IN THE BOX BREAKFAST SAUSAGE PATTIES

1 pound extra-lean ground pork or pork tenderloin, ground

2 teaspoons sugar

2 teaspoons pure maple syrup

½ teaspoon salt

¼ teaspoon ground black pepper

¼ teaspoon crushed red-pepper flakes

⅛ teaspoon garlic powder

IN a mixing bowl, combine the pork, sugar, maple syrup, salt, black pepper, red pepper, and garlic powder. With a fork, mix to blend well. Divide the mixture into 8 equal portions. One at a time, shape each portion into a ball and then flatten into a 4" patty on a sheet of waxed paper. Continue until all of the patties are formed.

Place the patties in a single layer or stack between sheets of waxed paper in an airtight plastic container. Refrigerate for up to 3 days.

MAKES 8, ENOUGH FOR 4 SERVINGS (2 PATTIES EACH)

Each serving: 155 calories, 24 g protein, 5 g carbohydrates, 4 g fat, 1 g sat. fat, trace fiber

DEL TACO: MACHO BACON AND EGG BURRITO

SAVE: 413 CALORIES, 40 G FAT, 12 G SAT. FAT

My friend Paige recently moved from Los Angeles to North Carolina to go back to school, which seems to be a trend among my friends right now. What is it about so many people suddenly switching career paths in their early to mid-thirties?

Anyway, I was talking to Paige on the phone the other night, and she was telling me about her new life. She's living alone; she doesn't know anyone; her classmates are a good 15 years younger than she is; and she's trying to get back into the swing of hitting the biology and chemistry books, which are prerequisites before she can even enter nursing school. If I were in her shoes, I'd be going insane. Yet she seemed very content . . . until food entered the conversation. Suddenly, she passionately blurted out, "I'm going nuts without Mexican food." I laughed. I've been in LA so long, I'd forgotten that we have so many Mexican food options, unlike other areas of the country.

Though I certainly can't help Paige with her class work, or age her fellow students any, I can provide her (and you) with this macho touch of "home."

> 1 large burrito-size flour tortilla (12") (see page 166)
>
> 3 slices center-cut bacon
>
> Olive oil spray
>
> 1 cup egg substitute
>
> 1 teaspoon taco seasoning
>
> 1 tablespoon + 2 teaspoons Del Taco Secret Sauce (opposite page)
>
> ¾ ounce (¼ cup + 2 tablespoons) finely shredded low-fat Cheddar cheese
>
> 1 cup finely shredded iceberg lettuce
>
> ½ cup chopped fresh tomatoes
>
> 1 tablespoon salsa verde, drained
>
> 1 tablespoon mild red taco sauce

Preheat the oven to 300°F. Wrap the tortilla in aluminum foil (it should remain flat and be completely covered). Bake for about 12 minutes, or until heated.

Meanwhile, lay the bacon slices side by side in a small nonstick skillet set over medium heat. Cook, flipping occasionally, for 4 to 6 minutes, or until cooked but not crisp. Transfer to a paper towel–lined plate to drain. Cover with a lid to keep warm.

Lightly mist a small nonstick skillet with oil spray. Set over medium heat. Pour in the egg substitute. Cook for 3 to 5 minutes, or until the egg substitute starts to set. With a spatula, scrape across the skillet to separate into chunks. Cook until the egg substitute is no longer runny. Sprinkle on the taco seasoning. Stir to blend.

Unwrap the tortilla and place it on a dinner plate, allowing it to drape over the sides. Spread the sauce, leaving about 1" bare on both ends, in an even strip (about 4" wide) running across the center. Cover the sauce evenly with the egg-substitute mixture. Top with the bacon, cheese, lettuce, and tomato. Drizzle on the salsa and then the taco sauce. Fold both bare ends over the filling ingredients. Roll the tortilla tightly, finishing it seam-side down on the plate.

MAKES 1 SERVING

617 calories, 41 g protein, 60 g carbohydrates, 20 g fat, 8 g sat. fat, 4 g fiber

Original Del Taco Macho Bacon and Egg Burrito: 1,030 calories, 40 g protein, 82 g carbohydrates, 60 g fat, 20 g sat. fat, 6 g fiber

DEL TACO SECRET SAUCE

¼ cup low-fat mayonnaise

2 tablespoons + 2 teaspoons fat-free half-and-half

1 teaspoon white vinegar

IN a small bowl, combine the mayonnaise and half-and-half. Whisk until smooth. Add the vinegar. Whisk until smooth. Cover with plastic wrap. Refrigerate for up to 3 days.

MAKES ABOUT ⅓ CUP, ENOUGH FOR 4 SERVINGS

Each serving: 32 calories, <1 g protein, 3 g carbohydrates, 2 g fat, 0 g sat. fat, 0 g fiber

CHICK-FIL-A: CHICKEN BISCUIT

SAVE: 104 CALORIES, 11 G FAT, 0.5 G SAT. FAT

Of all of the fast food restaurants I visited, Chick-fil-A and Burger King jumped out as polar opposites. Burger King's food is almost always the exact same size—even each onion ring within each order is virtually identical. Chick-fil-A, on the other hand, was hard to predict. No two Chick-n-Strips among a number of orders were uniform, and no two chicken fillets within a Chicken Biscuit were the same. The upside to that, though, is that this sandwich is very easy to make. Simply grab any 2-ounce piece of chicken and pound it until it's about a half-inch thick . . . or a bit thicker . . . or a bit thinner. Chances are, no matter what you do, somewhere across America, someone will be eating a similar sandwich prepared by Chick-fil-A.

> 2 ounces boneless, skinless chicken breast
>
> 1 teaspoon unbleached or all-purpose flour
>
> 1 teaspoon sugar
>
> $\frac{1}{4}$ teaspoon salt
>
> $\frac{1}{8}$ teaspoon ground black pepper
>
> $\frac{1}{8}$ teaspoon paprika
>
> Pinch of garlic powder
>
> Pinch of onion powder
>
> Pinch of cayenne
>
> Olive oil spray
>
> 1 egg white
>
> $1\frac{1}{2}$ teaspoons fat-free milk
>
> $2\frac{1}{2}$ teaspoons dry bread crumbs
>
> 1 warm Chick-fil-A Biscuit (page 182)
>
> 1 teaspoon light butter spread, divided

PLACE the chicken on a cutting board. Cover with a sheet of waxed paper. With the smooth side of a meat mallet, pound to an even $\frac{1}{2}$" thickness.

In a small resealable plastic bag, combine the flour, sugar, salt, black pepper, paprika, garlic powder, onion powder, and cayenne. Shake to mix well. Add the chicken. Shake to completely coat the chicken with the flour mixture. Place in the refrigerator for at least 10 minutes.

Preheat the oven to 450°F. Lightly mist a small nonstick baking sheet with oil spray. Set aside.

In a small shallow bowl, combine the egg white and milk. Beat lightly with a fork until smooth. Place the bread crumbs on a sheet of waxed paper set next to the bowl.

Dip the chicken into the egg-white mixture, being sure to coat completely. Allow any excess egg-white mixture to drip off. Dip into the bread crumbs to coat completely. Place on the reserved baking sheet. Lightly mist with oil spray.

Bake for 5 minutes. Carefully flip the chicken. Bake for 5 to 7 minutes, or until the breading is crisp and the chicken is no longer pink inside.

Cut the biscuit in half. Place on a plate. Spread the inside of each half with ½ teaspoon butter spread. Place the chicken on the biscuit bottom. Cover with the biscuit top.

MAKES 1 SERVING

316 calories, 22 g protein, 38 g carbohydrates, 8 g fat, 4 g sat. fat, 1 g fiber

Original Chick-fil-A Chicken Biscuit: 420 calories, 18 g protein, 44 g carbohydrates, 19 g fat, 4.5 g sat. fat, 2 g fiber

CHICK-FIL-A BISCUITS

Butter-flavored cooking spray

1 cup + 1 tablespoon unbleached flour + extra for sprinkling

1 teaspoon baking powder

½ teaspoon salt

¼ teaspoon baking soda

3 tablespoons cold light butter, cut into pieces

½ cup low-fat buttermilk

PREHEAT the oven to 425°F. Spray an 8" x 8" glass baking dish or metal non-stick pan with cooking spray. In a mixing bowl, combine 1 cup + 1 tablespoon flour, the baking powder, salt, and baking soda. With a pastry blender or a fork, mix to blend. Add the butter. Cut in the butter with the pastry blender or fork until crumbly. Add the buttermilk. Stir with a fork just until the mixture is moistened. The dough will be sticky.

Turn the dough out onto a lightly floured work surface. Lightly dust your hands with flour. Knead lightly, adding as little flour as possible, until the dough forms a rough ball. Pat it into a square that's about 6" x 6".

With a floured 3" round cookie cutter, cut 2 biscuits from the dough. Transfer to the prepared dish, placing the biscuits 1" apart. Reshape the remaining dough into a 6" x 3" rectangle. Cut another biscuit and place on the dish. Reshape the remaining dough to form 1 biscuit. (There should be no remaining scraps.) Place on the dish.

Bake for 15 to 19 minutes, or until lightly browned and no longer doughy inside. Allow to cool for a few minutes on a rack.

MAKES 4

Each biscuit: 158 calories, 5 g protein, 24 g carbohydrates, 5 g fat, 3 g sat. fat, 1 g fiber

 BEFORE YOU START This biscuit recipe calls for a 3" round cookie cutter. If you don't have one, you can substitute a clean empty 3" soup can or other empty can (cut off both ends) from your pantry.

MCDONALD'S: BACON, EGG, AND CHEESE BAGEL

SAVE: 225 CALORIES, 19 G FAT, 6 G SAT. FAT

When I started the research for this book, a number of fast food–loving friends told me that McDonald's Bacon, Egg, and Cheese Bagel was one of their favorite breakfast sandwiches. Months later, when I went to order it, I realized it was no longer listed on McDonald's menu (at least in my local area). I asked if they still served it, and they do, so I was excited to be able to remake it, but I had to call the corporate office to get the nutritional analysis since it wasn't listed on their Web site either. Regardless, I'm pleased to report that the sandwich has gotten the seal of approval from those who suggested I add it.

Olive oil spray

¼ cup egg substitute

1 slice center-cut bacon, halved

1 plain bagel (4")

2 slices (½ ounce each) 2% milk yellow American cheese

PREHEAT the oven to 325°F.

Lightly mist a nonstick loaf pan (8½" x 4½" x 2½") with oil spray. Pour in the egg substitute. Bake for 8 to 12 minutes, or until the egg substitute is set. Allow to cool for 3 minutes.

Meanwhile, lay the bacon slices side by side in a small nonstick skillet set over medium heat. Cook, flipping occasionally, for 4 to 6 minutes, or until cooked but not crisp. Transfer to a paper towel–lined plate to drain. Cover to keep warm.

At the same time, preheat a nonstick skillet over medium heat. Place the bagel top and bottom, cut-sides down, in the pan. Cook for 3 to 5 minutes, or until toasted.

Carefully remove the egg substitute from the pan. Fold into thirds as if you are folding a letter.

Place the bagel bottom on a plate. Top with 1 slice cheese, the bacon slices (side by side), the omelet, the remaining slice cheese, and the bagel top.

MAKES 1 SERVING

365 calories, 23 g protein, 49 g carbohydrates, 8 g fat, 4 g sat. fat, 2 g fiber

Original McDonald's Bacon, Egg, and Cheese Bagel: 590 calories, 28 g protein, 57 g carbohydrates, 27 g fat, 10 g sat. fat, 2 g fiber

MCDONALD'S: HASH BROWN

SAVE: 59 CALORIES, 6 G FAT, 1.5 G SAT. FAT

If you've perused this whole book, you may have noticed that I've suggested making McDonald's Hash Brown from fresh potatoes, but Sonic's Tater Tots from purchased preshredded potatoes (see page 120). Trial after trial of the Tater Tots made with fresh potatoes yielded inconsistent results. Trial after trial of the Hash Brown yielded virtual heaven in our hands. My testers and I were actually astounded at how well these came out. They not only tasted similar to McDonald's offering, but they were perfectly pick-up-able. In our opinions, that was key. Now, the key for you to perfectly duplicate them is to be sure to squeeze as much water from the potatoes as possible and not to wait too long between chopping the potatoes and getting them into the oven. But, if it's easier for you, you can always substitute store-bought preshredded potatoes in this recipe as well, though they may take a few minutes longer to cook.

> Olive oil spray
>
> 2 teaspoons egg substitute
>
> $\frac{1}{8}$ teaspoon salt
>
> 1 small russet potato (6 ounces), peeled and cut into $\frac{1}{2}$" cubes

PREHEAT the oven to 450°F. Lightly mist a small nonstick baking sheet with oil spray. Set aside.

In a small bowl, combine the egg substitute and salt. Set aside.

Place the potato in the bowl of a mini food processor fitted with a metal blade. Pulse into chunks that are slightly larger than shredded potatoes. (You can also grate the whole potato on a coarse shredder, but then the hash brown won't look exactly like McDonald's.) Using paper towels or clean hands, if you prefer, squeeze as much moisture from the potatoes as possible. (This is very important so the hash brown will not fall apart.) Measure $\frac{2}{3}$ cup of potatoes (about 3 ounces). Add to the egg-substitute mixture and stir to combine. Lay a sheet of waxed paper over a dinner plate. Spoon the potato mixture into the center. Shape into an oval about $4\frac{3}{4}$" long x $2\frac{1}{2}$" wide. Flip onto the reserved baking sheet. Reshape if necessary. Lightly mist with oil spray.

Bake for 10 to 12 minutes per side, or until crisp. Remove the hash brown from the oven. Allow to stand for 2 to 3 minutes.

MAKES 1 SERVING

81 calories, 3 g protein, 15 g carbohydrates, 2 g fat, trace sat. fat, 1 g fiber

Original McDonald's Hash Brown: 140 calories, 1 g protein, 15 g carbohydrates, 8 g fat, 1.5 g sat. fat, 2 g fiber

BURGER KING: FRENCH TOAST STICKS

SAVE: 114 CALORIES, 15 G FAT, 1.5 G SAT. FAT

I love that Burger King calls these scrumptious, delicious, decadent breakfast treats "French Toast Sticks." I personally find them to more closely resemble doughnuts. But I guess many more people can justify eating French Toast Sticks for breakfast than can justify eating Doughnut Sticks for breakfast.

As far as I'm concerned, the chef who created these wonderfully vanilla-y sticks is a genius. If you're like me, and you really don't feel very good about eating anything called or resembling doughnuts for breakfast (except on rare occasion, of course), this nonfried version parallels the sweet vanilla flavor with the hint of cinnamon found in Burger King's, but with 75 percent less fat and nearly a third fewer calories.

1/4 cup egg substitute

1/2 tablespoon vanilla extract

5 tablespoons confectioners' sugar

1/4 teaspoon ground cinnamon

2 teaspoons light butter

1 1/4 slices Hawaiian sweet bread, cut into five 1"-wide strips

Light pancake syrup (optional)

IN a shallow bowl, combine the egg substitute and vanilla. With a fork, mix to blend. Set aside next to the stove top.

On a sheet of waxed paper, combine the sugar and cinnamon. With a fork, mix to blend. Set aside next to the bowl.

Melt the butter in a nonstick skillet over medium heat. Working quickly with one bread strip at a time, dip each strip into the egg-substitute mixture just to coat. Do not soak the bread, or the sticks will be too soft to pick up. Transfer immediately to the sugar mixture to coat all sides. You may need to press the sugar into the strips. Place in the pan. Continue dipping and coating the remaining strips, placing them in the pan so that they don't touch the other strips. Cook for 3 to 5 minutes per side, or until golden brown. Serve with syrup, if desired.

MAKES 1 SERVING (5 STICKS)

276 calories, 7 g protein, 48 g carbohydrates, 5 g fat, 3 g sat. fat, 2 g fiber

Original Burger King French Toast Sticks (5 sticks): 390 calories, 6 g protein, 46 g carbohydrates, 20 g fat, 4.5 g sat. fat, 2 g fiber

STOP **BEFORE YOU START** You will not need to use all of the egg substitute and confectioners' sugar called for in the recipe. You'll need the excess to dip and coat the sticks easily, but the nutritional analysis is based on the average amount of these ingredients that actually adheres to the bread and is consumed.

DUNKIN' DONUTS: CRANBERRY ORANGE MUFFINS

SAVE: 72 CALORIES, 11 G FAT

I recently visited Oxford, Massachusetts, and the surrounding areas and was astounded by the number of Dunkin' Donuts restaurants that existed. Though I grew up watching those popular "It's time to make the doughnuts" commercials, I had no idea how popular this chain is. Near Boston, it felt like there was one on practically every corner. If you, like me, aren't from an area where they are so prevalent, let me assure you, you are totally missing out not sampling so many of their wonderful treats, including these Cranberry Orange Muffins.

Now if you are apprehensive about baking or are just plain a novice, don't despair. This recipe is a great choice even for first-time bakers. These muffins are so quick and simple that they don't even require a mixer.

Butter-flavored cooking spray

$^2/_3$ cup fresh or frozen cranberries, chopped

2 teaspoons + $^1/_2$ cup granulated sugar

1$^1/_2$ cups unbleached flour

1 tablespoon dried orange peel

2 teaspoons baking powder

1 teaspoon salt

2 egg whites, lightly beaten

1 teaspoon orange extract

1 teaspoon vanilla extract

$^3/_4$ cup low-fat buttermilk

$^1/_4$ cup fat-free vanilla yogurt

$^1/_4$ cup light butter, melted

1 tablespoon turbinado sugar

PREHEAT the oven to 400°F. Place 4 large muffin papers in 4 cups (3$^1/_2$" diameter) of a large muffin tin. Coat the insides of the papers with cooking spray.

In a small bowl, combine the cranberries with 2 teaspoons granulated sugar. Toss to coat. Set aside.

In a bowl, combine the flour, orange peel, baking powder, and salt. Mix to blend.

In a mixing bowl, combine the egg whites, orange extract, vanilla extract, and the remaining ½ cup granulated sugar. With a sturdy whisk or spatula, mix to blend well. Add the buttermilk, yogurt, and butter. Mix or stir to blend. Add the flour mixture. Stir just until none of the flour mixture is visible. Fold in the cranberry mixture. Dollop the batter evenly into the prepared cups. Sprinkle evenly with the turbinado sugar.

Bake for 25 to 30 minutes, or until a toothpick inserted in the center comes out dry (a few crumbs are okay). Allow to cool on a rack for 10 minutes. Serve warm or transfer to an airtight container and refrigerate for up to 1 day.

MAKES 4

Each muffin: 368 calories, 9 g protein, 68 g carbohydrates, 6 g fat, 4 g sat. fat, 2 g fiber

Original Dunkin' Donuts Cranberry Orange Muffin: 440 calories, 8 g protein, 66 g carbohydrates, 17 g fat, 3 g sat. fat, 3 g fiber

DRIVE-THRU Double or triple the recipe if you like, and then freeze any remaining muffins in a resealable plastic freezer bag. When you're ready for a morning treat or a snack, simply wrap a frozen muffin in aluminum foil so it is covered, then place it in a preheated 400°F oven for 10 minutes, or until it is warmed through.

EVEN BETTER Make 10 standard-size muffins instead of 4 jumbo ones. Follow the recipe instructions but use a standard-size muffin tin and divide the batter among 10 cups. Bake the muffins for 18 to 22 minutes, or until a toothpick inserted in the center comes out dry. Each standard-size muffin: 147 calories, 4 g protein, 27 g carbohydrates, 3 g fat, 2 g sat. fat, 1 g fiber. You'll save: 293 calories, 14 g fat, 1 g sat. fat.

BEFORE YOU START In order for your Cranberry Orange Muffins to look exactly like the ones at Dunkin' Donuts, you'll need 3½"-diameter muffin papers. They are most readily available at restaurant supply stores. If you are content without the papers, use a nonstick muffin tin and lightly mist the muffin cups directly with cooking spray.

Sparkling caramel-colored crystals of turbinado sugar are pretty sprinkled on the muffin tops. Look for it next to the granulated sugar in the supermarket. If you don't have any on hand, use granulated sugar instead.

DUNKIN' DONUTS: CORN MUFFINS

SAVE: 153 CALORIES, 15 G FAT, 2.5 G SAT. FAT

Early in my catering career, I was approached by a woman who wanted me to cater her parties, but to then pretend to be her friend at the party, while she took credit for the food. When she agreed to pay my teaching rate while I "helped her" prepare the food in addition to my catering rate for the party, I agreed. I quickly coined the service "ghost cooking."

Party after party she impressed her boyfriend, then later fiancé, with her talents in the kitchen. I always got such a kick out of it, as I wondered how she thought she could get away with lying to her fiancé about her cooking skills. How would he never find out that she could barely boil water? What would she do when she needed to cook for her in-laws?

After months of my playing along, she hired me for one last party just before the wedding. We served chili and corn muffins. She'd invited a group of her colleagues, friends, and her fiancé's friends for a casual Sunday night dinner. Though it was my last ghost-cooking assignment for her, it was my most memorable. She paid me a small fortune to make basic chili and simple corn muffins. I couldn't believe it.

I continued to cater more-traditional parties for her through her wedding . . . then her divorce—perhaps they didn't know everything about each other before getting married? But I still can't see a corn muffin without thinking about her and the lengths she went to to deceive. Fortunately, these muffins are very straightforward. In fact, they're so good and so low in fat that once you master them for breakfast, you, too, are likely to find yourself wanting to serve them with a pot of your favorite low-fat chili.

Butter-flavored cooking spray

1 1/4 cups unbleached flour

3/4 cup yellow cornmeal

2 teaspoons baking powder

1/2 teaspoon salt

3/4 cup sugar

1/2 cup fat-free vanilla yogurt

4 egg whites, lightly beaten

3/4 cup fat-free milk

1 tablespoon vanilla extract

1 tablespoon butter-flavored shortening, melted

PREHEAT the oven to 400°F. Place 5 large muffin papers in 5 cups (3½" diameter) of a large muffin tin. Coat the insides of the papers with cooking spray.

In a bowl, combine the flour, cornmeal, baking powder, and salt. Mix to blend. Set aside.

In a mixing bowl, combine the sugar, yogurt, and egg whites. With a sturdy whisk or spatula, whisk or mix to blend well. Add the milk, vanilla, and shortening. Whisk or stir to blend. Add the flour mixture. Stir just until none of the flour mixture is visible. Dollop the batter evenly into the prepared cups.

Bake for 28 to 30 minutes, or until a toothpick inserted in the center comes out dry (a few crumbs are okay). Allow to cool on a rack for 10 minutes. Serve warm or transfer to an airtight container and refrigerate for up to 1 day.

MAKES 5

> Each muffin: 357 calories, 10 g protein, 71 g carbohydrates, 3 g fat, 1 g sat. fat, 2 g fiber
>
> Original Dunkin' Donuts Corn Muffin: 510 calories, 8 g protein, 77 g carbohydrates, 18 g fat, 3.5 g sat. fat, 1 g fiber

DRIVE-THRU Double or triple the recipe if you like, and then freeze any remaining muffins in a resealable plastic freezer bag. When you're ready for a morning treat or a snack, simply wrap a frozen muffin in aluminum foil so it is covered, then place it in a preheated 400°F oven for 10 minutes, or until it is warmed through.

EVEN BETTER Make 10 standard-size muffins instead of 5 jumbo ones. Follow the instructions above, but use a standard-size muffin tin and divide the batter among 10 cups. Bake the muffins for 18 to 22 minutes, or until a toothpick inserted in the center comes out dry. Each standard-size muffin will have: 178 calories, 5 g protein, 36 g carbohydrates, 2 g fat, ‹1 g sat. fat, 1 g fiber. You'll save: 332 calories, 16 g fat, 2.5 g sat. fat.

BEFORE YOU START In order for your Corn Muffins to look exactly like the ones at Dunkin' Donuts, you'll need to hunt down 3½"-diameter muffin papers, which, by the way, might stick if not sprayed well. They can be found at most restaurant supply stores. If you are content without the papers, use a nonstick muffin tin and spray the muffin cups directly with cooking spray. Your muffins will be just as good.

WE SWEET YOU RIGHT

Even though I just may be the biggest chocolate lover on the planet, I find creating original recipes for fabulous low-fat desserts to be more challenging than creating recipes for any other category of food. In fact, years ago, after writing my first magazine article about desserts, I swore I would never write another one. Then I found myself faced with this chapter.

The challenge is straightforward: If I cook a burger and think it needs more salt, I can simply add it and retaste it. If I think muffins need more salt, I have to start from scratch. Though all the dessert recipes in this book are a breeze to make, getting them to that point—so you can achieve perfect consistency—can drive a gal a little wacky.

And then there's the fact that I have zero willpower when it comes to desserts (even failed ones in many cases), and for months, I found myself sitting over not-yet-perfected buckets of cookies, cakes, and brownies "not good enough to give away," but perfectly fine for me. It's a minor miracle that I'm still small enough to fit on the cover of this book. And I'm pretty sure you'll see why I say that after one bite of the Cinnabon.

What Goes Into the Perfect Dessert?

Fat Substitutes

A lot of people in search of lower-fat desserts swap baby food, pureed prunes, and/or applesauce for the butter or oil in their favorite baked goods. Some even swear by putting pureed beans in brownies, which is too horrifying a thought for me personally (I really don't like beans) to even consider for a minute. Others believe that light butter just plain doesn't work in baked goods. Heck, I've even seen packages of light butter with a note advising against substituting light butter in baked goods (my opinions on that later). Clearly, the opinions are quite mixed.

Yogurt

If you take a quick look at the ingredients in this chapter, you'll find that like most chefs, I favor certain ingredients. First, I use yogurt as a substitute in most of my cakes and muffins. It's been my personal experience after trying applesauce and other types of fruit purees that yogurt, in the right combinations, works best. Unfortunately, I can't provide any easy rule of thumb for knowing how much yogurt to substitute for fat—until I've perfected a recipe, I've found it's always a bit hit or miss—but again, after multiple attempts, 9 times out of 10, I find that yogurt gives consistently wonderful results.

Light Butter and Reduced-Fat Cream Cheese

Another ingredient that I consistently use is light butter—the type that's packaged in sticks just like regular butter or margarine. Yes, there is water added to it, which some argue will add excess moisture to your baked goods and ruin them. True, this is a possibility, but again, with some careful tweaking and mindful attention to compensating for the extra moisture, I often find light butter to be a friend, not a foe. Please note that light butter is different from light butter spread, which is sold in tubs. Though some recipes in this book do call for light butter spread, the two are, for the most part, not interchangeable. Likewise, in these recipes, 1/3-less-fat cream cheese (Neufchâtel) that is sold in blocks should not be replaced with any whipped or cream-cheese spreads that are sold in tubs.

MAKING MILKSHAKES

Did you ever notice that if you take a bowl of ice cream and mash it with a spoon until it softens, it then looks like you've already eaten some because it appears there's less there? Or have you ever eaten soft-serve frozen yogurt and found that whatever is left at the bottom of your cup looks noticeably smaller after it has melted?

I thought about experiences like that when I discovered (the hard way) that if you put 16 ounces of ice cream in a blender with 1/4 cup of milk and some chocolate syrup, you don't even have a 16-ounce shake by the time it's blended. (You might if the ingredients are extremely cold and you have a very high-powered or special blender, but typically you won't.) It was a huge challenge to figure out how to get some air back into the shakes since I didn't want to add so many calories from ice cream. Sadly, this is the only challenge I didn't conquer to my satisfaction.

Though I talked to two of the country's premier food scientists and did a slew of research and trials, the suggestions I received were not conducive to including them for use at home. A $500 blender was one solution. Adding maltodextrin was another, but I've found it is not quite as available as I'd like. So basically, I decided to stick to suggesting that you exercise portion control with the milkshake recipes.

Does the 31st ounce of a milkshake really satisfy anything that the first 8 ounces didn't? Too much of a good thing, or in the case of a milkshake, one might argue, a great thing, really can be a bad thing.

Egg Whites

Egg whites are another ingredient that you'll find in recipe after recipe. And with these, I do find the substitutions to correspond consistently; I almost always substitute two egg whites for one whole egg. Now, some people use egg substitutes, but I prefer not to. I think that because the consistency is thinner, egg substitutes alter my finished product ever so slightly. So I avoid them unless the original recipe was developed using them.

Ice Cream

You may notice that I suggest fat-free, sugar-free ice cream in the milkshake recipes. Though I've never been a proponent of the low-carb movement, I've sampled plenty of low-carb and sugar-free products, only to have horrible stomach pains afterward.

Vanilla fat-free, sugar-free ice cream has never had this effect on me, and I truly believe that it (or at least the brands at my local grocery store) tastes much more like real vanilla ice cream than any frozen yogurt found at the grocery store (though not necessarily the ones found at frozen-yogurt shops). Plus, fat-free, sugar-free ice cream provides some fiber, which makes you feel fuller and more satisfied with smaller amounts. Add that to the fact that it has fewer calories than others, and it was the perfect choice in my mind.

CINNABON: CLASSIC CINNAMON ROLL

SAVE: 371 CALORIES, 26 G FAT, 5 G SAT. FAT

Truth be told, this recipe is probably the most time-consuming recipe in this book (with the Pizza Hut Meat Lover's Hand-Tossed Style Pizza coming in second). But after the first bite, every person who's made it swears that they'd make it again . . . especially knowing the Drive-Thru option (see page 197). Even my friend Heather, who later revealed that she had never before made anything requiring yeast, swore it was much easier than she suspected it would be and worth the effort (we're close enough that she would have told me the truth).

Plus, it's the only recipe that I'll probably never admit how much I've actually eaten . . . they're just so good. Oops.

My version of the Cinnabon has also become the recipe in the book that I've used to prove to skeptics that, in fact, these recipes can be duplicated to satisfy cravings with a fraction of the fat and calories of their original counterparts. Though I believe many of the recipes truly duel the originals, this one happens to travel much better than many since it doesn't need to be hot. The rolls are just fine if they sit at room temperature for several hours. Imagine what a star you'll be if you show up at a brunch with a batch of these Cinnamon Rolls as your offering. (I'd recommend following the "Even Better" suggestions, see page 197, so they're more user-friendly and can be shared more easily.)

Butter-flavored cooking spray

2 tablespoons light butter from a stick, divided

1 cup fat-free milk

$\frac{1}{3}$ cup granulated sugar

$\frac{1}{4}$ cup artificially sweetened fat-free vanilla yogurt

1 egg + 1 egg white

1 package ($\frac{1}{4}$ ounce) active dry yeast

4 cups unbleached flour, divided + additional for work surface

1 teaspoon + 1 tablespoon ground cinnamon

$\frac{1}{2}$ teaspoon salt

3 tablespoons corn syrup

3 tablespoons packed brown sugar

$\frac{1}{2}$ teaspoon vanilla extract

1 recipe Cinnabon Frosting (page 197)

LIGHTLY mist a large bowl with cooking spray. Set aside 1 tablespoon butter to soften.

In a large microwavable measuring cup or a medium microwavable bowl, combine the milk, granulated sugar, and the remaining 1 tablespoon butter.

(continued)

Microwave on high power for 2 minutes, or until the milk is hot (130°F). Add the yogurt. Whisk until the sugar dissolves (some small lumps of yogurt may be visible). Add the egg and egg white. Whisk to beat well. Add the yeast. Whisk until dissolved.

In the bowl of a stand mixer fitted with the dough hook(s) or in a large mixing bowl, combine 2 cups flour, 1 teaspoon cinnamon, and the salt. Mix or stir by hand with a wooden spoon to blend. Add the milk mixture. Mix on medium power or stir vigorously to blend. The mixture will be very sticky. Add the remaining 2 cups flour, mixing or stirring until absorbed.

Turn the dough onto a floured work surface. (A plastic dough scraper or brittle plastic spatula is helpful for getting out all of the dough and starting the kneading.) Knead for about 5 minutes, or until smooth and elastic. Add scant amounts of flour as needed. The dough should be soft but not sticky. Place in the reserved bowl. Lightly mist with cooking spray. Cover the bowl tightly with plastic wrap. Allow to rise for about 1 hour, or until doubled in size.

Meanwhile, in a small bowl, combine the corn syrup, brown sugar, the remaining 1 tablespoon cinnamon, and the vanilla. Stir to blend well. Set aside.

When the dough has doubled, gently punch it down and place it on the lightly floured surface. Knead for about 1 minute. Dust lightly with flour. Cover and allow to rest for 10 minutes.

Lightly mist an 11" x 7" nonstick baking dish with cooking spray. Set aside.

Using your hands or a floured rolling pin, press or roll the dough into an 18" x 12" rectangle. With a butter knife, evenly spread the softened butter over the dough. Drizzle on the filling. With a knife or spatula, evenly spread it to the edges. Starting at one shorter side, roll the dough, jelly-roll fashion, into a tube, ending seam-side down. Cut into 8 equal pieces. Place, spiral-side up, in the reserved dish.

Cover the dish with a damp kitchen towel and place in a warm spot. Let the rolls rise another 30 minutes.

Preheat the oven to 350°F. Bake for 22 to 28 minutes, or until very lightly browned but slightly doughy in the center.

With a spatula, transfer one roll to a plate. Using a butter knife, spread 1½ table-spoons of frosting over the top and ½" down the sides. Repeat with the other 7 rolls.

MAKES 8

Each roll: 442 calories, 10 g protein, 88 g carbohydrates, 6 g fat, 3 g sat. fat, 3 g fiber

Original Cinnabon Classic Roll: 813 calories, 15 g protein, 117 g carbohydrates, 32 g fat, 8 g saturated fat, 4 g fiber

DRIVE-THRU To enjoy fresh rolls first thing in the morning, assemble the rolls the night before and then cover them loosely with plastic wrap instead of a damp towel. Refrigerate overnight and the rolls will rise while you sleep, so you can bake as soon as the oven is warm.

Or if you'd like to have the luxury of eating them whenever the mood strikes, consider making a batch or two and freezing them after baking and cooling. (Freeze the frosting separately.) Pack in an airtight plastic container. When you crave one, wrap it in aluminum foil and bake it in a preheated 250°F oven for 20 to 25 minutes, or until it is warmed through.

EVEN BETTER Make the dough following the recipe directions, but roll the dough out into a larger rectangle about 22½" x 11". Roll the dough starting with one of the longer ends. You'll end up with a roll that is 22½" long. Cut into 15 equal pieces. Place the rolls in a 13" x 9" nonstick baking dish. Bake for 18 to 22 minutes. You'll have 15 standard-size cinnamon rolls. Spoon 2 teaspoons of the frosting on top of each. Each roll will have 235 calories, 6 g protein, 47 g carbohydrates, 3 g fat, 2 g sat. fat, 1 g fiber. You'll save 578 calories, 29 g fat, 6 g sat. fat.

BEFORE YOU START Though this recipe requires a time span of several hours, only part of that is hands-on. They're the perfect lazy-weekend project, especially with kids in the kitchen. Each time you make the recipe, you'll develop more of a "feel" for the yeast dough. Or if you have a bread machine that can handle 2-pound loaves with a sweet-dough setting, prepare the dough in it by adding the ingredients in the manufacturer's suggested order.

CINNABON FROSTING

1½ cups confectioners' sugar

3 tablespoons reduced-fat (Neufchâtel) cream cheese from a block

3 tablespoons light butter from a stick, softened

½ tablespoon fat-free milk

1 teaspoon vanilla extract

IN a mixing bowl, combine the sugar, cream cheese, butter, milk, and vanilla. Mix on low speed with an electric mixer fitted with beaters or stir with a spoon for about 1 minute, or until combined. If using a mixer, increase the speed to high. Beat or stir vigorously for about 30 seconds or until smooth. Allow the frosting to set for at least 10 minutes. Place in an airtight plastic container. Refrigerate for up to 3 days. Just before using, stir well with a spoon.

MAKES ABOUT ¾ CUP, ENOUGH FOR 8 RESTAURANT-SIZE ROLLS OR 15 STANDARD-SIZE ROLLS

Each serving has: 119 calories, 1 g protein, 23 g carbohydrates, 3 g fat, 2 g sat. fat, trace fiber

STARBUCKS:
PUMPKIN POUND CAKE

SAVE: 64 CALORIES, 12 G FAT, 1.5 G SAT. FAT

This particular pumpkin pound cake recipe is very special to me because without it, I don't think I would have had a lot of the career opportunities I've had. Practically everyone who has ever tasted it has found it hard to believe that it's so low in fat. In fact, many people in the food and entertainment business had to watch me make it to believe it—and all those cooking demonstrations opened a lot of doors along the way! Over the years, I've found it to be one of those rare almost-fat-free baked goods that even people who swear they don't eat low-fat baked goods ask for time and time again.

It's incredibly moist, even compared with a full-fat recipe, and it holds up well if you want to try baking it in different size pans. (I've even baked it in teddy-bear-shaped muffin tins to serve to kids at Thanksgiving!)

Okay, enough buildup. I truly hope you enjoy it as much as I do.

Butter-flavored cooking spray

1½ cups unbleached flour

½ teaspoon ground cinnamon

½ teaspoon salt

½ teaspoon baking soda

½ teaspoon baking powder

¼ teaspoon ground cloves

¼ teaspoon ground nutmeg

1½ cups sugar

½ cup fat-free vanilla yogurt (not artificially sweetened)

3 egg whites

1 cup canned pumpkin

PREHEAT the oven to 350°F. Mist an 8½" x 4½" x 2½" nonstick loaf pan with cooking spray. Set aside.

Sift the flour, cinnamon, salt, baking soda, baking powder, cloves, and nutmeg into a mixing bowl. Set aside.

In a large mixing bowl, combine the sugar, yogurt, and egg whites. Using a sturdy whisk, mix until thoroughly blended. Stir in the pumpkin. Add the dry ingredients to the pumpkin mixture. Stir until no flour is visible. Pour into the reserved pan.

Bake for 55 to 60 minutes, or until a toothpick inserted into the center comes out dry (a few crumbs are okay). Cool in the pan on a rack for 10 minutes. Remove to the rack to cool completely. Cut into 8 slices. Wrap and refrigerate any leftovers for up to 3 days.

MAKES 8 SERVINGS

Each serving: 246 calories, 5 g protein, 57 g carbohydrates, trace fat, trace sat. fat, 2 g fiber

Original Starbucks Pumpkin Pound Cake (1 slice): 310 calories, 5 g protein, 47 g carbohydrates, 12 g fat, 1.5 g sat. fat, 2 g fiber

DRIVE-THRU This loaf freezes well. Wrap slices tightly in plastic wrap and then in aluminum foil. Or place the whole loaf in a resealable plastic freezer bag. Freeze for up to 2 months. Pull it from the freezer an hour or so before you're ready to eat it. Unwrap and then wrap in aluminum foil. Place in a preheated 400°F oven for 5 to 10 minutes, or until barely warmed.

BEFORE YOU START In order for this loaf to look exactly like that of Starbucks, it would need to be baked in a pan that measures 4" wide and 4" tall. After a great search, I found one in a restaurant supply store that is 16" x 4" x 4". However, I decided it would be best not to require special equipment that's just too large for home use anyway. So I developed the recipe for an 8½" x 4½" x 2½" loaf pan. If you cut the loaf into 8 slices, each will weigh precisely what the average Starbucks slice weighs. It will be slightly shorter, slightly narrower, and a bit thicker, but it will taste just as good ... I promise.

STARBUCKS: BANANA POUND CAKE

SAVE: 57 CALORIES, 11 G FAT, 10 G SAT. FAT

When I began writing this book, there was no doubt that I had to include the Starbucks Frappuccino (after all, it is a cultural icon, right?), but as I began my research for the drink, I realized how popular Starbucks baked goods are, too. Though I thought a lot of my friends were simply sneaking to Starbucks to grab a cup of coffee . . . and maybe even a date, it turns out that a couple of them have secret longings for Starbucks Banana Pound Cake. One bite and I could certainly see why.

Though I can't provide them with the social opportunities at our local chain, I can definitely present this alternative to quell at least one craving. I can't think of a better way to use up those overripe bananas, can you?

Butter-flavored cooking spray

2 cups unbleached flour

1 teaspoon baking soda

1 teaspoon salt

½ teaspoon baking powder

1 cup mashed very ripe bananas

1 cup sugar

2 egg whites

⅔ cup fat-free vanilla or banana yogurt (not artificially sweetened)

⅔ cup chopped walnuts

PREHEAT the oven to 350°F. Mist a 9" x 5" x 3" nonstick loaf pan with cooking spray. Set aside.

In a small bowl, combine the flour, baking soda, salt, and baking powder. Set aside.

In a large mixing bowl, combine the bananas, sugar, egg whites, and yogurt. Using a sturdy whisk or a spoon, mix until thoroughly blended. Add the flour mixture. Stir until no flour is visible. Stir in the nuts. Pour into the reserved pan.

Bake for 50 to 60 minutes, or until a toothpick inserted in the center comes out dry (crumbs are okay).

Cool in the pan on a rack for 10 minutes. Remove to the rack and cool completely. Cut into 8 slices. Serve warm or at room temperature. Wrap and refrigerate any leftovers for up to 3 days.

MAKES 8 SERVINGS

Each serving: 303 calories, 6 g protein, 56 g carbohydrates, 7 g fat, <1 g sat. fat, 2 g fiber

Original Starbucks Banana Pound Cake (1 slice): 360 calories, 4 g protein, 47 g carbohydrates, 18 g fat, 11 g sat. fat, 1 g fiber

DRIVE-THRU This loaf freezes incredibly well. Wrap slices tightly in plastic wrap and then in aluminum foil. Or place in a resealable plastic freezer bag. Freeze for up to 2 months. Pull it from the freezer an hour or so before you're ready to eat it. Remove it from the wrapping and then wrap in aluminum foil. Place in a preheated 400°F oven for 5 to 10 minutes, or until barely warmed.

BEFORE YOU START In order for this loaf to look exactly like that of Starbucks, it would need to be baked in a pan that is 4" wide and 4" tall. After a great search, I found one in a restaurant supply store that is 16" x 4" x 4". However, I decided it would be best not to require special equipment that's just too large for home use anyway. So I developed the recipe for a widely available 9" x 5" x 3" loaf pan. Each slice will weigh precisely what the average Starbucks slice weighs. It will be slightly shorter, slightly narrower, and a bit thicker, but it will taste just as good . . . I promise.

SUBWAY: OATMEAL RAISIN COOKIES

SAVE: 21 CALORIES, 4 G FAT

Ever since I first saw the Subway campaign starring weight-loss-success-story Jared, I've wondered exactly what he ate. I'm pretty sure he didn't have too many cookies. A number of my friends, however, swear by Subway's Oatmeal Raisin ones . . . especially now that they have this great alternative with half the fat.

> 1 cup unbleached flour
>
> ½ teaspoon ground cinnamon
>
> ½ teaspoon baking soda
>
> ½ teaspoon salt
>
> 1 stick (½ cup) light butter, softened
>
> ½ cup granulated sugar
>
> ½ cup packed brown sugar
>
> 1 egg white
>
> ½ teaspoon vanilla extract
>
> 1½ cups quick oats
>
> ½ cup raisins

PREHEAT the oven to 375°F. Line a baking sheet with parchment paper.

In a small bowl, combine the flour, cinnamon, baking soda, and salt.

In the large bowl of an electric mixer fitted with beaters, combine the butter, granulated sugar, and brown sugar. Beat for 2 minutes, or until smooth. Add the egg white and vanilla. Mix on medium speed until well blended.

Add the flour mixture. On low speed, beat until no flour is visible. Add the oats and raisins. Stir to incorporate.

Measure 2½ level tablespoons of the dough. Shape into a ball. Place on the reserved baking sheet. Lay a small sheet of waxed paper over the cookie. With your palm, flatten the ball into a 3¾" circle. Repeat rolling and pressing the dough so the cookies are not touching on the sheet. (Work in batches, if necessary.)

For softer cookies, bake for 8 minutes. For crisper Subway-style cookies, bake for 12 minutes. Cool for 5 minutes, then remove to the rack to cool completely.

MAKES 13

> Each cookie: 179 calories, 3 g protein, 34 g carbohydrates, 4 g fat, 3 g sat. fat, 1 g fiber
>
> Original Subway Oatmeal Raisin Cookie: 200 calories, 3 g protein, 30 g carbohydrates, 8 g fat, 3 g sat. fat, 2 g fiber

STEAK 'N SHAKE: CHOCOLATE MALT SHAKE (REGULAR)

SAVE: 90 CALORIES, 19 G FAT, 12 G SAT. FAT

Anyone who knows me knows I don't eat tofu. Don't do it. Won't do it . . . except in this recipe. I was looking for a way to cut calories from a milk-shake without using an exorbitant amount of ice cream. Well, in the process, one of my colleagues suggested that I use silken tofu. The thought immediately hor-rified me. But she swore that I wouldn't taste it and that it would add the bulk and smoothness I was seeking. She said that her 7-year-old daughter even refused to drink smoothies unless "the tofu is in there." I tried it and she was right . . . particularly in this recipe, where the malt definitely overpowers even the subtlest hint of tofu.

I know, I know . . . but just try it.

2 cups fat-free, sugar-free vanilla ice cream

½ cup light silken tofu

¼ cup fat-free milk

3 tablespoons malted milk powder

2 tablespoons chocolate syrup

⅓ cup aerosol fat-free refrigerated whipped topping

1 maraschino cherry

IN a milkshake maker or blender, combine the ice cream, tofu, milk, malted milk powder, and chocolate syrup. Place in the freezer for 10 minutes.

Blend on high power, stirring once or twice, for 30 to 90 seconds (depending upon the blender power), or until well mixed. Blend for another 20 seconds to aerate. Pour into a 20-ounce (2¼ cups) glass. Top with the whipped topping and the cherry.

MAKES 1 SERVING

670 calories, 25 g protein, 132 g carbohydrates, 3 g fat, 2 g sat. fat, 21 g fiber

Original Steak 'n Shake Regular Chocolate Malt Shake: 760 calories, 18 g protein, 130 g carbohydrates, 22 g fat, 14 g sat. fat, 2 g fiber

EVEN BETTER Even my reduced version has too many calories for a one-person snack. Try sharing it or simply make half the recipe. It takes only a couple of minutes to throw together, so you can make a more suitable size more frequently. The reduced version has only 335 calories, 13 g protein, 66 g carbohydrates, 2 g fat, 1 g sat. fat, 11 g fiber. You'll save 425 calories, 20 g fat, 13 g sat. fat.

MCDONALD'S: VANILLA TRIPLE THICK SHAKE (32-OUNCE)

SAVE: 147 CALORIES, 31 G FAT, 21 G SAT. FAT

I almost cut this recipe.

See, my goal in writing this book was to truly offer a scrumptious option for each dish that is lower in fat, lower in saturated fat, and lower in calories. I aspired to make each dish a "normal serving size" or at least to provide a simple "Even Better" option that is just as delicious and easy. Well, sure, I can tell you to split this one with 4 people and I'd be reaching that goal, but in this case, that just seemed like it may appear to be a cop-out. Divide one shake by 4?

After consulting with multiple food scientists, trying egg substitutes, dried egg whites, gelatins, puddings, tofu, protein shakes, meal-replacement shakes, various blender and milkshake blades, and double freezing to create enough volume to lower the calories in this shake, I realized that in no way have I copped out. Though I hope you agree, I know that I did what I could. And in the end, I decided that I needed to include this recipe, even though I am going to recommend that you do drink only one-fourth of it, because I want people to realize (I doubt most people do; I know I didn't) that the original version of this innocent-looking, amazing-tasting shake has 1,140 calories and 32 grams of fat—1,140 calories and 32 grams of fat (that's not a typo, I repeated it on purpose). That's about 300 calories and 5 grams of fat shy of what I consume in a day. It's more than a pint of ice cream. Heck, it's more than 2 pints of ice cream!

So I guess my contribution behind this recipe is a reminder: "Everything in moderation."

> 4³⁄₄ cups fat-free, sugar-free vanilla ice cream, divided
>
> 1 cup fat-free milk, divided
>
> 1 tablespoon vanilla extract, divided

IN a large freezer-proof glass or cup, combine 2¼ cups ice cream, ½ cup milk, and ½ tablespoon vanilla. Place in the freezer.

Meanwhile, in a blender jar, combine the remaining 2½ cups ice cream, ½ cup milk, and ½ tablespoon vanilla. Blend on high speed for 30 to 90 seconds (depending upon the blender power), or until mixed. (If overmixed, the mixture will get thinner.) Pour into a 32-ounce (4-cup) glass or cup. Set aside.

Immediately pour the freezer mixture into the blender. Blend on high speed for 30 to 90 seconds, or until just mixed. Add to the reserved mixture. Stir to mix. Serve with a straw.

S

N

L

MAKES 1 SERVING

993 calories, 38 g protein, 205 g carbohydrates, <1 g fat, <1 g sat. fat, 48 g fiber

Original McDonald's Vanilla Triple Thick Shake (32 ounces): 1,140 calories, 28 g protein, 178 g carbohydrates, 32 g fat, 22 g saturated fat, <1 g fiber

 BEFORE YOU START Do not substitute fat-free frozen yogurt for the fat-free ice cream unless you love the frozen yogurt and it has a pronounced vanilla taste. Most frozen yogurts have an aftertaste that will overpower the other ingredients.

Also, you should have a straw on hand.

EVEN BETTER This big shake is best shared—preferably, it will be served as 4 shakes (8 ounces each). Each shake will have 248 calories, 10 g protein, 51 g carbohydrates, trace fat, trace sat. fat, 12 g fiber. You'll save 892 calories, 32 g fat, 22 g sat. fat.

DAIRY QUEEN: CHOCOLATE CHIP
COOKIE DOUGH BLIZZARD
(MEDIUM)

SAVE: 209 CALORIES, 30 G FAT, 14 G SAT. FAT

It's apparently a Dairy Queen tradition that after your Blizzard is made, it must be turned upside down for you to view that it won't run out of the cup . . . or, I suppose, leave your hips for a very long time. If you exert the muscle necessary to mash the ice cream in my version (instead of just waiting for it to melt), you'll not only be able to continue the tradition of turning it upside down, you'll burn a few calories—maybe even build up your biceps—in the process. Please note, however, that you'll need to serve it in a Styrofoam cup to turn it upside down. It will slide out of a glass no matter how thick it is.

> 2¾ cups fat-free, sugar-free vanilla ice cream
>
> 2 tablespoons fat-free milk
>
> 1 teaspoon vanilla extract
>
> ¼ recipe Dairy Queen Blizzard Chocolate Chip Cookie Dough (opposite page)
>
> 1 tablespoon chocolate syrup

PLACE the ice cream in a mixing bowl. With a wooden spoon, mash until it is slightly softened and can be stirred. Add the milk and vanilla. Stir to blend well. Add the cookie dough. Stir to mix well. Quickly swirl in the chocolate syrup. Transfer the mixture to a 16-ounce (2-cup) Styrofoam cup. Serve with a spoon.

MAKES 1 SERVING

> 821 calories, 22g protein, 164 g carbohydrates, 10 g fat, 6 g sat. fat, 29 g fiber
>
> Original Dairy Queen Medium Chocolate Chip Cookie Dough Blizzard: 1,030 calories, 17 g protein, 150 g carbohydrates, 40 g fat, 20 g sat. fat, 0 g fiber

 DRIVE-THRU If you prepare one recipe of the cookie dough, you can have extra on hand when you feel a Blizzard craving coming. Shape the dough balls and place them, not touching, on a freezer-proof plate or tray. Freeze for about 1 hour, or until solid. Pack single serving amounts in small resealable plastic freezer bags.

 EVEN BETTER This is another recipe that, no matter how you scoop it, just doesn't qualify as a sensible serving. This is a good one to enjoy with a Blizzard buddy. Each half-Blizzard will have **410** calories, **11** g protein, **82** g carbohydrates, **5** g fat, **3** g sat. fat, **15** g fiber. You'll save **620** calories, **35** g fat, **17** g sat. fat.

BEFORE YOU START Do not attempt to bake the chocolate chip cookie dough mixture into cookies, since it's not a true cookie dough made with eggs.

Do not substitute fat-free frozen yogurt for the fat-free ice cream unless you love the frozen yogurt and it has a pronounced vanilla flavor. Most frozen yogurts have an after-taste that will overpower the other ingredients.

DAIRY QUEEN BLIZZARD CHOCOLATE CHIP COOKIE DOUGH

1/4 cup packed brown sugar

2 tablespoons granulated sugar

5 tablespoons light butter from a stick, softened

1/2 teaspoon vanilla extract

1/2 teaspoon salt

3/4 cup unbleached flour

2 tablespoons + 2 teaspoons mini semisweet chocolate morsels

IN a mixing bowl, combine the brown sugar, granulated sugar, and butter. Using electric beaters or a wooden spoon, mix until smooth. Stir in the vanilla and salt. Add the flour. Mix or stir until no flour is visible. Stir in the chips.

With a measuring spoon, scoop out level 1/4 teaspoonfuls. Place the balls in a single layer in a small plastic container lined with waxed paper. Store in the refrigerator for up to 1 week.

MAKES ABOUT 1 3/4 CUPS DOUGH, ENOUGH FOR 4 SERVINGS

Each serving: 249 calories, 4 g protein, 40 g carbohydrates, 10 g fat, 6 g sat. fat, 1 g fiber

STARBUCKS: MOCHA FRAPPUCCINO
BLENDED COFFEE (GRANDE)

SAVE: 179 CALORIES, 15 G FAT, 9 G SAT. FAT

Stock up on these ingredients and you'll save, save, save, save . . . save calories, save fat, save time standing in line at Starbucks, and save money—and lots of it. True, you won't be able to pick up a slice of your favorite Pumpkin Pound Cake or Banana Pound Cake, but if you turn to pages 198 and 200, respectively, and spend a few minutes, you can have it awaiting you in your freezer. Granted, if you also go to Starbucks to enhance your social life, I, unfortunately, have no offering for that.

> 2 tablespoons water
>
> $\frac{1}{2}$ tablespoon instant coffee
>
> 1 teaspoon sugar
>
> 20 ice cubes, divided
>
> $\frac{1}{2}$ cup fat-free half-and-half
>
> 2 tablespoons chocolate syrup
>
> $\frac{1}{3}$ cup aerosol fat-free whipped topping

IN a small microwavable bowl or cup, combine the water and coffee. Microwave on high power for 1 minute, or until the water is hot enough to dissolve the coffee. Add the sugar. Stir until the coffee and sugar are dissolved. Transfer to a mixing bowl. Add 6 ice cubes. Stir to accelerate melting the ice. When the ice is almost melted, add the half-and-half and chocolate syrup. Stir to mix. Pour into a blender jar. Add enough ice cubes for the liquid to reach the 16-ounce (2-cup) marker on the blender jar. Blend on high speed for 30 to 60 seconds, or until just slushy. Pour into a 16-ounce (2-cup) tumbler. Top with whipped topping. Serve with a straw.

MAKES 1 SERVING

241 calories, 5 g protein, 46 g carbohydrates, <1 g fat, trace sat. fat, 1 g fiber

Original Starbucks Grande Mocha Frappuccino Blended Coffee (16 ounces): 420 calories, 6 g protein, 61 g carbohydrates, 16 g fat, 10 g sat. fat, 0 g fiber

DAIRY QUEEN: BROWNIE EARTHQUAKE

SAVE: 239 CALORIES, 25 G FAT, 15 G SAT. FAT

Who wouldn't love Oreos and ice cream? It's a brilliant combo that I've been all too familiar with since college.

Years later, I was hanging out with my friend Mike and we were craving something decadent. The next thing I know, we were in my kitchen, scooping vanilla frozen yogurt into my blender. I then hesitated, surveying the skim milk and reduced-fat Oreos sitting on my counter. Mike got a worried look on his face and said, "Do you know what you're doing?" I chuckled and replied, "It's frozen yogurt and Oreos; how bad could it possibly be?" A few Oreos later, I was reminded of the great days at Smith College. So when I saw this dessert on Dairy Queen's menu, I immediately knew this amazing creation just had to be included.

> 1 Dairy Queen Brownie (page 210)
>
> 1$\frac{1}{2}$ tablespoons marshmallow creme
>
> $\frac{1}{2}$ teaspoon water
>
> 1$\frac{1}{2}$ cups fat-free vanilla ice cream
>
> 1 tablespoon fat-free hot fudge
>
> 1 reduced-fat chocolate sandwich cookie, crumbled
>
> $\frac{1}{4}$ cup aerosol fat-free whipped topping

CUT the brownie diagonally to form 2 triangles. Lay each triangle so that it rests on the opposite sides of a dessert or soup bowl that's wider at the top than at the bottom.

In a small bowl, combine the marshmallow and water, and stir until smooth.

Place the ice cream in a mixing bowl. With a wooden spoon, mash until it is slightly softened and can be stirred. Spoon into the reserved brownie bowl in a spiral motion to resemble soft-serve ice cream or simply mound it. Spoon the marshmallow evenly around the sides. Spoon the hot fudge on top. Sprinkle with the cookie crumbles. Top with whipped topping.

MAKES 1 SERVING

501 calories, 12 g protein, 107 g carbohydrates, 2 g fat, <1 g sat. fat, 5 g fiber

Original Dairy Queen Brownie Earthquake: 740 calories, 10 g protein, 112 g carbohydrates, 27 g fat, 16 g sat. fat, 0 g fiber

(STOP) BEFORE YOU START Dairy Queen's bowl is 2" high with a 4" diameter across the top and a 3$\frac{1}{2}$"-diameter base. I went to my cupboard and found a standard white porcelain soup bowl that was almost exactly this size, just slightly wider on top.

DRIVE-THRU Want Earthquakes in a hurry? Make a batch of brownies and store them in a resealable plastic freezer bag in the freezer for up to 2 months. They can be eaten directly from the freezer (they stay soft) when you are ready to serve them.

EVEN BETTER This sundae is perfectly designed to share with a friend. Use two bowls instead of one. Each serving will still have a brownie, ¾ of a cup of ice cream (more than a standard ½-cup serving), and plenty of toppings. Plus, it's always more fun to indulge with a "partner in crime." The result will be only **250** calories, **6 g** protein, **53 g** carbohydrates, **1 g** fat, trace sat. fat, **2 g** fiber. You'll save **490** calories, **26 g** of fat, and **16 g** of sat. fat over the one you'd buy at Dairy Queen.

DAIRY QUEEN BROWNIES

Butter-flavored cooking spray

¼ cup unbleached flour

½ cup cocoa powder

½ teaspoon baking powder

½ teaspoon salt

¼ cup unsweetened applesauce

1 teaspoon vanilla extract

4 egg whites

1 cup sugar

1 reduced-fat chocolate sandwich cookie, crumbled

PREHEAT the oven to 350°F. Lightly mist an 8" x 8" nonstick baking pan with cooking spray.

In a small bowl, combine the flour, cocoa, baking powder, and salt. With a fork, stir to mix. Set aside.

In a mixing bowl, combine the applesauce, vanilla, egg whites, and sugar. Using a sturdy whisk, mix until smooth. Add the flour mixture. Stir until no flour is visible. Pour into the reserved pan. Sprinkle evenly with the cookie crumbs.

Bake for 18 to 22 minutes, or until a toothpick inserted in the center comes out dry (a few crumbs are okay). Cool in the pan on a rack for 15 minutes. Refrigerate for 15 minutes before cutting into 16 squares.

Place brownies in an airtight plastic container in the freezer for up to 2 months.

MAKES 16

Each brownie: 71 calories, 2 g protein, 16 g carbohydrates, <1 g fat, trace sat. fat, 1 g fiber

RECIPES BY FAST FOOD CHAIN

Dunkin' Donuts Corn Muffins

Dunkin' Donuts Cranberry Orange
Muffins

*El Pollo Loco Cheese Quesadilla

*El Pollo Loco Macaroni and Cheese

*Fatburger Turkeyburger

*Hardee's Big Hot Ham 'N' Cheese

*Hardee's Charbroiled Chicken
Sandwich

Hardee's ⅓-Lb Western Bacon
Thickburger

*In-N-Out Burger Double-Double with
Onion

*Jack in the Box Bacon Ultimate
Cheeseburger

*Jack in the Box Extreme Sausage
Sandwich

Jack in the Box Fish and Chips

*Jack in the Box Onion Rings

*KFC Original Recipe Chicken Breast

*KFC Popcorn Chicken

*KFC Twister

*Long John Silver's Crunchy Shrimp
Basket

*Long John Silver's Lobster Crab
Cakes

*McDonald's Bacon, Egg, and Cheese
Bagel

*McDonald's Big Mac

*McDonald's Egg McMuffin

*McDonald's Filet-O-Fish

McDonald's French Fries

*McDonald's Hash Brown

*McDonald's McChicken Sandwich

*McDonald's Vanilla Triple Thick Shake

*Original Tommy's Burger

Papa John's Hawaiian BBQ Chicken
Original Crust Pizza

Pizza Hut Meat Lover's Hand-Tossed
Style Pizza

Pizza Hut Supreme Personal Pan Pizza

Popeyes Cajun Battered Fries

*Popeyes Popcorn Shrimp Po' Boy

Sbarro Stuffed Pepperoni Pizza

Sonic Country-Fried Steak Sandwich

*Sonic Grilled Chicken Wrap

Sonic Tater Tots

Starbucks Banana Pound Cake

*Starbucks Mocha Frappuccino
Blended Coffee

Starbucks Pumpkin Pound Cake

*Steak 'n Shake Chocolate Malt Shake

*Steak 'n Shake Frisco Melt

*Subway Chipotle Southwest Cheese
Steak

*Subway Meatball Marinara

*Subway Oatmeal Raisin Cookies

*Subway Turkey Breast and Bacon
Melt Wrap

*Taco Bell Double Decker Taco
Supreme

*Taco Bell Mexican Pizza

*Taco Bell Nachos Supreme

*Taco Bell Soft Taco Supreme

*Wendy's Big Bacon Classic

*Wendy's Spicy Chicken Fillet

*White Castle Fish Nibblers

*White Castle Slyders

SOURCES

Throughout this book, I've advised you to seek the ingredients you like best when preparing your fast food restaurant favorites at home. However, for those who find such information helpful, I've also included a guide to the brands I used in creating these recipes. Regional differences, where applicable, are noted throughout.

Dairy and Freezer

Fat-free half-and-half: Land O'Lakes Fat-Free Half-and-Half

Fat-free, sugar-free ice cream: Dreyer's (West Coast)/ Edy's (East Coast) No Sugar Added Fat-Free Vanilla

Fat-free whipped topping: Reddi-Wip Fat-Free Dairy Whipped Topping

Light butter: Land O'Lakes Light Butter

Light butter spread: Land O'Lakes Light Butter with Canola Oil (tub-style)

Light cream cheese: Philadelphia ⅓ Less Fat Than Cream Cheese (Neufchâtel Cheese)

Low-fat Cheddar cheese: Cabot's 75% Light Yellow or White Cheddar

Low-fat mozzarella cheese: Precious Low-Fat Mozzarella (West Coast)/Sorrento Part-Skim Mozzarella (East Coast)

Preshredded potatoes: Simply Potatoes Shredded Hash Browns

Meat and Seafood

96% lean ground beef can generally be found at most Trader Joe's stores and select grocery store chains.

Imitation Lobster: Louis Kemp Lobster Delights

Turkey pepperoni: Hormel Turkey Pepperoni

Grocery Aisles

Chocolate syrup: Hershey's Chocolate Syrup

Cocoa powder: Hershey's Cocoa

Extra virgin olive oil: Spectrum Naturals Organic Italian Extra Virgin Olive Oil (or any other Spectrum Naturals Extra Virgin Olive Oil Variety)

Light mayonnaise: Best Foods Light Mayonnaise (West Coast)/Hellmann's Light Mayonnaise (East Coast)

Low-fat mayonnaise: Best Foods Reduced-Fat Mayonnaise (West Coast)/Hellmann's Reduced-Fat Mayonnaise (East Coast)

Malted milk powder: Carnation Original Malted Milk

Nacho cheese sauce: Taco Bell Nacho Cheese Sauce

Panko: Found in the international section of most major grocery stores (often next to the tempura batter)

Ranch dressing mix: Hidden Valley The Original Ranch Salad Dressing and Seasoning Mix

Reduced-fat chocolate sandwich cookies: Reduced-Fat Oreo Chocolate Sandwich Cookies

Refried beans: Taco Bell Home Originals Fat-Free Refried Beans

Semisweet mini chocolate chips: Nestlé Real Semi-Sweet Chocolate Mini Morsels

Taco seasoning: Simply Organic Southwest Taco Seasoning

Tortilla chips: Frito Lay Baked Tostitos

TRADEMARKS

"Arby's" is a registered trademark of Arby's, Inc.

"Back Yard Burgers" is a registered trademark of BYB Properties, Inc.

"Blimpie Reuben" and "Blimpie Ultimate Club" are registered trademarks of Blimpie International, Inc.

"Burger King," "BK Big Fish," and "Chicken Tenders" are registered trademarks of Burger King Brand, Inc.

"Carl's Jr." and "The Six Dollar Burger" are registered trademarks of CKE Restaurants, Inc.

"Chick-fil-A," "Chick-fil-A Chicken Biscuit," and "Chick-n-Strips" are registered trademarks of CFA Properties, Inc.

"Church's Chicken" is a registered trademark of Cajun Operating Company, under license by Cajun Funding Corp.

"Cinnabon" is a registered trademark of Cinnabon, Inc.

"Dairy Queen," "Brownie Earthquake," and "Chocolate Chip Cookie Dough Blizzard" are registered trademarks of Am.D.Q. Corp.

"Domino's," "Domino's Deep Dish," and "America's Favorite Feast" are registered trademarks of Domino's Pizza L.L.C.

"Dunkin' Donuts" is a registered trademark of Dunkin' Donuts Incorporated.

"El Pollo Loco" is a registered trademark of American Securities Capital Partners, L.P.

ACKNOWLEDGMENTS

Having written for magazines for years, I embarked upon this book thinking I knew how long it would take. Boy was I wrong, and if it weren't for so many people, there's no way I would be sleeping even today. To everyone mentioned below and all of my family, friends, and colleagues, I am eternally grateful.

To my assistants, Stephanie Farrell and Danielle Boulé, who are more like culinary angels than assistants. They're both ultimate pros, who never lost their smiles or enthusiasm . . . even while picking, sorting, weighing, and counting each individual piece of topping off pizza after pizza after pizza.

To my sister-in-law, Jenny Alder, who introduced me to Ben Roter at Rodale. And to Ben, who then introduced me to his most incredibly professional and talented team. The entire Rodale clan has truly been such a joy. To editors Margot Schupf, Shea Zukowski, and Miriam Backes (and the little "kickboxer" in Miriam's tummy), who contributed brilliant idea after brilliant idea and were always available to collaborate. To test-kitchen wizard Jo Ann Brader, who has more food solutions than anyone I've ever met. To recipe editor Sharon Sanders, who dedicated weekend after weekend to simplifying my renditions, so that others could undoubtedly re-create them. To publicists Cathy Gruhn and Meghan Phillips, who spent more time and energy brainstorming and meeting with me in the first few months after acquisition than most publicists (from what I've heard) spend even through the launch. To designer Carol Angstadt, who, along with Shea, made the cover shoot a blast. To Steve Murphy, who is clearly the glue of the company and is revered like no other. And did I mention that they're all really fun people who I can't wait to work with again? (I'm serious; they're the best!)

To Jessica Guff and Lauren Lexton, who independently thought that I should compile and expand upon the makeovers I'd been doing in magazines to create this book. And to Jessica, for instantly believing in me enough to put me on *Good Morning America.*

To the whole team at *Muscle & Fitness* and American Media Inc., who gave me a forum for my "Recipe Dr." column, which eventually inspired this book.

To recipe testers Danielle Boulé, Stephanie Farrell, and Gail Gillman, who pitched in countless hours and brainpower.

To photographer Ben Fink and makeup artist Linda Lockwood, who are really cool people (and not only because they made me look good).

To Jamie Nehasil, who let me overtake his bachelor kitchen in Nashville to create and test many of the regional recipes. And to his colleagues at Tri Star Sports and Entertainment Group who helped equip his kitchen.

To the folks at Cuisinart (food processor) and KitchenAid (electric mixer) who generously provided me with the absolute best equipment available. And to the folks at Zojirushi who enabled me to crank out Cinnabons in no time using their Home Bakery Supreme Bread Machine (it's one of the few that has a 2-pound capacity and a sweet dough setting).

To fellow writer and friend Shanti Sosienski, who conceived the title and rescued the book from being called *Big Girls Don't Fry* or *Home Is Where the Hamburger Is.* (I wasn't really going to use those titles, but you get the point.)

To my parents, Benjamin and Toni Simone, who taught me I could do anything . . . and more. To my sister, Leslie Simone, and my godmother, Florence Putnam, who are (and have always been) my biggest cheerleaders. And to everyone else in my family—I'm so blessed.

To all of my friends for supporting me through the process, even when I was ranting about the number of menu items that changed. And a special thanks to those who contributed their brains (to help select recipes), their taste buds, and/or their cooking abilities to retest the recipes: Alana Burton, Christina Calandra, Tony Dimond, Jim Eber, Steve Farrell, Gail Gillman, Alexandra Gudmundsson, Eric Hammarlund, Heather Haque, Tas Haque, Julie Jaynes, Leigh Klein, Grace Kung, Lauren Lexton, Michelle Miller, Chris Nielsen, Jeff O'Connell, Kristine Oller, Becky Postmus, Helene Pretsky, Erik Runnels, Lara Scatamacchia, Scott Sherman, Rita and Josh Sostrin, Tucker Taylor, Rochelle Travers, Jerry Whitworth, Cara Williams, Tiffany Wong, and Chuck Young.

And last but not least, to Brian Taylor, who provided the much-needed (and treasured) distraction and support throughout the process of writing this book.

INDEX

Underscored page references indicate boxed text.

C